Ballroom

Dress, Body, Culture

Series Editor: **Joanne B. Eicher**, *Regents' Professor, University of Minnesota*

Advisory Board:
Ruth Barnes, *Ashmolean Museum, University of Oxford*
James Hall, *University of Illinois at Chicago*
Ted Polhemus, *Curator, "Street Style" Exhibition, Victoria and Albert Museum*
Griselda Pollock, *University of Leeds*
Valerie Steele, *The Museum at the Fashion Institute of Technology*
Lou Taylor, *University of Brighton*
John Wright, *University of Minnesota*

Books in this provocative series seek to articulate the connections between culture and dress which is defined here in its broadest possible sense as any modification or supplement to the body. Interdisciplinary in approach, the series highlights the dialogue between identity and dress, cosmetics, coiffure and body alternations as manifested in practices as varied as plastic surgery, tattooing, and ritual scarification. The series aims, in particular, to analyze the meaning of dress in relation to popular culture and gender issues and will include works grounded in anthropology, sociology, history, art history, literature, and folklore.

ISSN: 1360-466X

Previously published in the Series

Linda B. Arthur, *Undressing Religion: Commitment and Conversion from a Cross-Cultural Perspective*
William J.F. Keenan, *Dressed to Impress: Looking the Part*
Joanne Entwistle and Elizabeth Wilson, *Body Dressing*
Leigh Summers, *Bound to Please: A History of the Victorian Corset*
Paul Hodkinson, *Goth: Identity, Style and Subculture*
Michael Carter, *Fashion Classics from Carlyle to Barthes*
Sandra Niessen, Ann Marie Leshkowich and Carla Jones, *Re-Orienting Fashion: The Globalization of Asian Dress*
Kim K. P. Johnson, Susan J. Torntore and Joanne B. Eicher, *Fashion Foundations: Early Writings on Fashion and Dress*
Helen Bradley Foster and Donald Clay Johnson, *Wedding Dress Across Cultures*
Eugenia Paulicelli, *Fashion under Fascism: Beyond the Black Shirt*
Charlotte Suthrell, *Unzipping Gender: Sex, Cross-Dressing and Culture*
Yuniya Kawamura, *The Japanese Revolution in Paris Fashion*
Ruth Barcan, *Nudity: A Cultural Anatomy*
Samantha Holland, *Alternative Femininities: Body, Age and Identity*
Alexandra Palmer and Hazel Clark, *Old Clothes, New Looks: Second Hand Fashion*
Yuniya Kawamura, *Fashion-ology: An Introduction to Fashion Studies*
Regina A. Root, *The Latin American Fashion Reader*
Linda Welters and Patricia A. Cunningham, *Twentieth-Century American Fashion*
Jennifer Craik, *Uniforms Exposed: From Conformity to Transgression*
Alison L. Goodrum, *The National Fabric: Fashion, Britishness, Globalization*
Annette Lynch and Mitchell D. Strauss, *Changing Fashion: A Critical Introduction to Trend Analysis and Meaning*
Marybeth C. Stalp, *Quilting: The Fabric of Everyday Life*

Ballroom

Culture and Costume in Competitive Dance

Jonathan S. Marion

BERG

Oxford • New York

English edition
First published in 2008 by
Berg
Editorial offices:
First Floor, Angel Court, 81 St Clements Street, Oxford OX4 1AW, UK
175 Fifth Avenue, New York, NY 10010, USA

Berg is the imprint of Oxford International Publishers Ltd.

Library of Congress Cataloging-in-Publication Data

Marion, Jonathan S.
    Ballroom : culture and costume in competitive dance / Jonathan S. Marion.
—English ed.
        p. cm.—(Dress, body, culture, ISSN 1360-466X)
    Includes bibliographical references and index.
    ISBN-13: 978-1-84520-799-1 (cloth)
    ISBN-10: 1-84520-799-8 (cloth)
    ISBN-13: 978-1-84520-800-4 (pbk.)
    ISBN-10: 1-84520-800-5 (pbk.)
    1. Ballroom dancing—Social aspects. 2. Dance costume. I. Title.

GV1751.M29 2008
793.33—dc22

                                                    2008007436

British Library Cataloguing-in-Publication Data

A catalogue record for this book is available from the British Library.

ISBN 978 1 84520 799 1 (Cloth)
          978 1 84520 800 4 (Paper)

Typeset by JS Typesetting Ltd, Porthcawl, Mid Glamorgan
Printed in the United Kingdom by Biddles Ltd, King's Lynn

www.bergpublishers.com

CONTENTS

LIST OF TABLES AND ILLUSTRATIONS

TABLES

ILLUSTRATIONS

ACKNOWLEDGEMENTS

This project would not have been possible without the support, advice, guidance and contributions of a great many people. Direct financial support for the research upon which this text is based came from the World Federation of Ballroom Dancers, the Department of Anthropology at the University of California, San Diego, in the form of an F.G. Bailey Fellowship, from Nina Seattle, and from one other party who wished to remain unnamed. Research of this type and magnitude would also not have been possible without the in-kind support of the many competitions that granted me official access to conduct my research, and I gratefully acknowledge the access I was accorded by: Blackpool Dance Festival (2002–2003, 2005); California Open (2002–2003); Can-Am Dancesport Gala (2002–2003); Colorado Star Ball (2001); Crystal Palace DanceSport Cup (2003); Desert Classic (2002–2003, 2005); Embassy Ball (2002–2003); Emerald Ball (2002–2007); Empire State Dancesport Championship (2002); Feinda - Italian Open (2003); German Open Championship (2002); Golden State Challenge (2002–2006); Holiday Dance Classic (2001, 2003); Intercontinental Dancesport Festival (2002); Ohio Star Ball (2001–2002); Pacific Dancesport (courtesy of Donald Johnson in 2002); San Diego Dancesport Championships (2004, 2007); San Francisco Open (2002); Seattle Star Ball (2004); Southern California Amateur DanceSport Championships (2003); Southwest Regional Dance Championships (2002–2003); Star Championships (2003); Unique Dance-O-Rama (2003); USABDA National Championships (2001–2002); United States DanceSport Championships (2001–2007); and Yankee Classic (2001, 2004–2005), and I especially want to thank competition organizers Wayne Eng, Ann Harding, Tom Hicks and Thomas Murdock for their ongoing interest, assistance, support and facilitation throughout my research.

The studios that granted me official access, deserving no less thanks, are: Arthur Murray (Boston and Paoli); Champion Ballroom (San Diego); Dance Options (Cheam); Fred Astaire (Boston); Kaiser's Dance Academy (Brooklyn); Metronome Ballroom (San Francisco); Dancesport Academy of New England (Brookline); The Semley Studio (Norbury); Starlight Dance Academy (Streatham); Stopford's Dance and Fitness Center (Mitcham); Viva Dance (Thornhill); and the ÅS dancesport club (Århus). Good friends in the dance world who have shared their feelings, experiences, homes and hotel rooms along the way include F.J. and Catherine Abaya, JT Thomas, Jim Gray and Sunnie Page, Larinda McRaven, Dawn Smart, and Felipe and Carolina Telona (as well as their parents). Likewise, my experiences within the world of competitive ballroom dancing demand thanks to my various partners – Amy, Erin, Renee, Janelle, Stacey, Krista, Leslie and Andrea – and coaches – Yolanda Vargas, Donald Johnson and Katarzyna Kozak, as well as the ballroom photographers who allowed me to shoot alongside them: Chris Hansen, Dore and Park West.

This book would not be what it is without the input, advice and support of a great many people including: Steven Parish for overseeing the dissertation research upon which this text is based; Joel Robbins for advice on the proposal that led to this book; Becky Carpenter for her invaluable feedback on the first iteration of this manuscript; David Marion for helpful suggestions on the introductory materials; Devin Flaherty and Kristin Bronowicki – students in my Spring 2007 'Anthropology of Perform-ance' class at the University of California, San Diego – and the anonymous reviewers of both the proposal and manuscript for this book for the critical suggestions for which this text is undoubtedly better; and Nara Cox for her assistance in indexing the final manuscript. Robert Bunnett deserves more credit than I can possibly express for his generous and unflagging support in finalizing the materials presented in this book, including numerous challenges, questions and suggestions for which this text is far the richer. Most of all I owe my ongoing gratitude to Dress, Body, Culture series editor Joanne Eicher for her initial interest in my writing such a book and her ongoing support throughout that sometimes trying process, and to Hannah Shakespeare – I could not have wished for a more supportive, informative and accommodating editor.

I must also extend my gratitude to the many members of the ballroom world who sat down to talk with me and answered what must have seemed an endless string of questions, and without whom this project could never have come to fruition. To each and every one of them, I again say 'thank you'.

Finally, while many others contributed to this work – and without whom I would surely have fallen short of what I have accomplished – any part of these materials that strikes the reader as unclear or erroneous are solely my own responsibility.

PROLOGUE

This is a book about the culture of competitive ballroom dancing. It is not therefore a book about ballroom dress and costuming per se, but about a culture where dress and costume matter greatly and in myriad ways. This book is also about much more than competitive ballroom dancing. It is a book about people, their activities, values and lives. In particular, this book examines how participation in competitive ballroom dancing involves dancers in transnational systems of aesthetics, social networks and cultural codes that work through both body and mind.

Interestingly, this is not the book that my research was initially intended to support. Indeed my original research interests concerned the constructions of personal and collective meanings and identities within the context of competitive ballroom and salsa dancing, and these are topics that I continue to explore. Yet when asked about the most interesting things I have found in the course of my research, it is only partly in jest that I say 'that I know what ruching is'. The point here is not, of course, about ruching, or godets, or tulle, but the fact that amid my ballroom research these terms became part of my vocabulary – despite not being my subject! Perhaps even more tellingly, while recently visiting the production facility of Doré Designs,[1] I correctly guessed which professional ballroom competitor 'went with' a faxed-in dress design. The underlying point being that dress and costume are part and parcel of ballroom culture.

Within this context, then, the materials presented here are directed towards four complementary ends:

1. Using an activity of increasing mainstream popularity and media attention to introduce, illustrate and explore a variety of significant issues and considerations within the social sciences, with a strong emphasis on the relationships between the body, dress and culture.
2. Analysing how ballroom dance, as an activity, serves as a site of cultural life and identity – an ever-more important consideration in the face of the increasing social and informational interchanges of globalization.
3. Exploring (a) activity as a site of culture, and (b) how cultures can and do work through both body and mind by utilizing materials gathered in six countries, including numerous dancers from far further abroad.

4. Using a visually familiar activity to explicate how culture mediates aesthetic values and bodily practices, and how cultural practices give rise to unintended as well as intended consequences.

Taken together, the materials presented here provide an analytic look into the culture of competitive ballroom dancing. The reader is presented with an overview and history for perspective and context, and since this book focuses on competitive ballroom dancing, an outline of ballroom judging allows the reader to proceed with confidence through the rest of the book. As a complex activity linked together through cultural norms highlighting ballroom bodies and costumes,[2] competitive ballroom is spectacle, art, sport, festival and more. Beyond these complexities, this book takes us into the personal lives of the dancesport competitors, judges, spectators, vendors and participants, and discusses the effects of gender, intimacy, relationships and the important human experiences which go into living the dancesport life.[3]

THE STRUCTURE OF THIS BOOK

Increasing calls for greater ethnographic reflexivity within all forms of ethnographic explication (e.g. Ruby 2000) have come in response to the crisis in representation noted by Marcus and Fischer (1986), and it is along these lines that the extended introductory chapter explains my various roles and involvements that provided the materials for this book. In order not to draw too much attention away from the ballroom culture and community that are the focus of this text, I have elected to lay out my own journey into ballroom – as dancer, anthropologist and photographer – at the outset. I hope that this description assists in understanding my frames of reference for this work and thus helps the reader to evaluate my observations and analysis.

The remainder of the book is broken up into four complementary sections. Part I sets up the remaining sections by first introducing the reader to contemporary competitive ballroom dancing as it is practised around the world today in Chapter 1, followed by sketches of the history and background that underlie these contemporary performances and practices in Chapter 2, while Chapter 3 provides an overview of ballroom judging. Part II looks at dancesport as what John MacAloon (1984) has termed a 'metagenre' in his work on the Olympics, and in this vein I examine how the competitive ballroom culture is based upon and incorporates elements of spectacle in Chapter 4, art in Chapter 5 and sport in Chapter 6. Shifting from the sociocultural field of dancesport, Part III focuses on ballroom competitions themselves – the specific 'events' where the practices and performances of dancesport are most on display and in their most concentrated forms. Specifically, Chapter 7 examines ballroom competitions as both festivals and celebrations, while Chapter 8 focuses on ballroom competitions as rituals. Finally, Part IV explores both the intended and the unintended outcomes of the sociocultural values, practices and aesthetics outlined in Parts II and III. Chapter 9 highlights the general costs, consequences and outcomes of ballroom costuming and conduct, Chapter 10 focuses on the performances of gender implicit to dancesport, and Chapter 11 wraps up this section by considering what it thus means to live a 'dancesport life'.

While each part of this book, even each chapter, can be productively read and analysed separately, Parts II and III do build on a basic understanding of the different divisions and practices that are explained in Part I, just as Part IV addresses both the intended and unintended outcomes of the sociocultural behaviours, values and practices examined and discussed in Parts II and III. Overall then, specific chapters can stand largely on their own as far as content, analysis and discussion are concerned, but, read together, each chapter contributes to a deeper and more robust understanding of the overlapping and intersecting variable of dress, body and culture in competitive ballroom dancing, and how participation is implicated in meaning, being and doing. Finally, the concluding remarks foreground the complex intersections of spectacle, art, sport, festival, celebration, ritual, performance, costuming and gender within dancesport, highlighting some of the ways in which the intersections of dress, body and culture discussed in this book are about much more than ballroom alone.

INTRODUCTION

GETTING STARTED

After completing my BA in 1994, I spent fourteen months working as a volunteer on an Israeli kibbutz. Based on that experience, when I first started graduate school at the University of California, San Diego (UCSD), in 1998, I was planning to write my dissertation on gender relations in contemporary kibbutzim.[1] At that time I had hardly taken a step of any type of dance in my life, and was rather disinterested in dance altogether. Attending a religious conference in Los Angeles in 1997, however, I met a woman from Toronto with whom I fell in love and who, at the time, was very 'into' what she referred to as 'Spanish dancing' – which turned out to be salsa.[2] The first time I visited her in Toronto she tried teaching me the basic steps of salsa and, when that proved too far beyond my abilities, the basics of merengue, before taking me to a salsa club that night. I recall being very impressed by one of the couples I saw dancing there, but, unlike many stories of people who fall in love with some type of dancing the first time they see it, this was not the case for me. As I remember it, my only 'achievement' for that entire night was managing to stumble my way, literally, through one merengue.

Lacking both aptitude and genuine interest, I nevertheless decided that I needed to learn salsa in order to impress the woman I had fallen in love with and so, on my return to San Diego, I searched the local phone book for a studio to take lessons. Several advertisements mentioned salsa, and I started calling, explaining that I was a complete beginner interested in learning salsa. One studio that seemed relatively near had an attractive introductory offer, and the person answering the phone, who turned out to be the studio manager, said that he could schedule a lesson for me with his professional competition partner the very next day. The next day I drove to the studio and, after finding a parking space, walked across the street, opened the door, and found myself at the bottom of a wide staircase going up to a high second floor[3] from which I could hear music playing. Little did I know where those steps would eventually lead.

They changed my life. Not through any instant revelation or miraculous transformation, but because it was the first of many steps that, in later years, saw me become: (1) a regular in the San Diego salsa scene; (2) a member of the UCSD Ballroom Club; (3) first a member and then co-captain of the UCSD DanceSport

Team; (4) an amateur ballroom competitor; (5) a ballroom dance photographer (first recreationally and later as a part-time professional); (6) co-administrator for Dance-Forums.com, the largest and most active English-language online dance discussion forum in the world; and (7) a PhD the dissertation research for which was ballroom-based. At that time all of this was still far in the future, and I have since realized that while there may be people who are even less naturally gifted dancers than I am, they are few in number! In 1997, however, ballroom was an unknown activity to me.

Knowing what I do now, how I chose to start my involvement with dance was far from ideal. People regularly visit and compare several health clubs before becoming a member, just as purchasing a new camera or computer is likely to involve some background research (be it online, via personal recommendations or through various review magazines). It is an interesting and odd element of ballroom dancing then (at least in the United States) that so many people, especially many who would otherwise be cautious in almost any other arena, seem to just take what they are told – and sold – at face value. While the marketing and selling of dance is another subject altogether, I note it at this point to situate myself, at least initially, as one of those new dance students who did not even know what questions to ask.

After six months of lessons I started going to some of the most popular salsa clubs in town, where I realized that what I had been taught in the studio did not match what people were dancing in the clubs, and so I soon stopped taking lessons. While taking lessons, however, I had been exposed to a wide range of ballroom dances (almost exclusively American-style) and, over time, my interest in dancing started snowballing. By the time I started my graduate work at UCSD in the fall of 1998, going to salsa clubs a couple of nights a week was part of my regular routine. Although I cannot put a specific date on it, somewhere along the way dancing had stopped being something done to impress someone else and become something that I wanted to do for myself – my interest in dancing had shifted from being instrumentally and extrinsically motivated to a much deeper intrinsic motivation. I continued dancing mostly salsa that year, but also started taking some of the recreational ballroom classes offered on campus, and the next year tried out for the formation-routine-based UCSD DanceSport team.[4] I started my first year as a member of the 'Show Team' (effectively junior varsity), before becoming an alternate and finally a member of the 'Competition Team' (effectively varsity). Team involvement included practices from 9 to 11 p.m. every Monday, Tuesday and Thursday evenings, on top of which I also started working with two partners on a few different 'couples routines'.[5]

By this point I had three weekly team practices, practised with my various partners during additional weeknights and weekend hours, and was going out to various salsa clubs at least twice a week. Dance was becoming a bigger and bigger part of my life, engaging more and more of my overall interest and attention. Although I was now becoming more involved with ballroom, at the time salsa was still my primary focus. And, while I had stray thoughts about shifting my research focus to include dance,

I still planned on pursuing my interests about gender relations in contemporary kibbutzim for my dissertation.

Around this time, and before I had started to prepare my dissertation proposal, cultural anthropologist Marco Moskowitz accompanied me to 'Questions', a San Diego salsa club.[6] This was Moskowitz's first exposure to salsa dancing, and he came away from it enthusiastically encouraging me to adopt salsa as the subject of my dissertation. Among the comments he made was that 'it's an entirely different culture, right here under our noses, that most people don't even know about!' While Moskowitz's heady enthusiasm contributed to my eventual shift in research topics, the more telling point is that even without being able to identify much of the culture, it was already clear to me that there was a culture here to be recognized. Soon afterwards I bumped into another colleague, Laura Stanley, at 'Sport Spot', another San Diego salsa club, where she was attending the birthday party of Henrietta, a work colleague and a regular in the San Diego salsa scene. Like Moskowitz, Stanley was unfamiliar with the salsa society and readily conceded that the birthday celebration she was attending was transpiring within a community with its own cultural rules and identity. When I first mentioned the possibility of shifting my dissertation research, the notion of a salsa culture also resonated for departmental colleagues Julie Pockrandt and Julie Monteleone, who had experience with salsa in Costa Rica and Chile respectively.

At this time I was a teaching assistant for Tanya Luhrmann; she thought that the ballroom angle, rather than salsa, could be a fruitful focus. Since salsa was then my main personal interest, I somewhat shelved the whole idea – until the evening of Sunday, 13 February 2000, when Bradd Shore was in town to give a departmental colloquium the next afternoon. That evening Luhrmann hosted a dinner for Shore with the UCSD psychological anthropology students and faculty. After dinner, when we were all sitting around the living room chatting, Shore began asking each of us about our fieldwork. When he reached me, I discussed my original kibbutz project, but then mentioned my inkling to do something on salsa and ballroom. One concern was whether the academic community would take such a topic seriously or would consider it as too 'fluffy'. As we briefly discussed some of the issues involved Shore seemed excited by the possibilities, and it was this reaction that first convinced me that such a project might actually have significant academic merit. So I went back to the drawing board, did background research on dance theory in the social sciences, and found some rich background materials pertinent to theorizing about the intersectionality of person, culture and society.

In the spring of 2000 I conducted some preliminary research in order to confirm my intuition that dance served as a source of personally salient deep meanings – meanings that served as filters for other non-dance-related aspects of many dancers' lives (Marion 2000) – and I started identifying possible directions for more in-depth research. A General Theory course with Roy D'Andrade in the autumn of 2000, followed by several quarters of independent study with Steven Parish, eventually gave rise to my dissertation proposal. After defending my dissertation proposal on 15 June 2001, I conducted my first official field research the following week in Denver at the Colorado Star Ball. Over the following years my research took me to studios, clubs and competitions throughout the USA, Canada, Denmark, England, Germany and Italy, as well as into contact – both in person and on-line – with numerous dancers from even further abroad.

ENTERING THE FIELD

As someone whose participation in ballroom dancing preceded my anthropological interest in it, it is difficult to isolate a single point of entry.[7] Various entries into 'the field' could be said to include the first time I went to a salsa club, or took a lesson at a dance studio, danced socially, visited the UCSD dance club, tried out for the UCSD ballroom team, saw an actual ballroom competition, first competed, took photographs of ballroom dancers, sold my photos, and had my photographs published in *Dance Beat*.[8] In some ways each of these was itself an entry, testimony to the non-dichotomous natures of culture and community – in other words, that saying a person belongs (or not) to any given culture or community is not the same thing as saying that everyone is either entirely an insider or an outsider, or that all belongings are the same. Each of my 'entries' thus provided a new frame of participation and reference to the ballroom community, as then did my entries as an anthropologist. Each entry, however, whether as dancer or anthropologist, offered its own insights into the nature of the community.

Now, years later, I still remember my first ballroom studio visit, and while I only vaguely remember getting there, I vividly recall opening one of the tall, wood double doors, and looking up the long, wide, carpeted stairs leading upwards. Reaching the top of the stairs I faced a large reception counter directly in front of me with the studio opening up to my left in the form of a long hardwood floor with a fully mirrored wall on one side. I do not remember meeting my first ballroom teacher, but she quickly became a regular fixture in my daily life, setting the stage to this day for many of my perspectives, experiences and perceptions about partner dancing. Many of the concepts and techniques to which I was soon exposed and which I now take for granted, at the time struck me as being near superhuman, utterly incomprehensible, or both, and my early efforts involved seemingly endless struggles with even the most rudimentary issues of timing and 'weight change'. Indeed, for over two months I struggled to understand even the basic timing of the music, just as it eluded me how I could be doing anything but standing 'over' my foot. It was only over time, with practice and experience, that standing 'over' and on the 'inside' of my foot made sense, just as issues such as timing, footwork, and weight distribution emerged as additional layers of understanding and execution. Each such element thus represented deeper entry into the culture, community and practice of dance, testifying to the very values, norms and skills constitutive of belonging.

The 2001 Colorado Star Ball in Denver provided my first 'official' visit to a ballroom competition, as well as my first 'dissertation research' interview with Sam Sodano,[9] a ballroom judge and the organizer of several ballroom competitions, including the Ohio Star Ball – the site of the long-time PBS series Championship Ballroom Dancing and (starting in 2005) America's Ballroom Challenge. The following month I attended the 2001 United States Amateur Ballroom Dance Association (USABDA) National Championships[10] in Salt Lake City, Utah, where I began to learn the who's who of the US amateur rankings. Then, in September 2001, I attended the 2001 United States DanceSport Championship (USDSC) held in Miami, Florida. This was the first really large and international competition I had been to and, in many ways, this event served as the threshold for my entry into the ballroom world as an anthropologist. The number of competitors and their skill levels eclipsed anything I had seen to date. Still new to both ballroom and to my own status as an anthropologist, I was intimidated by the idea of approaching many of the dancers and coaches I wished to interview. Fortunately, competition director Tom Murdoch and head registrar Pat Traymore facilitated my efforts, asking specified competitors, as they were checking in, if they would be willing to be interviewed by me.

If the sheer scope and scale of the 2001 USDSC in many ways marked my first full entry into the ballroom world as a social scientist, my first research visit to London and then Blackpool, England, in May 2002, and my visit to the German Open Championships in Mannheim in August 2002, also represented points of significant entry, signalling, as they did, transitions in my fieldwork and research into the larger, European-based world scene of competitive ballroom dancing. Both my own dancing and my research signalled the importance of expanding my research into the broader world circuit, with even local competitions and interviews typically pointing to wider scales of activity in referencing various top dancers, coaches and competitions. For instance, local teachers would reference national finalists who, in turn, might then reference world finalists in exactly the same way. What quickly became apparent, mandating a more global focus, was the simple truth that the world-class dancers, coaches, adjudicators and competitions ultimately defined competitive ballroom dancing for all ballroom dancers and localities.

As such, my first visit to the elite competitive studios in London the week before Blackpool, and Blackpool itself – which is the most important ballroom competition in the world – marked an entry into the international, 'world circuit' of competitive ballroom in a way that my previous research had not. Tellingly, however, my entry into the world-level scene was not discontinuous with my existing dancing and research experiences; the practices and rules of ballroom studios and dancing resonated with my US experiences and knowledge, just as many of the people I knew from the United States participated in the international scene as well. Confirming the contextualizing nature of the world-level practices, the magnitude and level of Blackpool (the most prestigious ballroom event in the world) thus served as a point of both deeper and wider entry, but not a categorically different entry.

A last point regarding field 'entries' concerns an unanticipated outcome of my first research trip to London in May 2002. Attending the 2002 Desert Classic in Palm Desert, California, a widely travelled ballroom coach told me that one of his couples had walked round a corner at a competition in London preceding Blackpool and, seeing me standing down the hallway, 'freaked out, and turned around, and went back the way they had come'. 'They just don't understand who you are or what you are doing', Zack elaborated, 'and it weirded them out to keep seeing you everywhere.' In response I arranged for a brief editorial blurb in *Dance Beat*, the most widely read ballroom publication in the United States, hoping that a brief note would increase familiarity with me and my research, thereby mitigating future apprehension such as Zack had described. Most importantly, however, I started pursuing my ballroom photography more actively, a topic deserving its own introduction and treatment.

PHOTOGRAPHY

Before my first trip to Blackpool I realized that given the nature of ballroom dancing, I would want and need pictures for future publications. Having worked as a commercial portrait photographer the year before starting graduate school, I had camera equipment sitting in the back of a closet, and realized how much easier it would be to take my own photos rather than tracking down and securing permissions from others. Not then knowing that my trip to Blackpool would be but my first, I dug my cameras out of the closet and started shooting ballroom for the first time at the 2002 Emerald Ball (in Los Angeles), two weeks before leaving for England. As cultural anthropologist Barbara Anderson points out, however, 'if there is an axiom applicable to fieldwork in general it is that the worst troubles will arise in the most problematic contexts' (Anderson 1990: 110). My experience was no different, with both of my camera bodies breaking immediately after my arrival in England and my fully equipped camera bag only providing a rather cumbersome fifty-pound weight. Yet that one experience aside, photography proved to be an invaluable passport to fieldwork for me.

Almost all fieldwork involves the need to find some way to 'fit in', and this sometimes daunting task is often far from straightforward. While my own dancing provided entry into some facets of the culture and community of competitive ballroom dancing, this same avenue of access presented concomitant complications. Amidst the often widespread insinuations, innuendos and accusations about political marking and results invited by the subjective nature of ballroom judging,[11] I wanted to avoid contributing even an appearance of impropriety. Thus, although I could have waited until after I had danced to interview any of the judges judging my events, misimpressions were still possible if competitors from my events were to see me spending over an hour privately conversing with one of the adjudicators who had been deciding between us just hours before. Wishing to avoid even the appearance of such impropriety I elected to limit my competitions to select local events where I never interviewed judges.

It was at the many events where I was not competing – and thus lacked 'competitor' as a recognized role – that photography came to serve as a sociocultural passport, providing me with a recognizable (and valued) role within the ballroom community. Seen as a 'photographer'[12] it 'made sense' to dancers to see me throughout the competitive circuit and, amid the image-driven culture of competitive ballroom, photographs provided me with a culturally valuable currency with which I could repay dancers I had interviewed. As I interviewed more and more competitors, however, I did not want to come into conflict with or undercut the official event photographers contracted for each event, so I explained who I was and what I was doing to the various photographers, making sure it was all right to shoot at 'their' events. While I experienced mixed degrees of acceptance from the different photography companies, all allowed me to shoot, which, in turn, continued to facilitate my 'belonging'. In an industry that privileges image and appearance as integral elements of competitors' standings and success, photography thus provided a powerful point of cultural entry and acceptance, facilitating interactions with dancers and dress vendors alike, as well as unpacking cultural understandings – for instance, discovering why different dancers liked certain photographs provided rich data on aesthetic values and standards.

ETHNOGRAPHIC SETTINGS

The settings for my research can be broken up in several ways that suggest and offer different analytical perspectives. Here I provide brief sketches of the types of studios, camps, clubs and competitions within which my observations occurred and regarding which my analysis generated. While each location had its own unique nuances and character, there were just as certainly consistencies of structure and operation across the different settings (and types of settings). No two studios, clubs or competitions are identical, yet even newcomers would not mistake a competition for a studio given the distinct characteristics which constitute the various settings for ballroom dancing. These characteristics differentiate one setting from another at the same time as they are constitutive elements of the larger ballroom scene. The following descriptions should thus be read as representative of the most common features and characteristics of their respective settings and not as comprehensive definitions or all-inclusive descriptions.

STUDIOS

The key physical ingredients of a ballroom studio are a good-sized[13] hardwood floor and ballroom music, and most also have at least one quite sizeable mirror.

Such fundamental elements aside, a reception desk or counter, seating (at least for changing shoes, although usually also sufficient for a certain modicum of social interaction as well) are also regular physical features of the ballroom studio. Typical personnel include: receptionist, manager, owner and dance instructors, and even in the smallest of studios, where all of these roles might be filled by the same person, each role – with its different objectives and primary responsibilities – is somehow met. Beyond physical and personnel considerations, studios have cycles and rhythms of student traffic. Sometimes these patterns are daily, with the morning and early afternoon hours seeing the fewest and most dedicated dancers on the floor, with more recreational dancers trickling in and starting to fill the studio floor as they get off work in the early evening, and only the most serious of competitors left practising late into the night and early hours of the next morning.

Other patterns involve weekly and monthly studio schedules of weekly group classes, social dance parties and competitive practice rounds, each attracting its own core group of (at times overlapping) participants. In more socially based studios, annual patterns and cycles of studio-based activity are closely linked to non-dance-related annual cycles such as holidays and summer vacations, contrasting with the annual activity cycles at more competition-based studios which are closely predicated on the scheduling of various competitions. Despite often wide variation in studio practices, however, there are also great and regular similarities in both the physical and social structures between all the studios I have visited, whether for fieldwork or my own dancing. After all, the physical and social structures of all studios are geared (albeit in varying degrees) towards the common purpose of developing and exercising ballroom dancing.

CAMPS

Geared towards the same physical activity and purposes as ballroom studios (improving dancers' ballroom dance skills), dance camps, like studios, require the physical ingredients of a dance floor and ballroom music. Unlike ballroom studios, however, where more time is often spent in practice than in lessons, mirrors are seldom present in ballroom camps and the daily schedule is built around group lessons.[14] And whereas dance studios are locations dedicated to the activity of dancing, dance camps occur at a variety of venues including non-dance-specific locations (e.g. mainstream hotels). Most ballroom camps last from three to five days, so there is daily cyclicality at best (i.e. similar schedules for each day of the camp) and none of the longer-term cycles that emerge from the year-round nature of studios. Similarly, the fleeting nature of dance camps minimizes both the importance and the opportunity of knowing and understanding who the assembled people (e.g. organizers, staff, teachers and dancers) are, and of developing social relationships with them.

CLUBS

A somewhat misleading term, 'dance club', can refer to both physical structures and social organizations. Physical dance clubs, like studios, have floor space for dancing and dance music. Unlike dance studios, however, the dominant common purpose of such establishments is social interaction and dancing, not necessarily the development of dancing skills. While studios can also be sites of social interaction, and dance clubs can be sites of skill development, the focus is different. Where studios offer bright lighting and mirrors for self-evaluation and adjustment, dance clubs seldom have mirrors and inevitably offer dimmer lighting designed to facilitate social interaction. Similarly, where the largest percentage of time spent at the studio is typically dedicated to lessons and practice, dance clubs are about dancing *with* other people rather than improving one's own dancing.[15] The amount of space and the density of bodies in that space are typically quite different between studios and clubs too. While studios can be crowded and clubs nearly empty, the social emphasis at clubs regularly elicits far tighter concentrations of physical bodies.[16] The focus and structure of clubs also gives rise to an additional set of roles largely absent from the studio setting, such as DJs, live bands, security, bartenders and servers. Different from physical dance clubs are the social ones which, as social organizations, lack physical elements such as floors built specifically for dancing. Also, as social organizations such 'dance clubs' may have meetings, outings and events that have nothing to do with dancing. As dance clubs, however, the majority of the time spent together is most often in social dancing, whether through group outings to various studio social parties or through club-sponsored social dances. Whether physical or social, however, dance clubs are primarily about social dancing.[17]

COMPETITIONS

Dance competitions are far and away the most complex ethnographic sites I have explored.[18] Focal points of social, cultural and individual variables, competitions involve concentrations of personnel, roles, regulations and values absent from my other research venues. Competitors, audience, adjudicators, scrutineers, runners, deck captains, registrars, chairmen (of judges), MCs, DJs and vendors – for dresses, shoes, accessories, videos and photographs – are all competition regulars. Similarly, the set-up of dance flooring, tables and seats, an on-deck area, lighting, registration, vending booths and musical equipment (just to name a few such examples) illustrates the level of organization required for (even relatively small) competitions. The scheduling of numerous competitive events, judging assignments, and the various rules and regulations for eligibility, costuming and age categories are just some of the myriad complexities that underlie and constitute competitions. Although brief – lasting from half a day on the short end to eight days on the longest – competitions are of central importance and significance to competitive ballroom dancing.

As pointed out elsewhere (Marion 2005b: 20), competitions are key to competitive dance in the same way as elections are to politics and the Olympics to sports: just as political elections are not the day-to-day events of political life nor the Olympic Games the day-to-day events of sports, they are still centrally salient and orienting to politics and sports. Just because elections do not happen daily does not mean that much (if not most) of regular politicking does not take place either in relation to, or under the umbrella of, election-related considerations. If nothing else, elections set the stage for those engaged in non-election-related day-to-day politics, and the Olympic Games fit this same general model, serving as a point of orientation while being a rare event in day-to-day athletics. Indeed, the (relative) rareness of elections and the Olympic Games is part of what makes them focal. If elections were held every other day, the stakes involved in who won simply could not be as significant, and if the Olympic Games were contested every four weeks instead of every four years, the drive, prestige, and importance of being an Olympic champion simply could not be as great or as widely encompassing. As with politics or the Olympics, the relative scarcity of ballroom competitions – at least as a ratio of time spent in the activity – plays an important role in establishing competitions' social and cultural significance within ballroom dance.[19]

WHERE IS THERE?

So where do I do my fieldwork?[20] The most typical answer I give, as I have noted elsewhere (Marion 2005a), is 'in the international competitive ballroom circuit' or 'with the community of competitive ballroom dancers'. While places such as studios and competitions are physical features and contexts for the ballroom community, they are not conterminous with the dance-sport culture. Similarly, there is an annual calendar of ongoing, year-round events of varying prestige and implications which provides temporal structure to the competition circuit, but here, too, the ballroom culture and community are greater than the collection of dates involved. Even the membership base is ever-fluctuating, with different people filling activity-specific roles. Overall then, while there are regular locations, times and people involved in the competitive ballroom circuit, none of these defines, constitutes or situates the competitive ballroom community. Indeed the majority of people who take ballroom classes never become members of the competitive community. Rather, as this book illustrates, it is both chosen participation and commitment to activity-specific aesthetics and standards that demarcate the membership of the competitive circuit. Though not perfectly, to be sure, competitive ballroom dancers still share common activity-based goals, values and understandings of visual and bodily aesthetics and standards.

Doing fieldwork among the fluctuating population, events and locations of ballroom life presented a variety of logistical, methodological and theoretical challenges, not the least of which was the need to continuously *re-enter* the field, negotiating access anew for each city, studio, and competition. Unlike logistics for more stable fieldwork 'sites', arrangements for travel and housing required ongoing exploration and scheduling, exerting a continuing toll in time, effort and money. The extent of such expenses are theoretically significant, however, pinpointing very real aspects of the serious dance-sport scene, wherein annual expenses for elite competitors can reach US$100,000 and above annually. Certainly ongoing travel, airports, hotel lobbies, ballrooms and living out of continuously repacked suitcases are not the prototypical features of ethnographic fieldwork, but in the translocal world of competitive ballroom these features were of central theoretical (and not just logistical) consideration. Insofar as widespread travel and exposure are fundamental features of dancesport living, they emerge as theoretically central and methodologically imperative to doing research with such a mobile and translocal community, especially as 'it is only in their translocality that the social networks, action systems, and embodied identities of the competitive ballroom scene can really be appreciated' (Marion 2005a: 19).

While there are differences between studio communities, and even between the subcultures of different studios, all such differences transpire under a wider umbrella of ballroom culture (Marion 2005b). Even though a newcomer may not automatically be accepted as a studio insider, his or her dancing will still be recognized for what it is, marking them as a dancer of 'X' proficiency level. The widespread circulation of coaches and students between various studios and competitions are all part of a wider circuit, expanded even further via internationally produced and circulated instructional manuals, videos, DVDs and online media. Values and identities are always contextual, which means that ballroom competitors, coaches, studios, adjudicators and competitions are all contingent upon their place within a field of activity replete with all its constituent practices, values, negotiations of agency and power, and constructions of meaning and identity that transcend geographic positioning. As all this helps to make clear then, there is not always a simple 'where' to fieldwork. The overlooking and under-theorizing of 'locations' that do not fit traditional models of 'place', unfortunately and unnecessarily leaves open critical methodological concerns, undermining both the empirical and theoretical contributions possible from such research. This book is a step in the opposite direction; it looks carefully – and finds that the 'how', 'who' and 'what' defining the 'where' cannot always be said to be 'there'.

PART I
SETTING THE STAGE

1 WHAT IS COMPETITIVE BALLROOM DANCE?

WHAT IS 'BALLROOM'?

The Oxford Dictionary of Dance provides the following entry for 'ballroom dance':

ballroom dance. Social dance usually performed by couples in dance halls or at social gatherings. During the 20th century these dances came to be performed widely in competitions, which flourished in Britain and America following the First World War. In 1929 the Official Board of Ballroom Dancing was founded and by the 1930s standardization of training and levels of expertise had been established. Today Britain leads the world in ballroom dancing, and the annual Open British Championship is the most important competition. Standard ballroom dances include the waltz, Viennese waltz, foxtrot, tango, lindy, Charleston, and the quickstep. Latin American dances such as the rumba, samba, paso doble, and cha-cha-cha are also part of the ballroom repertoire. (Craine and Mackrell 2000: 49)

That is the entry in its entirety. At the very least this is an overly simplistic definition, ignoring myriad national, local and situational uses and understandings of what constitutes 'ballroom'. In some cases 'ballroom' is used as a gloss for many varieties of partnered dancing including Waltz, Foxtrot, Cha Cha, Rumba, Lindy Hop, Salsa, Night Club Two Step, Hustle, Argentine Tango, West Coast Swing, and many more – and indeed many US ballroom studios offer classes in all of these dances. But 'ballroom' is also used with much tighter meaning, referencing only the dances included in multi-dance competitive events such as International Standard and International Latin throughout Europe, to which American Smooth and American Rhythm are added in the United States, and New Vogue in Australia. Similarly, few members of the contemporary ballroom community, if any, would classify Lindy (short for Lindy Hop) as a ballroom dance regardless of its historical role as the basis for American style East Coast Swing and International style Jive.

The Oxford Dictionary of Dance entry also entirely ignores broad articulations between dance and society, such as the historical connections between ballroom dancing, class, style and social mores. In her overview to the Library of Congress collection for Western social dance, for instance, Elizabeth Aldrich offers up the following much more contextually complete historical synopsis for ballroom dancing:

> For centuries, in Europe and wherever Europeans have settled, the ballroom was the perfect setting for men and women to demonstrate their dancing abilities, to show their awareness of the latest fashions, and to display their mastery of polite behavior – qualities required for acceptance in society. The importance of dance and appropriate conduct was echoed in manuals that date back to the early Renaissance, to a time when courtiers, gentry, and wealthy citizens were fortunate enough to have a private dancing master or to have taken advantage of the skills of itinerant masters who traveled from one court to another.
>
> The grandeur of the Baroque court of King Louis XIV and his court at the Palace of Versailles set the stage for a new style of dance that would spread to royal courts throughout Europe. With the development of a dance notation system, published in 1700 by dancing master Raoul-Auger Feuillet, French court dance could be taught in every palace and manor house. By the end of the eighteenth century, when ideals of democracy swept through nations, group dances gained popularity, so dance instruction manuals, as well as etiquette books, were published to enlighten a growing middle class of Europeans and European colonists, especially those in the Americas. (Aldrich 1998: electronic document)

As Aldrich's entry makes pointedly clear, ballroom dancing has always been about more than just ballrooms or dancing.

Modern ballroom dancing thus has its roots in fifteenth- century Europe, amidst the rise of chivalry and the increasing popularity of dance within the French royal court. In particular, the 1533 marriage of Catherine de' Medici to Henri, duc d'Orléans brought Italian dancing masters into the employ of the French monarchy (Hammond 2000: 144–45), where Catherine often held extravagant balls as both royal celebrations and political displays. By the early fifteenth century dance masters were thus recognized as expert authorities on both proper social behaviour and dance (Hammond 2000: 141–42), and early dance books, such as Arbeau's *Orchesography* (1589), were concerned with providing instruction in both dance technique and social mores.[1] This linking of class and ballroom dancing has proved to be an enduring image in the collective Western psyche, serving as an accepted part of social rearing and development in many parts of Europe and as the foundation for cotillion programmes throughout the United States – programmes which teach both dance and social etiquette. Historical foundations notwithstanding, the ballroom dancing of years gone by is not that of today. The *term* 'ballroom' is now typically used to describe a formalized style of partnered dancing, namely the major dances and styles taught in ballroom studios and contested at ballroom dance competitions.

My original research plans included both the social and the competitive wings of ballroom dancing, but eventually ended up focusing on competitive ballroom – also known as dancesport. Early on I made a point of interviewing the more prominent dancers and dance personas I encountered, recognizing that relative to social dancers they would be harder to come by, track down and arrange to interview later on. As I had access to many social dancers on campus and at local dance studios that was, in a way, untrue of the elite competitors and judges, but my thinking was essentially an informal and imprecise calculus of scarcity. On this basis, I prioritized opportunities to interview the most highly placed ballroom personnel whenever possible, but in so doing came to recognize sizeable and significant differences between the social and competitive ballroom scenes and circuits.

Additionally, and especially since the issue of identity construction was one of my central interests, this was explored more fully among competitive ballroom dancers for whom ballroom dancing was often more centrally contextualizing and defining of 'self'. There are certainly also social ballroom dancers for whom ballroom dancing does play a key role in their personal and collective identifications, just as there are competitive ballroom dancers for whom ballroom dancing does not play such a role. Yet the underlying point remains that, on average, competitive dancers dedicate more time, energy, resources and greater personal investment into their dancing and, as such, serve as a more efficacious population for exploring chosen commitment systems and identity constructions. Few dancers start out as competitive dancers, however, and it is for this reason that the variety of ballroom studios where dancers start dancing (including the many social dances and functions that are typical of such studios) remained important to my exploration of competitive ballroom dancing.

Centring my research in North America and Western Europe should not be misread as dismissing the very significant, sizeable, and active ballroom communities in other locales throughout Eastern Europe, Asia and Australia. When initially formulating this project I was unsure of the geographic scope and the interconnectedness of various elements of the ballroom scene and circuit. It was only during my preliminary research that I came to realize that the US ballroom scene could not be fully appreciated and understood save in reference to the European scene. In the same way that the local student looks to their instructor for a model of good dancing, so too does the local instructor look to a more accomplished dancer, and so on up. It is in exactly this way that the best dancers in the United States set the models for students who will never even hear of them. But it is also exactly in this way that the best dancers in the United States look to, contest with, and evaluate themselves relative to the best on the worldwide circuit – based in Europe, and in England in particular (but perhaps less so today than in years past) – in order to set their own goals and marks. Similarly, many of the teachers, coaches and adjudicators who help mould and direct the competitive US ballroom scene are not products of the US ballroom scene themselves, while even those who are not transplants (of other competitive scenes) have almost inevitably still had experiences with, and exposure to, many non-US influences during their own formative periods. As such, the US ballroom scene – including current trends, changing social positioning, aesthetic values, and ongoing politics – cannot be adequately understood nor explicated save in relation to the larger worldwide scene and its Western European base (as well as growing influence from Eastern Europe and Russia).

THE MAJOR DIVISIONS OF BALLROOM

Starting out as one of the social graces expected of the European upper classes, then, 'Ballroom' is now an umbrella term for a style of lead-and-follow-based partner dancing that is danced both competitively – under the name 'dancesport' (also seen as Dancesport or DanceSport) – and socially. First formalized in Europe, ballroom is still considered part of a well-rounded social graces and upbringing throughout Europe and is still regularly offered in schools or as a 'cultured' elective alongside musical instruction. While sometimes used to refer to the whole range of partnered dances, including Lindy Hop, Nightclub Two Step, West Coast Swing, Hustle, Merengue, Salsa, and Argentine Tango, this is not the understanding typical among competitive ballroom dancers. The most common and prominent division within the international circuit of ballroom dancing (both competitive and social) is that between the traditional Ballroom dances (also known as the Standard or Modern dances) of Waltz, Tango, Viennese Waltz, Foxtrot and Quickstep, and the Latin dances[2] (also sometimes known as Latin American) of Cha Cha (also known as cha cha cha), Samba, Rumba, Paso Doble and Jive.

Some countries have additional divisions which, like Ballroom and Latin, are also danced both socially and competitively. In Australia, for instance, there are New Vogue and Street Latin categories. The United States, by contrast, has two divisions, Smooth and Rhythm, corresponding to the International Style Ballroom and Latin divisions respectively. The American Smooth dances consist of Waltz, Tango, Foxtrot and Viennese Waltz, but these dances differ from their International-style counterparts in slight differences in tempi and, far more significantly, in allowing partners to separate from one another while dancing. Indeed, the name 'Smooth' is meant to signal the premium this style places on smoothly moving in and out of the closed dance frame of Standard. The American Rhythm dances consist of Cha Cha, Rumba, Swing, Bolero, and Mambo. The American Cha Cha and Rumba have traditionally varied in technique and tempi from their International-style counterparts, and the American Rumba also differs in basic timing and basic step pattern. The differences between the competitive International and the American Cha Cha have been have been decreasing, however, especially as more and more internationally trained dancers start to cross back and forth and compete in the American Rhythm division.

Figure 1.1 shows each of the four styles described, Table 1.1 illustrates how the different categories are most typically viewed, compared and contrasted in relation

1.1. International Standard, American Smooth, International Latin and American Rhythm ballroom styles – as danced at the 2006 United States DanceSport Championships, Hollywood Beach, FL by: US Professional Standard Champions Jonathan Wilkins and Katusha Demidova (top left); US Professional Smooth Champions Ben Ermis and Shalene Archer-Ermis (top right); US Professional Latin Champions Andrei Gavriline and Elena Kryuchkova (bottom left); and US Professional Rhythm Champions Tony Dovolani and Elena Grinenko (bottom right). ©2006 Jonathan S. Marion

to each other among active competitors in the United States, and Table 1.2 depicts the specific dances assigned to each: [3]

Beyond these four styles are International 10-Dance, comprising the five Standard and five Latin dances combined, and American 9-Dance consisting of the four smooth dances and the five rhythm dances. Additional categories such as Theatre Arts, Exhibition, Cabaret, Classic Showdance and Latin American Showdance are more open-ended and allow for varying degree of lifts and suchlike. In the end, however, it is the basic styles depicted in Figure 1.1 and Tables 1.1 and 1.2 that shape the dominant contours of dancesport.

Table 1.1   Ballroom Styles

	International Style	*American Style*
Ballroom	Standard/Modern	Smooth
Latin	Latin	Rhythm

Table 1.2   Dominant Model of Dances by Style

Standard *(International)*	*Latin* *(International)*	*Smooth* *(US)*	*Rhythm* *(US)*
Waltz	Cha Cha	Waltz	Cha Cha
Tango	Samba	Tango	Rumba
Viennese Waltz	Rumba	Foxtrot	East Coast Swing
Foxtrot	Paso Doble	Viennese Waltz	Bolero
Quickstep	Jive		Mambo

Beyond these larger categorical divisions, however, the ballroom landscape is also shaped – albeit on a far smaller scale – by many ballroom-related organizations, publications and websites that are all also part of the overall ballroom scene. In general, then, my research focuses on the competitive ballroom circuit (including the American and International styles) and many of the organizations, publications and websites that are part and parcel of the competitive circuit. Far from being located in any one place, this ballroom 'scene' is best understood as a highly interconnected grouping and institutionalization of people, places, understandings, values and practices that are relatively stable if still somewhat malleable.

The Major Structural Divisions of Ballroom ... or Not   Where 'International' and 'American' differentiate between different *styles* of ballroom dancing, 'Professional', 'Amateur' and 'Pro-Am' distinguish the participants by structural divisions, respectively pairing professionals, amateurs and an amateur with a professional. Who is or is not a professional is an often contentious subject and the classificatory schemes vary from country to country under the auspices of national representative bodies of the World Dance Council (WDC). With an even larger participant base than the WDC, the International DanceSport Federation (IDSF) and its national member bodies represent 'amateur' dancers.[4] Overall these two structural divisions run parallel to each other, with most major competitions holding both amateur and professional events in the different styles, with today's amateur champions typically emerging as tomorrow's professional champions. While the professional and amateur division is worldwide, Pro-Am is a primarily American division (although beginning to gain in some international markets as well) pairing amateurs with professionals (typically student and teacher). While these structural divisions are significant in many respects, what counts and is judged as good dancing and costuming – be it Latin, Standard, Rhythm or Smooth – is only slightly nuanced across these participant bases.

'BALLROOM' AS CULTURE

Both in conducting my research and in speaking to others about it, I kept hearing people mention the 'subculture' I was studying.[5] From a regional perspective this may makes sense; Bostonian dancers are a subset of Bostonians, for instance, just as Japanese dancers are clearly a subset of Japanese. Yet whatever else cultures may be – and the definitions and understandings of this have been wide ranging indeed – they are shared.

As such, I would contend that cultures are recognized as the largest such shared units with subcultures representing more specific subsets of sharing. So, yes, Bostonian and Japanese dancers are, as dancers, subsets of Bostonians and Japanese. Yet by the same token, these same individuals could also be recognized – as Bostonians and Japanese – as subsets of dancers.

Ballroom dancers from the United States, Japan, Australia, Denmark, Germany, Italy, South Africa and Finland do *not* represent a subset of any larger shared system,[6] and, in point of fact, ballroom dance *is* what is shared. In this light, it is just as reasonable to speak of Danish dancers or Australian dancers as subsets of ballroom dancers as of Danes or Australians. In the course of explaining my project to dancers, for instance, I would often suggest that 'In the same way that an anthropologist might have gone to an island and lived with a tribe for a year or two and studied various elements of the social structure, cultural norms, and personality development within that culture that I am doing the same type of project for the "tribe" of ballroom dancers' (Marion 2005a: 18).

An oversimplification to be sure, yet this model resonated for most, eliciting several comments of 'we really are a tribe, aren't we?', with some taking it even a step further, adding 'with war paint and everything' (regarding their competition make-up). As an institutionalization of action, ballroom dance informs the meanings of bodily movement, display and performance – including the clothing, grooming and costuming with which those bodies are presented. Lacking a fixed location, the ballroom community is still a site of both personal and collective identity formation, of cultural norms and values.

I do not mean to suggest that ballroom dancers be thought of only or entirely as ballroom dancers, but I do think that relegating their self-selected and self-affirmed status as ballroom dancers to a secondary status – as being a subset of something else – is equally wide of the mark. Holland and Quinn's (1987) conceptualization of each person as an individual nexus of overlapping cultures well describes the situation represented by ballroom dance; each dancer is simultaneously a member of their national culture and of the ballroom culture in distinct but also inextricably interrelated ways.[7] It is against this background that I contend that ballroom dance is more accurately understood as (and thus termed) a culture than a subculture.

As Benedict Anderson (1991) has pointed out, imagining is a necessary constitutive element of group membership. And how could it be otherwise? No one, after all, feels like a member of a community to which they do not think they belong. While necessary, however, imagining alone is not sufficient for group membership since distinct social groups achieve their distinction by way of group specific appraisals, norms, values, action systems, techniques. Thus, while ballroom classes, lessons, studios, workshops, competitions (and other such venues) do teach dance steps, patterns and techniques, they simultaneously inculcate frames of reference and action that go much deeper then imagining alone. It is not by random happenstance, after all, that dancers from disparate countries can easily dance with one another in the absence of a shared verbal language.

While always taking place within larger social contexts, dance is a socially levelling and formative arena of human activity of great potency (Spencer 1985: 28), and it is exactly this phenomenon that makes dance so efficacious in generating its own collectivities (Hanna 1988). This dynamic is especially telling of (contemporary) competitive ballroom which resists conventional locality-based models and understandings of community. My observations from North America and Europe reveal that, while ballroom may vary both locally and individually, there is a larger ballroom culture, a culture with its own social rules and languages, codes and hierarchies (Savigliano 1998: 105–8), and stars and celebrities (e.g. Sumner 1906: 12) that remain opaque to the 'outsider'. Yet how could it be otherwise? Competitive ballroom is far from a spontaneous activity, but a deliberate institutionalization of practices[8] and values that take effort.

The larger ballroom community is thus best viewed, examined and understood according to Stromberg's (1986) notion of commitment systems as chosen cultural systems. Eclipsing Anderson's (1991) conceptualization of self-constitutive imagination, Stromberg's model accounts for the generation of both belief and action (1986: 90), which is especially informative of the multiplex nature of performative activity-based communities such as those of bodybuilding (e.g. Bolin 2004), beauty pageants (e.g. Banet-Weiser 1999), surfing (e.g. Ford and Brown 2006) and dancesport. The specific people who will be at the studio, at a practice, at a performance, or at a competition on a given night may be – and often are – highly variable. At the same time, however, across time there is constancy of both community and culture: the same people do come back, in what Skinner calls the 'cyclical properties of human interaction systems' (1985: 289). Perhaps even more importantly, there are predictable patterns of activity – Skinner's 'spatial patterning of human interactions' (1985: 288) – which undergird McMains's contention that the ballroom community 'is created by replication of common circumstances rather than by actual shared experience of the entire group' (2006: 13).

Despite this book's focus on ballroom dance, then, it is about far more than just dancing. Dances, after all, do not dance themselves. Just as it is people and not cultures that act,[9] so too is it persons who dance. Dancing is intentional, deliberate,[10] and takes work.[11] As such, the performative aspect of dance both reflects and shapes the sociocultural norms and meanings that articulate personal and collective participation, involvement, and belonging. Just as Marta Savigliano recognizes the nomadicism of Argentine Tango dancers (Savigliano 1998: 105), ballroom dance communities can also be described as translocal, intermittent, recurring, overlapping, floating, drifting, mobile and migratory. Understanding such communities is of ever-growing importance as they testify to the experience(s) of culture, community and identity in modernity, where the primacy of geographic locality recedes in the face of ever-expanding physical and conceptual mobility.[12] Ballroom communities do exist, albeit not in customary geographic or temporal locals. They are social arenas in which community and identity are confirmed. They are 'places' where people live lives and forge identities. As complex, hybrid cultures, ballroom communities resist standard models – they exhibit elements of ritual, ceremony, leisure, performance, exhibition, pageant and competition. Each of these elements is integral to understanding ballroom communities but – especially when considered separately – all fall far short of capturing the flavour of this lived world.

Insofar as imagining is generative of communities (Anderson 1991), ballroom communities are no exception; yet this is only part of the picture. Dancing, as Savigliano points out, 'starts out way before the actual dancing' (Savigliano 1998: 105), and even the briefest assessment reveals distinct norms, values, action systems, techniques and patterns of appraisals across ballroom dance classes, lessons, studios, workshops and competitions. Despite postmodern emphasis on local explication,[13] it is not by chance that ballroom dancers from different countries, and speaking different languages, can successfully dance with each other at their first meeting. As my observations from the United States, Canada, Denmark, England, Germany and Italy clearly illustrate, while always subject to both local and individual variation, there is a ballroom culture – a culture of dance with its own social rules.[14] Ballroom communities also have their own 'language' – terms and usages that remain opaque to the 'outsider'. So, too, do they have their own codes and hierarchies,[15] as well as stars and celebrities.[16] All of this makes sense since ballroom dancing is not a spontaneous activity but, rather, one that needs to be understood – including all the associated ramifications – as an institutionalization of action.[17]

Peter Stromberg's notion of a commitment system as a chosen cultural system (Stromberg 1986) – particularly informative for communities often defined by their diversity[18] – well suits the translocal ballroom community. Going beyond Anderson's notion of self-generative imagination, Stromberg's idea of commitment is directly generative of both belief and action (e.g. Stromberg 1986: 90). This dynamic is important in understanding ballroom communities, which are simultaneously mobile and nontransient.[19] The individuals present at a given competition or studio on any night are always highly variable, yet over time the same 'faces' appear over and over. Perhaps most telling, however, is that for many people, belonging to these communities matters. Membership, however conceptualized and defined by both self and others, constitutes, in F.G. Bailey's words, 'the only valid self' (Bailey 1993: 26). As such, the models, norms and values associated with ballroom dancing – despite their lack of grounding in geographical coordinates – are not experienced as separate or disparate from other facets of life. This is of particular significance when considering the importance and communicativeness of *physical culture*.[20] Indeed, it is precisely in this way that dance factors into the construction bodily practices' identifications such as those of gender (see, especially, Chapter 9).[21] For the moment, however, I want to examine further the nature of the ballroom community as a translocal one.

TRANSLOCAL

More than just multi-sited (e.g. Marcus 1986, 1995; Gupta and Ferguson 1997), the ballroom community is *translocal*.[22] Dancers, studios and competitions alike are all 'connected with one another in such ways that the relationships between them are as important ... as the relationships within them' (Hannerz 2003: 207). The 'site' of such research, as Hannerz notes, is as much in the 'translocal linkages' as the locations themselves, and 'these linkages make the multi-site study something different from a mere comparative study of localities' (2003: 207). Thus, while multi-sited fieldwork typically requires choosing among an array of locations (Hannerz 2003: 207), it is in the 'networks of relationships' (Hannerz 2003: 205) between studios and competitions that ballroom culture is lived. Like Hannerz's foreign correspondents, ballroom lives are implicated in 'patterns of collaboration, competition and division of labor, which organize their daily activities' (Hannerz 2003: 205). The patterns and practices of day-to-day ballroom life are thus informed by larger sociocultural forces, always contextualized by standards, institutions, networks and events transcending specific localities.

As Hannerz notes, a key challenge of establishing interpersonal rapport in a 'modern, multi-site field comes not so much from deepening particular interactions as from the identification of common acquaintances – from placing the ethnographer in the translocal network of relationships' (Hannerz 2003: 209). An important facet of becoming accepted as a ballroom insider – rather than 'that guy doing a school paper on us' – included establishing networks of interactions, histories and common acquaintances with dancers, judges, vendors and organizers. Yet this dynamic is indicative of the nature of translocal communities; far from being a unique dilemma for me as an anthropologist, it served as a means of experiencing how sociocultural networking establishes belonging in such communities. Lacking any 'native' locations, ballroom dancers regularly encounter and interact with 'strangers' within their own community (Hannerz 2003: 211). Quite significantly, then, it is by 'turning the combinations of sites into coherent fields' and making locations into cultural sites (Hannerz 2003: 211) that those who travel most widely within the ballroom world play the largest role in establishing ballroom locations as 'translocalities' (Appadurai 1995).

An important point to make here is that while most of my interviews were in English, the site of my fieldwork was far from monolingual, like most translocal fieldwork settings (Marcus 1995: 101). If English is the most widely used language across ballroom venues, it is far from the only one. Dance lessons, practices and competitions are often home to a plethora of languages, with popular studios and competitions representing multiplexed soundscapes of intersecting tongues. Indeed many dancers and coaches are polyglots extraordinaire, particularly among the elite competitors who may well live in, dance for, and have partners from countries other than their own. Multiple languages are often the norm for the international ballroom circuit rather than the exception. When I met the newly partnered couple of Rebecca and Zack in Cervia, Italy, for instance, they conversed in a combination of five languages. Each knew English, Russian and Italian, and each also understood the other's Polish or Slovenian. While it was utterly beyond my limited linguistic skills to understand Rebecca and Zack's various conversations, these same exchanges made the translinguistic nature of ballroom blatantly obvious and clear to me, a dynamic which in turn feeds back into and further cements the translocal nature of the values, aesthetics and practices of the competitive ballroom culture and community.

As a translocal (and translingual) social arena wherein personal and collective identities are forged, challenged and confirmed, the ballroom community resists customary geographic positioning. Ballroom dancers from Japan, Germany, Russia, Denmark, England, the United States, and beyond, can easily partner one another because of translocally shared models and standards. Extensive travel by top coaches and competitors, and wide circulation of information media via ballroom websites, videos and publications, only amplifies the translocality of information, models and standards for ballroom dancing. Whether explicitly recognized by members of the ballroom community or not, participants are implicitly aware of the shared standards for dancing, partnering, instruction, performance, competition and judging that transcend national differences. Predicated on their shared purposes and activities the physical layouts of studious and competitions are relatively standardized, which makes and marks ballroom dancing and settings as translocally consistent (relatively speaking) to the ballroom insider.

BALLROOM AS METAGENRE

Ballroom exhibits elements of ritual, ceremony, leisure, performance, exhibition, pageant, competition and belonging, and, as a complex hybrid culture, something is lost in any attempt to understand ballroom in the absence of any one of these elements.[23] Yet when considered separately each element falls far short of adequately illustrating, revealing, or understanding the flavour of the lived world of ballroom. Based on the modern Olympic movement, MacAloon's conceptualization of 'metagenres' as unique linkages of the symbolic actions of spectacle, festival, ritual and game (MacAloon 1984: 241–59, 275–8) well suits ballroom. Like the Olympics, ballroom is a nexus of overlapping webs of meaning and relations. Turner, too, recognized that the cultural forms inherent in the performance of the 'great genres' – ritual, carnival, drama and spectacle – are 'orchestrations of media' that colour the messages they convey (Turner 1987: 23–4).[24]

The gender roles performed in competitive ballroom dancing (see Chapter 9), illustrate how the ballroom community exemplifies exhibiting qualities, dynamics, systems and orchestrations of spectacle, festival, ritual and game, as well as those pertaining to ceremony, leisure, performance, exhibition, pageant and competition, thus ballroom culture exemplifies MacAloon's concept of metagenre. Like the cultures of the Olympics, rodeo and the circus (e.g. Offen 2000), ballroom culture functions as a nexus of experience, meaning and lives representing loci of social systems, models and actors.

While part of what makes ballroom interesting and compelling is this multiplex nature – including all the overlap and feedback between the various facets and aspects involved – there is also something to be gained, for analytical purposes, in trying to consider some of the more prominent elements individually. While different permutations could be equally viable, I will focus on the dominant elements of dance as spectacle, art and sport in Part II, as festival, celebration and ritual in Part III, and as costs, consequences and outcomes in Part IV. Before moving on to these topics, however, a little background on the history of competitive ballroom dance seems in order.

2 A BRIEF HISTORY OF BALLROOM

Beyond a general ancestry in the French court dances of the sixteenth century, this chapter highlights major dance organizations salient to contemporary dancesport and introduces the Blackpool Dance Festival, the longest running and most prestigious ballroom competition in the world. While the culture of ballroom, including its dressed uses of the body are the theme of this book, the overlapping histories and developments between these various ballroom organizations establish the very parameters of dancesport, sanctioning the competitions and championships where the standards of dancesport are asserted, demonstrated, contested and displayed. These organizations (and their histories) thus contextualize contemporary practices as the governing bodies for competition-related practices such as competitor eligibility and costuming restrictions. The overall culture of competitive ballroom represents socially constructed values and products that work through both mind and body alike, and the organizations discussed in this chapter play a powerful role in shaping the dancesport landscape.

EARLY ORIGINS

As noted in Chapter 1, ballroom dancing has never only been about dancing. Originating in Europe in the fifteenth century, and evolving alongside chivalry, ballroom dancing became increasingly popular in the French royal court, where ornate balls served as ideally conspicuous displays of royal ostentation and political power. Such balls linked class and dance, with dance masters being recognized as authorities and experts not just of dance but of proper social behaviour as well (Hammond 2000: 141–2). The late sixteenth century thus saw Italian dancing masters (then considered the best) regularly employed by the French monarchy (Hammond 2000: 144–5) with early books on dance, like Arbeau's *Orchesography* (1589), providing instruction on dance technique and social mores alike. Reaching its height in the Baroque court of King Louis XIV at the Palace of Versailles, this new style of dancing quickly spread throughout the European royal courts, especially after dance master

Raoul-Auger Feuillet developed and published a system of dance notation in 1700 (Aldrich 1998).

This linking of class and dance has proved to be an enduring image in ballroom dancing. Responding to early twentieth century concerns about the baseness of dance, for instance, in their 1914 instruction manual Vernon and Irene Castle note that 'dancing, properly executed, is neither vulgar nor immodest, but, on the contrary, the personification of refinement, grace, and modesty' (1914: 18). Also making explicit this connection between ballroom dance and proper manners, the subtitle to Helene Davis's 1923 *Guide to Dancing* reads 'Complete Guide to Dancing Ball Room Etiquette and Quadrille Call Book' and the first six sections (preface excluded) are about: Deportment; Etiquette for the Ballroom; Introductions; Asking a Lady to Dance; The Bow; and The Curtsy. It is in this tradition that ballroom training continues to be cast as an appropriate element of proper social rearing and development in many parts of Europe and, to a lesser extent, in the United States (for example, via cotillion programmes). Yet as both Picart (2006) and McMains (2006) have recently pointed out, the class associations of ballroom get manipulated for economic gain, with the cultural capital of ballroom 'class' being leveraged against the economic capital of dance students and patrons.

ORGANIZATIONS

While a distinct topic in its own right, the structural dynamics of ballroom dance provides the frame upon which contemporary ballroom standards and practices are draped. Enduring links between class and ballroom dance not withstanding, today's ballroom dancing is not that of the French royal court of the sixteenth century, and it is the history and development of various ballroom-related organizations that best situate contemporary dancesport. Accordingly, this chapter introduces prominent organizations (albeit far from comprehensively) that shaped the historical development of contemporary competitive ballroom dancing. Beyond their historical significance, the overlapping memberships, structures, regulations and influences of these groups continue to function as telling components of the social landscape of my fieldwork and of ballroom dance.

In large part, responding to a lack of any umbrella-level coordination and setting the foundation for the current shape of ballroom dancing, 'the first *Dancing Times* Conference was called for Wednesday, May 12th [1920], at the Grafton Galleries in London' (Richardson 1945: 41). Bringing ballroom teachers together for the first time (Richardson 1945: 45), it was at this event that M. Maurice proposed that 'the basic steps ... should be standardized' so that all teachers would teach the same and each dancer could combine the steps for themselves (Richardson 1945: 43), and Major Cecil Taylor suggested a committee be formed to decide what steps would be recognized (Richardson 1945: 44). This committee provided the first codification of acceptable steps on Sunday, 10 October 1920 at the second *Dancing Times* Conference, with a further committee issuing a report in October of 1921 that provided the first efforts to codify basic technique (Richardson 1945: 47). While this was the first attempt to coordinate the various teachers, there were other organizations already on the scene, the most significant of which was the Imperial Society of Teachers of Dancing (ISTD).

IMPERIAL SOCIETY OF TEACHERS OF DANCING

Originally formed at Hotel Cecil in Covent Garden as The Imperial Society of Dance Teachers on 25 July 1904, and with its current structure dating to 1924, the name was changed to the Imperial Society of Teachers of Dancing in 1925, and was incorporated in 1945.[1] Now an educational charity, the ISTD's chief objective is 'to educate the public in the art of dancing in all of its forms' (ISTD website), which it attempts to do via fourfold efforts to: promote knowledge of dance; maintain and improve teaching standards; qualify and examine teachers; and provide technique-based syllabi to train professional dancers (http://www.istd.org/about.html). Producing books, tapes, videos, a bi-monthly magazine and extensive website, the ISTD is divided into twelve divisions which test over 250,000 dancers per year. While only two of the twelve ISTD faculties focus on ballroom dancing (Modern Ballroom and Latin American Dance), these two divisions both play central roles in developing contemporary ballroom dancing.

The Ballroom branch of the ISTD was formed in 1924 and was responsible for codifying ballroom technique including terms familiar to today's ballroom competitors such as: 'body sway, contrary body movement, rise and fall, and foot-work' (Richardson 1945: 60). Perhaps of greatest significance was a committee of the ISTD's Modern Ballroom division, headed by Alex Moore, which produced the *Technique of Ballroom Dancing*, later updated editions of which are broadly considered to be the definitive norm for International Standard and it remains the most widely distributed dance manual. Examinations in technique for amateur dancers in the form of Bronze, Silver, and Gold 'Medal Tests' were adopted in 1932 (Richardson 1945: 99), and this structure is still in use throughout much of the ballroom world.

The Latin division of ballroom was a later addition, both to the English dance scene overall and to the ISTD. It was introduced into the English dance scene during the 1930s by the accomplished French dancer and teacher, Monsieur Pierre, who was involved in the formation of the initial Latin American Faculty of the ISTD in 1946.[2] Now only one of many international organizations offering examinations and instructor certification in ballroom dancing, ISTD certification is still often viewed as the golden standard carrying the most cultural capital. Given the translocal nature of dancesport, ISTD certification remains the most widely acclaimed and respected certification available, especially for International-style ballroom (Standard and Latin).

WORLD DANCE COUNCIL

Originally known as the International Council of Ballroom Dancing (ICBD), and later, until 1 June 2006, as the World Dance and Dance Sport Council (WD&DSC), the World Dance Council (WDC) was initially created by representatives from twelve countries in Edinburgh, Scotland, on 22 September 1950.[3] As the world governing body for professional Dance Sport, the WDC aims 'to encourage and promote dancing through its membership' (WDC website). It currently comprises over fifty member bodies – most of which are national governing bodies for professional dancesport – and is split into two sections, one dedicated to professional Dance Sport and one to dance schools and teachers. Perhaps the most notable role played by the WDC in the ballroom world today is the awarding of the Professional European and World Titles in Ballroom, Latin American, 10-Dance, Classic Showdance and South American Showdance. The 'awarding' of these championships is actually twofold since the WDC also decides which competitions will get to host the various professional European and world titles in a given year, long before these titles are eventually won by and then awarded to the competitors.

INTERNATIONAL DANCESPORT FEDERATION

The first international amateur dancers association, the Federation Internationale de Danse pour Amateurs (FIDA),[4] was formed between amateur associations from Austria, Czechoslovakia, Denmark, England, France, Germany, Holland, Switzerland and Yugoslavia in Prague on 10 December 1935, with the amateur associations from the Baltic States, Belgium, Canada, Italy and Norway all joining soon after.[5] This early organization was 'very active', and in conjunction with Germany's RPG,[6] organized the first official World Championship – between 15 countries – in 1936 in Bad Nauheim, Germany. The FIDA conducted 'all international competitions' until the start of World War II in 1939, when all such international activities ceased; the FIDA was reconstituted by Austria, Belgium, Denmark, France, Italy and Yugoslavia in July 1953 in Velden, Austria,[7] but as a result of internal conflicts and divergent agendas from the professionals in Austria, Germany and Switzerland, which first manifested in January 1956, the FIDA ceased to exist in 1964.

The instantiation of a second international amateur association, the International Council of Amateur Dancers (ICAD) took place on 12 May 1957, with initial members including Austria, Denmark, England, Germany, Italy, Switzerland, France and the Netherlands; these were soon followed by Belgium, Norway, Sweden and Yugoslavia. Unfortunately many of the schisms that led to the eventual demise of the FIDA also plagued the ICAD until Detlef Hegemann became president in 1965. Hegemann initiated efforts to set up a joint committee between the ICAD and the ICBD to act as a forum for resolving the ongoing tensions between amateurs and professionals, and such a committee was formed with the signing of the 'Bremen Agreement' (named for the German city where it was signed) on 3 October 1965.

In order to further the recognition of competitive ballroom dancing as a sport, especially amidst efforts to gain recognition from the International Olympic Committee (IOC), the ICAD changed its name to the International DanceSport Federation (IDSF) on 11 November 1990. Many national amateur organizations from Eastern Europe and Asia joined the IDSF in 1991, and this large influx helped add momentum to the IDSF's efforts for IOC recognition. In 1992 the IDSF formally applied for recognition by the IOC, receiving provisional recognition on 6 April 1995, and achieving full IOC recognition on 4 September 1997. As the largest ballroom organization in the world with eighty-four National Member Federations (fifty-nine recognized by their respective National Olympic Committees), the IDSF now represents more than 4 million dancers, and is generally recognized as the undisputed governing body for all international amateur dancesport competition.[8]

NATIONAL DANCE COUNCIL OF AMERICA

Originally the National Council of Dance Teachers Organization (NCDTO), the National Dance Council of America (NDCA) was formed as a non-profit educational organization in 1948.[9] Responsible for overseeing professional dancing throughout the United States, the NDCA became a member of WD&DSC (now WDC) in 1962, it started certifying scrutineers in 1973, signed the North American Treaty (of cooperation) with the Canadian Dance Teachers Association in 1981,[10] and became a member of the Asian-Pacific Council in 1986.[11] The NDCA is composed of full, affiliate and associate member organizations, and serves as the coordinating and oversight committee for professional dancing and dance instruction that sanctions and sets standards for professional competitions in America. Additionally, as the WDC-recognized body for governing professional ballroom activity in the United States, the NDCA sets the procedures and is responsible for selecting the dancers and adjudicators who represent the States at WDC-sanctioned professional world championships. Organizations with full NDCA membership are limited to 'professional dance teacher organizations' and have six votes in all NDCA matters, with affiliate membership status for other dance-related organizations (i.e. non-professional dance teacher organizations). Meetings of representative delegates from each member organization and the executive committee take place twice yearly in order 'to discuss affairs, programs and problems related to the dance industry' (www. ndca.org).

USA DANCE

Originally based in New York, the United States Amateur Ballroom Dancers Association (USABDA) was formed in 1965 to facilitate the inclusion of ballroom into the Olympic Games. Now renamed USA Dance, the group strives to promote and develop both social and competitive ballroom dancing.[12] The USABDA's first national elections took place in 1979; local chapters, the backbone of USABDA's current structure, were started in several regions over the following years as 'efforts were made to bring all other amateur ballroom dance organizations into USABDA' (USA Dance). In 1985 the USABDA was granted tax-exempt status by the Internal Revenue Service and, in 1987, unification efforts culminated in an election which placed all American amateurs under the same umbrella and USABDA was recognized by the IDSF as the official governing body for amateur ballroom dancing in the United States.

Following the 1997 recognition of the IDSF by the IOC, in 1999 the USABDA was recognized as an Affiliate member of the United States Olympic Committee (USOC), which also included recognition 'as the National Governing Body of DanceSport in the United States'. On the competitive front, USA Dance runs local, regional and national competitions, including the National Amateur DanceSport Championships where US representatives to the IDSF World DanceSport Championships and the World Games are chosen.[13] The organization is also highly active in promoting social dancing, and its greatest success has come in providing affordable access to both social and competitive dancing. With the stated aim of generating 'a pool of world-class DanceSport athletes that will dominate the international world of dance in the years ahead' (USA Dance), USA Dance's ambitious outreach endeavours, especially to younger dancers, has also sometimes seemed to contradict its goal 'for everyone to ballroom dance', since the same resources cannot be fully committed simultaneously to both competitive training and subsidies, on the one hand, and social outreach and expansion on the other. As a volunteer-driven not-for-profit organization, USA Dance has been faced with a difficult challenge in trying to balance both interests.

BLACKPOOL

The history of the Empress Ballroom at the Winter Gardens, Blackpool – the location of the most prestigious ballroom competition in the world – is central to the history of competitive ballroom dance.[14] The ballroom was completed in the summer of 1896, and during World War I the Winter Gardens were opened up to nearby naval and military personnel, with the Empress Ballroom itself being utilized by the Admiralty to support assembly of the R.33 airship in 1918. Ten years after the Treaty of Versailles, in 1929, extensive renovations approximated the current design. There is debate regarding the original idea for the Blackpool Dance Festival, although it is generally considered to have been the idea of either Harry Wood or Nelson Sharples. The first Blackpool Dance Festival took place during the Easter week of 1920, prior to the development and codification of Modern and Latin ballroom dancing, and was a 'contest' between the new sequence dances Waltz, Two Step and Foxtrot, with one danced each day and one selected 'winner' on the fourth day. Amateur competitions of waltz and foxtrot were introduced in 1923. Following a shift in management in 1927, there was a break in the regular running of the festival until 1929.

The first British Professional and Amateur Championships took place in 1931 based on 250 preliminary heats and around forty district finals danced around England to advance to the Amateur Championships. The following year, 1932, saw the introduction of formation team dancing (at the time termed 'pattern dancing'), with nearly 5,000 spectators present for a tie-breaking dance-off in the professional event (Richardson 1945: 95). Another turning point came in 1934 when the reigning Danish Amateur Champions, Ravn Petersen and Anna Peterson, became the first 'Continental' couple to compete at Blackpool; they were placed fourth (Richardson 1945: 100). By 1936, the number of non-English amateur competitors had swelled, although the Danes continued to lead the way with the then Danish Champions, Niels Boels Rasmussen and Lise Pehrssen, being placed third (Richardson 1945: 104). The skating system of judging was introduced in 1937, and the same system is now used in competitions worldwide. In the following year, 1938, the event attracted close to 7,000 spectators, and participants in the amateur contest included the reigning champions from France, Czechoslovakia and Germany, as well as the Danish Champions, who ended up as runners-up (Richardson 1945: 109).

During World War II a limited festival was held in 1940 prior to a five-year suspension for the remainder of the war. The festival returned in 1946 and continued to develop; by 1953 it played host to the North of England Amateur and Professional Championships, a Ballroom Formation Dancing Competition, the British Amateur and Professional Championships, and a Professional Exhibition Competition. Although there was a notable Danish involvement starting in 1934, the real foreign influx came in the 1950s with the provision of special seating for foreigners in the south balcony. This arrangement lasted until 1980, by which time the foreign participation far exceeded this configuration. International involvement continued to swell, and in recent years has involved the participation of over fifty countries. Also significant was the introduction of an Amateur Latin event in 1961 followed by a professional event in 1962, both of which became championships in 1964. The British National Championships were first held in 1975 as the British Closed Dance Festival – the name later being changed to the British Open Blackpool Dance Festival in response to the continuing influx of foreign competitors.

NOT JUST ALPHABET SOUP

The organizations introduced in this chapter represent the structure within which dancesport is enacted. More than just an 'alphabet soup', the plethora of acronyms – ISTD, WDC, IDSF, NDCA, USABDA and the like – have significance for ballroom competitors. If the organizations names and histories are irrelevant for most beginning competitors, the organizations themselves still determine the very nature of what constitutes competitive ballroom dance. Yet the acronyms themselves are more than just alphabet soup as most seasoned competitors are familiar with the intertwining and multilayered framework generated by the various organizations. The international scope of the ballroom framework since very early on is noteworthy, as is the centralizing role these organizations exert on ballroom standards and procedures. It is not by accident that the rumba I learn in San Diego is the same dance that others learn in Poland, South Africa, Russia and Australia.

To help put the subject matter of this chapter in perspective, Table 2.1 shows the current World, US and UK governing bodies for dancesport. The NDCA and BDC, are currently just two of the fifty national organizations with full WDC

Table 2.1   Governing Dancesport Bodies

	Professional	*Amateur*
World	World Dance Council (WDC)	International DanceSport Federation (IDSF)
USA	National Dance Council of America (NDCA)	USA Dance
UK	British Dance Council (BDC)	English Amateur Dancesport Association (EADA)

membership, while the EADA and USA Dance are just two of the seventy-six national organizations with full IDSF membership (fifty-nine of which had recognition from their respective National Olympic Committees).

Yet, if international ballroom organizations and competitions (of which Blackpool is pre-eminent) represent the framework within which contemporary ballroom dance continues to develop, they do not represent either the form or substance of ballroom dancing. For that we need to look at the dancing itself, at what is assessed and evaluated in dancesport, for the conceptual and evaluative matrices within which ballroom culture is lived. How dancesport is performed, the nature of ballroom competitions, and the costs, consequences and outcomes of ballroom life all take place in dialogue with the aesthetic values and standards of competitive ballroom dancing, so it is to the dancing itself that I turn in the next chapter.

3 JUDGING BALLROOM DANCE

Chapter 1 provided an overview of dancesport as it is danced today, including the different styles and divisions, the translocal nature of the ballroom culture and community, and some of the key sociopolitical dynamics of competitive ballroom dancing. Chapter 2 then provided a brief history of ballroom dance, including some of the key governing organizations through which it developed. As important as this background and context are, however, they do not describe the actual practices and qualities being assessed in the dancing itself – they are not what it is that is actually being judged in competitive ballroom dancing. What is being judged matters; not just for those who are competing, but also for understanding the aesthetics, values and standards that undergird the practices of dancesport. Ideas about costuming, dress and bodies within the competitive ballroom world (the topics of this book) matter, and can only be fully appreciated within the context of the aesthetic standards that contextualize and frame competitive ballroom dancing.

WHAT IS BEING ASSESSED AND EVALUATED?

So what are judges actually looking at and evaluating in ballroom competitions? In his excellent on-line article *How a Dance Competition is Judged* (1996), Dan Radler mentions: (1) posture; (2) timing; (3) line; (4) hold; (5) poise; (6) togetherness; (7) musicality and expression; (8) presentation; (9) power; (10) foot and leg action; (11) shape; (12) lead and follow; (13) floor craft; and (14) intangibles. While all of these variables may be 'givens' among those with sufficient dancesport experience, those less familiar with the ballroom scene often fail to recognize these wide-ranging variables factoring into judges' assessments. At one major competition, for instance, the friends and family of a competing couple, seated in front of me, proved to be entirely unaware of the many dynamics assessed and involved in judges' marks. When their couple did not place highly, the group verbalized their feelings that the judging was 'clearly rigged', attributing this bias to their couple's not being 'circuit regulars'. Yet speaking with these people made it quite evident that they were unfamiliar with the myriad variables involved. When I mentioned items such as foot placement and foot pressure, their surprised response was: 'They [the judges] look at such things?'[1]

POSTURE

Improving both 'balance and control' posture makes dancers 'look elegant and exude confidence' (Radler 1996). This helps dancers not only to move in a visually pleasing manner, but also to look the part while standing still. Most people can rotate in place in a circle, but it is the balance, control and poise with which they do it – all of which are posture-based, that helps to set the dancer apart from the non-dancer.[2] Perhaps the most striking display I saw of this dynamic took place on my first visit to Blackpool in May 2003. Never having been to Blackpool before, I took the train up from London the day before in order to get 'the lay of the land'. After settling myself in at the bed and breakfast where I was staying, I went for a walk to get my bearings, see what the area was like, and generally orient myself with the competition venue and surroundings. Nothing really stood out in my mind as I got the sense of a somewhat quaint resort town, now past its prime.

All of that changed the very next day, however, as thousands of ballroom competitors from around the world arrived in Blackpool, and literally overnight almost everyone in the vicinity of the Winter Gardens – the facility where the competition is held – seemed to have perfect posture. Far from being a minor and hardly noted detail, the contrast in just under twenty-four hours was as striking as it was remarkable. Where on the previous day the teenagers queuing in front of me for pizza slouched, settling heavily down into one hip, the dancesport teenagers in line the very next day stood straight, tall and elongated, all fully at ease and engaged in playful banter with their peers while waiting to be seated. Where on the first day the adults sitting on the outdoor benches had slightly rounded shoulders and mildly dropped chins, the next day the dancesport adults seated on the outdoor benches all sat straight and erect, with their chins parallel to the ground and not tilted down towards it. Of course not all the dancers at Blackpool had perfect posture, and some dancers clearly have much better posture than others. Yet the relative impression of perfect posture drastically stood out to me, especially in contrast to the regular English townspeople of the proceeding day.[3]

Dancers are not, of course, born with superior posture, but in the course of learning ballroom dancing the alignment of one's body 'blocks' – head, shoulders, torso and hips – are mechanical fundamentals. Furthermore, the stacked alignment of these elements is trained, drilled and practised, not as static posing but as a process of active alignment in order to facilitate proper ballroom movement. Dancers are trained to move around their spines as it were, using the spine as a cylindrical fulcrum *around which* to twist and turn without distorting its vertical alignment. While some dancers' tricks and posed 'lines' may briefly violate this principle, it is only briefly and specifically as a point of contrast. Similarly, almost all tilting and bending is, when carefully analysed, actually movement that hinges at dancers' knees or hips without actually disrupting spinal alignment. Perhaps no dance better showcases dancers' posture in motion than the quickstep, as shown in Figure 3.1,

3.1. Posture in Motion – as danced by World and Blackpool Professional Standard Finalists Dominico Soale and Gioia Cerosoli doing the quickstep at the 2005 Embassy Ball Dancesport Championships, Irvine, CA (then World and Blackpool Amateur Standard Champions). ©2005 Jonathan S. Marion

where even when airborne, and progressing at great velocity, proper posture is maintained throughout.

TIMING

Timing matters simply because dancesport (like most forms of dance) is about bodily movement in relation to sound, rhythm and music. As such, movement to music that does not correspond to ballroom conventions is visually and conceptually jarring to those familiar with the genre. How someone moves in relation to the music is an inherent part of what marks a dance – say, a rumba – and differentiates it from another, such as a mambo. The prescribed coordination of movement to music is a key ballroom aesthetic, an integral element of judgement and evaluation.

Importantly, timing can be either a simple or a complex element to be judged. Not a lot of expertise is needed to differentiate between dancers completely off-time versus others who are on-time. But not all dancers who are 'on-time' accomplish this to the same extent. A powerful example was presented to me when I asked Fraser, one of the top Latin coaches in the world, why he had placed the reigning world champion third at a specific competition. His response was as straightforward as it was telling: 'Sure he danced great', I was told, 'but he used the same rhythm the entire time, whereas Kent used all three timings'.[4] If a coach respected worldwide can criticize the timing of a reigning world champion, it almost goes without saying that timing is not a simple 'right versus wrong' factor for evaluating dancesport.[5]

LINE

Related to but different from posture, line references the stretch and extension from toe to head to fingertips. Line is not just the upright carriage of posture; it includes the extension of arms and hands, legs and feet, in the various pictures produced in dancing. Is a dancer's arm extended, but their wrist and hand awkwardly dropped, needlessly disrupting the line of their arm? Does a dancer perform a kick, but without toes pointed to properly extend the leg line through the foot? Such physically small yet visually powerful elements are 'line'. Note, for example, how Anna points her foot to extend the line of her left leg; and how Jonathan makes a perfectly horizontal line with his arms and shoulders in the left frame of Figure 3.2. Similarly, the right frame

3.2. Examples of 'line' in International Latin – as danced by Professional Latin competitors Jonathan Roberts and Anna Trebunskaya (both of *Dancing with the Stars* in the US) at the 2004 Emerald Ball Dancesport Championships, Los Angeles, CA. ©2004 Jonathan S. Marion

3.3. Example of 'line' in American Smooth – as danced by US Professional Smooth finalists Hunter and Maria Johnson at the 2004 United States DanceSport Championships, Hollywood Beach, FL. ©2004 Jonathan S. Marion

captures how Anna pushes and elongates all the way through her toes in extending her body into Jonathan as he twists and compresses into a complementary line.

The same dynamics are implicated in all the different ballroom styles, as illustrated in Figure 3.3. Note, for instance, the extension from Maria's right foot, on the floor, all the way through her pointed left toe, and the extension of her right arm and wrist, in opposition to her left arm connection with Hunter. Similarly, note the 'X'-like shaping of Hunter's body, as he extends from his right foot through his pointed left fingers and the stretch of his body from his left toe through his right arm connection with Maria. Also note how, as a couple, Hunter and Maria generate several other sets of common lines: there is an almost seamless line starting with the point of Hunter's left toe and extending all the way, through his connection with Maria, and out through the extension of her right arm and wrist; the curve of Maria's and Hunter's backs closely parallel each other; and the extension from Hunter's right foot through his left hand provides a rough approximation of Maria's extended leg line.

HOLD

Hold is the visual aspect of the dancers' frame. The same dropped shoulders that compromise the communicative efficiency of the dancers' frame also breaks the shape of their hold and bodily positioning relative to one another. Even with proper posture and good line, an improper hold in closed dance position disrupts the continuity of a couple's silhouette, thus generating a less pleasant and 'messier' appearance and shape.[6] Proper hold maintains the frame between partners even as their combined shapes twist, tilt, rotate and shape for added visual impact.

POISE

For Radler (1996), poise refers to 'the stretch of the woman's body upwards and outwards and leftwards into the man's right arm to achieve balance and connection with his frame, as well as to project outwards to the audience'. This dynamic is clearly seen in the two frames of Figure 3.4. The left frame, provides a full body perspective and illustrates how Katusha's stretch 'up and out' to her left fills her back into Jonathan's right hand at the same time as it brings her ribs and torso into even greater contact and compression with his body, thereby enhancing their ability to move and function as a unit on the dance floor. The right frame provides a tighter depiction of proper poise, showing how Anna's 'up and out' stretch to her left fills

3.4. Examples of 'poise' – as danced by US National Professional Standard Champions, and World and Blackpool Professional Standard finalists Jonathan Wilkinson and Katusha Demidova at the 2006 USDSC, Hollywood Beach, FL (left); and US Professional Standard finalists and World and Blackpool Professional Standard finalists Victor Fung and Anna Mikhed at the 2005 Emerald Ball Dancesport Championships, Los Angeles, CA. ©2005 and 2006 Jonathan S. Marion

the frame provided by Victor's right arm while generating closer contact, connection and compression through their torsos.

From what I have seen in the ballroom world, however, I think that there is also a broader understanding and usage of poise – in practice even if not in formalized definition – that concerns a certain bearing, calmness and composure in all situations and at all times. One prominent and common example of this dynamic concerns collisions on the competition floor. What of the person who is collided with through no fault of their own?[7] The fact that they were involved in this collision does not affect them, in itself, but how they handle themselves in response to such a collision matters greatly. The couple that gets flustered and lets the collision disrupt their performance exhibits poor poise, whereas the competitor who recovers quickly and continues with aplomb – as if nothing untoward had happened – exhibits excellent poise. All other factors being equal in the two couples' dancing, the couple demonstrating the better poise in this manner gains the edge in the judges' eyes by demonstrating better command of themselves and their dancing.

Even when the competing itself is over, however, poise can still factor into a dancer's long-term success, as the case of amateur competitor Francesca makes all too clear. When Francesca was announced in second place at a national competition she had expected to win, she did little to hide her disgust with her placing as she walked across the floor to accept her position and stood in the line-up as the runner-up. Her lack of poise in this situation has cost Francesca greatly as, ever since, she has consistently been placed lower than her dancing would seem to merit according to both a number of judges as well as several of her competitive peers.

TOGETHERNESS

Togetherness refers to the integration of movement, action, focus and feeling between partners. More than just the lack of gapping in the connection between leader and follower, togetherness also refers to partners' attention to and focus on each other. Even when dancing the same routines, with perfect timing and perfect technique, partners may individually look like great dancers but lack the appearance of a partnership – in other words, they just look like exceptional dancers dancing next to each other but without the unity of a couple At first blush the non-dancer might think 'but they aren't even looking at each other!,' while the more seasoned ballroom insider sees something quite different, recognizing an almost palpable unity and melding of the dancers' actions and movements and the mutual focus and feeling of their dancing. Togetherness then is a shared focus between partners and a supreme awareness of each other, both in relation to one another as partners and to themselves as a partnership – a mutually constituted unit of ballroom dancing. Ultimately, the thousands of hours of floor time invested in lessons and practices are as much about developing togetherness as they are about the other facets of dance factoring into judges' evaluations.

MUSICALITY AND EXPRESSION

More than just timing (but upon which it is built), musicality involves characterizing music through movement. Every song sounds different and evokes different feelings and moods, so that the dancer who dances in exactly the same way regardless of the song fails to demonstrate musicality, no matter how technically perfect his or her movement may be. Musicality starts with choreography that matches musical phrasings, but goes much further than this, playing on the particular flavour and accents of any given piece of music. Closely related to such musicality is expression – the ability of a dancer to use their body, in conjunction with the music, in a manner that accentuates the character of each dance. By way of description, Radler provides the following three examples of such musicality and expression: 'for instance, in foxtrot, the stealing of time from one step to allow another to hover; or a quick speed of turn in an otherwise slow rumba; or the snap of a head to suddenly freeze and then melt into slowness in tango' (1996).

PRESENTATION

More than image alone, presentation involves the flavour which competitors project through their dancing to audience members and judges alike. Do the competitors make their dance look effortless or difficult? Do they make it look as though they enjoy dancing? Do they appear comfortable and confident on the dance floor? These are the types of elements which, although far too many and too difficult to delineate specifically, an observer can still easily recognize and evaluate in a competitor's dancing. By way of example, the shots of Steven and Eulia in Figure 3.5 come from the 2004 US Professional National Smooth Championship. The sheer ease, enjoyment, joy and exuberance expressed here give no hint that this event – their national title competition – was taking place on a small floor in a makeshift ballroom. The hotel had just reopened after hurricane Frances (with hurricane Ivan on the way) and, as a result, the main stadium and competition floor had not yet been set up.

POWER

Power is the energy *in* a dancer's movement; not the energy expended in executing that movement. Far from muscular exertion, power is primarily built through proper technique. Most obvious as speed, power also shows up in longer strides in the moving dances. To illustrate the proper harnessing and channelling of energy, Radler comments: 'Powerful movement is an asset in waltz or foxtrot, but only if it is channeled into the correct swing of the body, and not just by taking big steps' (1996). Figure 3.6 shows exactly the dynamic that Radler has in mind, as it is clearly the swing of William and Allesandra's bodies that are generating their abundantly evident power, not their steps – as the side-by-side positioning of each of their feet makes abundantly clear.

3.5. Presentation in action (fun on the floor) – as danced by US National Professional Smooth finalists Steven Dougherty and Eulia Baranovsky at the 2004 United States DanceSport Championships, Hollywood beach, FL. ©2004 Jonathan S. Marion

FOOT AND LEG ACTION

Foot and leg action are, perhaps, among the most opaque judging criteria to those who are non-dancers or are just beginning dancers. Where the untrained eye may decide that a certain dancer's leg movements look 'better' to them, but often cannot pinpoint how or why, the knowledgeable dancer quickly takes note of myriad elements including: turned out or parallel foot placements depending on the dance; use of the inside edge of the foot in striding; pointing the foot onto the outside edge during a line; taking toe leads in the Latin and Rhythm dances but heel leads in the standard and smooth dances; proper use of ankle rise; and the proper articulation of toes, ankles, knees and hips. Although really best appreciated in the dynamic of movement, the quality of Ieveta's and Yulia's foot and leg use and action are still evident in Figure 3.7, particularly in the visible foot pressure maintained into the floor through the full extension of leg, foot and ankle.

SHAPE

Shape is actually a combination of two elements. First, shape is concerned with the visual contours characteristic of each dance, and it is in this way that many

3.6. Power in action – as danced by World and Blackpool Professional Standard Finalists William Pino and Alessandra Buchiarelli at the 2005 Blackpool British Open Championships, Blackpool, England. ©2005 Jonathan S. Marion

dancers comment on being able to look at and 'tell right away what dance they are doing based on the shapes of their arms and legs'. Radler provides a more specific example of exactly this element, asking: 'in Paso Doble does the man create the visual appearance of maneuvering his cape? Does the lady simulate the billowing flow of the cape through space?' (Radler 1996). The other aspect of shape concerns the functional contouring of the dancers' bodies needed to facilitate proper dancing. Again providing a specific example, Radler provides an illustrative question, asking: 'in foxtrot, does the man use the appropriate shape on outside partner steps to enable body contact to be maintained?' (Radler 1996). Where the ballroom outsider might only see a pleasing line (or not, depending on their personal tastes), a quick glimpse (be it in person, photograph or video) is typically enough for the ballroom insider to determine what dance a couple is executing.

Where the ballroom outsider might only see a pleasing line, the briefest glimpse at Figure 3.8 is enough for the ballroom insider to know that these couples are dancing a Samba and Paso Doble respectively. Paul and Olga's 'Shadow Samba Roll' (Figure 3.8, left), and Eugene and Maria's flamenco-inspired Paso Doble element (right) are

3.7. Foot use – as danced by World Professional 10-Dance Vice Champions, Gherman Mustuc and Iveta Lukosiute, practising at the 2005 United States DanceSport Championships, Hollywood beach, FL (left); and World and Blackpool Professional Latin Finalist, and US Professional Latin Champion, Yulia Zagoruychenko at the 2006 United States DanceSport Championships, Hollywood beach, FL (right). ©2006 Jonathan S. Marion

each unmistakable 'shapes' to those familiar with dancesport. This obvious depiction is Radler's first use of 'shape', while his second – that of functional shape – is visible in Paul's shaping, which invites and allows Olga to maintain body contact without stepping on or into him as they both progress back towards their right sides while in rotation towards their left sides.

LEAD AND FOLLOW

Proper leading and following is based on clear communication being provided by the leader at the appropriate time and responsive execution on the part of the follower. More specifically, lead and follow is the information being provided by the leader and being received by the follower. As Radler asks, is it the leader's body that is requesting certain actions from the follower, or is the leader only using hands and arms in attempting to communicate what is wanted? Similarly, is the follower sensitive and responsive to the leader's movements and suggestions, or is extra assistance required of the leader? More than any other judged element, lead and follow is what differentiates partnered dancing from all other genres of dance.

3.8. Examples of Latin 'shape' – US and British Professional Latin National Finalists, Paul Richardson and Olga Rodionova, dancing a "Samba Roll" in shadow position at the 2005 British Open Championships, Blackpool, England (left); US Amateur National Latin National Champions, and World and Blackpool Amateur Latin Finalists, Eugene Katsevman and Maria Manusova demonstrating the flamenco inspired elements of the Paso Doble at the 2005 British Open Championships, Blackpool, England (right). ©2005 Jonathan S. Marion

FLOORCRAFT

Floorcraft is a couple's ability to use the floor effectively and execute their dancing in 'traffic'– that is, among other dancers, including following the established counterclockwise 'line of dance' around the floor for the travelling dances (all Standard and Smooth dances, plus Samba and Paso Doble from the Latin programme). As Radler relates, proper floorcraft is demonstrated both in the ability to avoid collisions but also in the ability to continue the flow of one's dance even when blocked by other couples. I do, however, disagree with Radler's suggestion that good floorcraft demonstrates choreographic command. Many lower-level competitors, for example, compete without set choreography, simply leading and following their limited repertoire of syllabus figures. And, in a related vein, because social ballroom dances almost always involve larger numbers of couples on the floor and of more disparate levels, floorcraft can be all the more important in these situations. Similarly, whether it is in salsa, swing, or Argentine tango – where most of the dancing is social lead and follow – floorcraft is critical. What Radler does suggest, and which in some ways actually proves my point, is that floorcraft demonstrates 'the ability of the man to choose and lead figures extrinsic to their usual work when the necessity presents itself'.

INTANGIBLES

In describing the last of his variables, 'intangibles', Radler includes 'basically whether they look like "dancers"'. While not specified in Radler's article, it is important to realize that such evaluations come into play long before dancers have started dancing. At the very least, judges start to evaluate the couples as soon as they step onto the floor. Even more commonly, judges will begin to evaluate dancers in their vicinity, and it is neither uncommon nor unlikely that a judge would start to make an assessment as soon as a competitor enters the ballroom. Is a dancer sitting in a slovenly way at a table? Are the dancers late onto the floor because they had not got their shoes on? Do dancers seem disorganized as they are getting ready? Are partners fighting as they rehearse on the side? Any of these things will start to influence a judge's assessment, suggesting – as they do – a lack of professionalism, confidence and competence.

A contrasting image can be made by the dancer behaving in a calm and un-ruffled manner before taking the floor, and this can be achieved in a number of ways. Perhaps the dancer is brushing his shoes, making last-minute grooming adjust-ments, stretching or quietly rehearsing in a very workmanlike manner? Perhaps she is conversing with fellow competitors in a seemingly relaxed manner? Perhaps partners are standing with their heads down, in quiet meditation or prayer? Good or bad, judges are likely to notice such elements and start forming an opinion before the dancers take to the floor.

None of this means that judges have (necessarily) made any decisions yet. But has a couple caught the judges' attention already, and if so, in what manner? How is a judge likely to proceed, especially with numerous couples on the floor, all of whom need to be assessed and evaluated in some 90 seconds? In large competitions couples are split into multiple 'heats' (also known as 'rounds') in order to provide sufficient space to dance, as well as a chance for the judges to assess each couple. Competitions such as Blackpool can have over 300 couples in the most popular events, requiring an entire morning of heats just to complete the first preliminary round. Even at much smaller events there may not be enough time to assess the actual dancing of everyone on the floor. If, for instance, there are twelve couples in a heat (which is common), 90 seconds of music may mean that only seven seconds are available for each couple to be examined by each judge. Yet this is not what earlier rounds are really about. Earlier rounds ask for judges to recall those dancers who they want to see advanced into the next round, when they can take a closer look. Good dancing can certainly persuade a judge, but it is rarely quite so clear or simple. Perhaps there are too many couples on the floor to assess in the allotted time? Or perhaps a couple's position on the floor makes them hard to see? This is where having caught a judge's attention in a positive manner can work to dancers' advantage. Whether the judge actively looks for them on the floor or 'passes' them on to the next round – where supposedly a closer look can be taken – this is where a positive pre-dance impression can pay telling dividends.

A final and significant point is that there is no weighted formula for the judging criteria discussed in this chapter. Instead, each judge's marks reflect his or her subjective prioritization of the variables involved. For many, this situation calls into question the legitimacy of ballroom 'judging', a topic discussed at greater length in Chapter 5 which considers ballroom as sport.

PART II
PERFORMING DANCESPORT

4 BALLROOM AS SPECTACLE

As the photographs in Chapter 3 begin to suggest, in many ways the dancesport world is quite quintessentially 'the society of the spectacle' (Baudelaire 1964). Unlike social ballroom, dancesport is meant to be displayed. Dancesport's performance of social dance is far from social dancing itself as McMains has noted (2006). Big shapes, lines and easily 'readable' timing therefore become important as competitors' movements and actions need to be clear to judges and spectators fifty or more feet away. Tight-fitting clothing, open backs and bare legs help make body actions visible, just as performance make-up is intended to design a beyond-everyday look that shows well under bright stage lighting. While many competitors wear 'cover-ups' until it is their time to dance – precisely to make the biggest impact with the unveiling of their costumes – there are always enough dancers coming and going to create a moving scatter of colour, cut and texture. Adding to the spectacular nature of dancesport, these points of fast-moving colour are offset against spectators' attire ranging from edgy looks and leather to the classiest of evening gowns and tuxedos (further discussed below and in Chapter 9).

Being noticed amongst this ongoing visual display is tantamount to success in competitive dancing since audiences do not cheer and judges do not mark couples that go unnoticed or fail to hold attention. The couple that dances in a small, 'timid', compact manner suitable to a social situation might not even be noted if 'lost' in the middle of the floor among a multitude of powerfully active couples. Likewise, conditions vary, and a dancer's darkly coloured dress can become a liability in a dark ballroom with a dark-coloured floor, whereas it would have easily stood out in a bright ballroom against a light-coloured floor. Being noticed thus becomes the first priority of competitive dancing – with grooming, choreography and costuming all intended to help couples stand out. Dancers' hair cuts, hair colour, make-up and costume choices are all important. Ruffles, fringes and feathers in an unending variation of colours, cuts and fabrics – almost always encrusted with an abundance of rhinestones in a dizzying array of patterns and colours – are par for the course, and all for the express purpose of drawing notice and attention from both judges and spectators alike.

Bright lights, often in mixtures of blue, red and white illuminate the floor, and glint brightly off the rhinestones, sequins and metallic threads of competitors' costumes. The flash, sparkle, colour and movement of competitors in motion stands out all the more vividly as the lighting around the rest of the room is typically dimmed during competition. Adding to this atmosphere is an MC[1] behind a podium on a raised dais, upon which a scrutineer[2] and DJ are also typically located. The judges forming the panel for each event stand around the periphery of the competition floor dressed in suits, tuxedos or elegant gowns, with pens and clipboards in hand,[3] as the judges not on the active panel typically sit at especially reserved tables. Competitors in the next event line up in the 'on-deck' area[4] according to numerical order, waiting their turn. Those competing later may be warming-up or practising beside the on-deck area, in the back of the room or in a nearby hallway. Up until the final, couples are called by numbers pinned to the gentleman's back, and in the final round couples may be called out by name as well, sometimes with each dancing a brief 30-second introductory dance. After the penultimate dance of their event (Bolero in Rhythm, Foxtrot in Smooth and Standard, and Paso Doble in Latin), the finalists are again often introduced by name, each couple stepping forward and taking a bow as their names are called.

In the US the majority of competitions are financially driven by the pro–am circuit of students dancing with a professional partner (typically their teacher). Almost all the competition venues are elegant hotels and resorts, with the competition events themselves taking place in what are, at times, quite elegantly appointed ballrooms – Figure 4.1 illustrating a typical scene. While the afternoon sessions are often more casual affairs with not too many audience members, aside from competitors, in-structors, family, and friends, the evening sessions tend to be much more formal with fresh white tablecloths (changed since the afternoon session), centrepieces on all the tables around the room, and cushioned chairs lined up facing the ballroom floor. If some of the European competitions are less elegant, more sportsmanlike affairs – taking place in athletic halls and the like – other European events are the

4.1. IDSF Grand Slam (Standard) – Part of the IDSF's premiere series, drawing a large field and diverse international field of competitors showcasing the top amateur dancers in the world, at the 2004 USDSC in Hollywood Beach, FL. ©2004 Jonathan S. Marion

4.2. Empress Ballroom at the Winter Gardens – 2005 Blackpool Professional Latin finalists receiving a standing ovation, seen here facing the ground floor, first balcony and second balcony of the ballroom's west promenade. ©2005 Jonathan S. Marion

epitome of class and distinction, such as: 'the International',[5] for which the quarter-final, semi-final and final rounds are danced in London's Royal Albert Hall; the Star,[6] which was danced in the fresco-covered ballroom of the Blackpool Tower; and the British Open, which is danced in the Empress Ballroom of the Blackpool Winter Gardens (Figure 4.2) and where the evening sessions are danced to a live band.

Adding to the spectacle of the competitive ballroom, multiple couples are dancing their routines simultaneously. Unlike performance numbers – with a clear focus on one couple (as seen in figure-skating) or a coordinated routine between a larger group of dancers – there is something different happening wherever one looks on the floor during a competition. Since there is no coordination in choreography between competitors, the routines that each couple have meticulously crafted and practised can be disrupted in an instant by the movement and positioning of others on the floor (Figure 4.3). And, since there is no coordination in costuming between competitors, that 'great new white dress', which was meant to stand out on a traditionally darker ballroom floor,[7] may backfire if five of the six finalists have the same idea.

Apart from the lack of coordination in costuming and choreography between competitors, each venue is also different so there can be many unknowns for potential competitors. What size will the floor be and how 'fast' or 'slow'?[8] How bright or dark will the lighting and the ballroom be? Are there practice facilities available? Will there be time to practice on the competition floor in advance, and if so, when? How many other couples will one be dancing against, and which ones? What music will be played for each dance in each round?

While each of these variables may not seem like the stuff of spectacle on its own, taken together they amplify the here-and-now/in-the-moment energy of ballroom

4.3. Where do I look? – Multiple couples dancing their routines simultaneously at the 2007 Blackpool Dance Festival. ©2007 Jonathan S. Marion

competitions. Different from dance performances in known settings (and to known music), there is always something of an 'anything can happen' feel and dynamic to dancesport. Even the best dancing is subject to collisions, accidents and injuries on the floor – and not just bumps and bruises. Although thankfully infrequent, slipped kneecaps, concussions and scalp wounds requiring more than a few stitches at the nearest emergency room are inevitable over a period of time, especially when linked to the lack of systematic coordination between competitors actively vying for yet-to-be-determined outcomes; but all these factors contribute to the mix of dynamic sights and sounds that make up the spectacle of competitive ballroom dance.

THE 'MYTHIC' IN DANCE

Just as Barthes says of wrestling, ballroom competitions can be seen as 'the spectacle of excess' (1957: 15). It is not only the thousands upon thousands of dollars spent in costuming, shoes, rhinestones and feathers, or even the stage-style lighting and music, which are in excess, but the very movements, postures and facial expressions of the dancers as they dance. In their need to stand out from across a crowded floor, it is in their on-floor movement and performance that ballroom dancers – like the wrestlers for Barthes – often 'offer excessive gestures, exploited to the limit of their meaning' (1957: 16).[9] To assume that it is only in motion that dancers express their dance would be a mistake, however, as their costuming – the explicit topic of Chapter 8 – is itself communicative of the underlying 'mythology'.

To translate Barthes into the ballroom again, his observation that 'as soon as the adversaries are in the ring, the public is overwhelmed with the obviousness of their roles' (1957: 17) is equally applicable just by substituting 'on the floor' for 'in the ring'. Admittedly there are differences as dancers are less sequestered from the audience than wrestlers are, but the underlying idea holds true: as dancers step onto the floor, their costuming already informs the audience of their roles. This 'informing', however, is not done in a subtle way. Tuxedos, full-length ball gowns, short dresses with deeply plunging necklines, and suchlike, provide overwhelmingly obvious messages about gender roles and types, just as dancers' physiques and posture provide overwhelmingly obvious messages about physical grace and ease. There should be no doubt, then, that 'each physical type expresses to excess the part which has been assigned to the contestant' (Barthes 1957: 17).[10] While it is thus true that the dancers' dressed body, like the wrestlers' physique, 'therefore constitutes a basic sign' (Barthes 1957: 18), this is still only part of the picture.

Just as it is the wrestlers who are wrestling, not their audience, so too it is the dancers who are dancing and not their audience. This is important because, although audience members may dance themselves, it is not the *act* of dancing itself that they are participating in as spectators. Certainly their own experiences with dancing may deepen their appreciation and their ability to empathize with the feel of dancing, but their primary experience of dance, as an audience member, is not of dancing – it is of the image of dancing. As such, I find Barthes' assertion (made in reference to wrestling) fully applicable for ballroom: 'what the public wants is *the image* of passion, not passion itself' (1957: 18; emphasis added). The ballroom audience wants to *see* the flirtation between partners in their cha cha and the romance between them in their rumba, their elegance in their waltz and their passion in their tango. The point here is that it is what the dancers convey and what the audience *sees in the dancing* that matters – not the reality of flirtation, romance, elegance or passion between dance partners. It is this dynamic 'voluntary ostentation of the spectacle' (Barthes 1957: 19) that audience members often watch for, notice and care about *as* audience members, and why audience opinions and tastes may, at times, clash with the results handed down by the judges.

THE GLAMOUR OF IT ALL

Thus, much of the mythic in dance rests on the glamour of it – the images it conjures and evokes. 'Glamour', as Wilson notes, 'is the result of work and effort – artfully concealed of course' (2007: 100), and this is both its boon and its bane within dancesport. Because 'glamour depends on what is withheld, on secrecy, hints, and the hidden' (Wilson 2007: 100), the dancer who shows the extent of their efforts fails to move us. Similarly, much of dancesport's glamour hinges on its costuming. The tuxedo and ball gown of a Standard couple suggest refinement, social stature, reserve, class and comportment seemingly at odds with the immense physical (and emotional) efforts and energies expended in ballroom competition. As Bolin has noted, for instance, 'restrictive clothing, such as ... *ankle-length dresses, high heels* along with sanctions against the exposure of particular body surfaces has historically imprisoned women's bodies and prevented hem from exploring extra-domestic options such as exercise and athletics' (1998: 191; emphasis added); yet in dancesport it is ankle-length dresses (in Smooth and Standard) and high heels that are the vehicle for women's physical exertion and athleticism. The connotations of dancesport costuming thus recruit the myth of ease and effortlessness, building dancesport's glamour by belying the underlying effort.

In noting that 'the elitism of glamour sends a message that we cannot all be glamorous. We can aspire to, but we will never reach the stars', Wilson (2007: 100) identifies the promise and the cost of ballroom glamour. The idealized image of ballroom can be inspirational, engaging spectators' attention and driving dancers to aspire to greater and greater heights. Such mythic inspiration collapses if 'the stars' are ever reached, and it is this ever-out-of reach dynamic of glamour that McMains (2006) casts as the economic con-game driving the US dancesport industry.[11] Certainly false promises are made in the name of sales, and within certain circles emotionally manipulative sales tactics are central elements of instructors' training. Yet the physical ease, social grace, improved athleticism and social opportunities offered up by the dancesport industry are not unachievable – only unrealizable at this mythic level insofar as reality is always grittier than idealized imagery. Because most spectators are dancers themselves (albeit across widely different levels), there is more of what Coleridge (1817) so famously phrased 'the willing suspension of disbelief for the moment, which constitutes poetic faith'.

Thus, while there is admittedly little glamour in waking at 5 a.m. for a hair appointment and then dancing for hours in costuming already soaked with sweat by 9 a.m., the glamour is not in the execution but in the performance and presentation. Completely wet-costumed or not, from the edge of the floor the competitor may still look like a princess, evoking flights of fancy and inspiring the efforts of others. More importantly, ballroom is danced *as one's self*, meaning that one's ballroom costume is not about performing as someone else, but as a more glamorous facet of *self*. 'Glamour' as Wilson notes, 'is about the individual' (2007: 105). Thus, whether it is the newcomer who only sees and experiences the allure, or the experienced competitor who appreciates the efforts underlying execution, what looks glamorous, *is* glamorous (even if only in the viewing). The glamour is in the spectacle of it all – in the movement, swirl, sparkle and shine of ballroom dancing.

SPECTACLE WRIT SMALL

The spectacle-driven facet of competitive ballroom is not, however, solely confined to the level of grand-scale 'mythic' performances and competitions. Smaller, day-to-day and personal-level conduct, practices and interactions fall under this same umbrella. Many individual dancers, couples and studios go out of their way to showcase and feature their successes. And, while hard earned results are important substantive credentials, both results and popularity confer an element of personal spectacle-like status as well. Many of the more elite dancers are thus the subjects of varying degrees of hero-worship, despite the fact that many are actually very humble and generous with their time. At the 2005 USDSC, for instance, I was standing near Bob Powers, the thirteen-times US National Professional Rhythm Champion, when two younger women approached him to express what great fans they were. Despite Bob's exceedingly gracious manner, the almost tongue-tied demeanour of these two women is far from exceptional as many newcomers to the competitive scene find personal heroes among their favourite dancers.

Individual dancers and coaches of past and present thus emerge as spectacles-writ-small in many instances, with people flocking to particular studio workshops or competition venues in order to see 'X'. Many dancers downplay these 'heroesque' images, leaving their dance-based status unannounced among those who might not know but would clearly be impressed if they did know. Other dancers, however, play up their spectacle status via various forms of conspicuousness and ostentation. Yet, even for those dancers who do not make a point of being personal spectacles, a certain element of personal recognition and impression is an important element of dancers' sociocultural/sociopolitical progress and promotion. Regarding professional ballet dancers, Wulff notes that 'transnational experience and exposure are regarded as desirable for dancers' development and reputation' (1998: 40), and this is equally true in dancesport. 'Being seen', one of the important yet intangible judging criteria discussed in Chapter 3, depends on competitors' conspicuous presence across a wide-ranging circuit of competitions and events.

RETIREMENTS

It is in a related vein that, beyond whatever personal and sentimental reasons may be in play, there is also cultural inertia such that specific competitions typically serve as the retirement venues for the more highly ranked competitors. In the United States, for example, most professional national champions announce their retirement at one of two events – the USDSC or the Ohio Star Ball. Similarly, dancers who have been among the most competitively successful on the international stage may choose Blackpool (usually after the Wednesday night team match event), or some other prominent world-class competition, to announce their retirement. The 2002 German Open Championships in Mannheim, Germany, for example, was the venue chosen by four-times Blackpool Professional Latin champions Jukka Haapalainen and Sirpa Suutari to announce their retirement from the competition floor; this was accompanied by a multi-dance show that had been prearranged with the event organizers, yet not listed in the event programme, so coming as a surprise to most of the audience.

PERFORMING SPECTACLE

If ballroom competitions are a spectacle of sights, sounds and movement, they are also performances by dancers, officials and audience members alike. Unlike many other Western dance forms, ballroom dancing is not a 'staged' dance style. Ballroom audiences are not seated at a distance from the dancers. Similarly, their seating area is dimmed relative to the competition floor, but not in the dark. This means that the dancers can easily see and interact with the audience, and such interaction is regularly part and parcel of ballroom competitions, as can be clearly seen in Figure 4.4. Spectators stand as well as sit, and most events sell standing-room-only tickets as well as specific seats. Applause and cheering during the dancing is not only

4.4. Dancer–audience proximity and interaction – as danced by World and Blackpool Professional Latin Finalists and US Professional Latin Champions Maxim Kozhevnikov and Yulia Zagoruychenko at the 2007 Emerald Ball Dancesport Championships in Los Angeles, CA. ©2007 Jonathan S. Marion

expected but actively encouraged and appreciated, and still photography during the competition is par for the course.[10]

Competitors, officials and audience members all have roles that they perform as regular parts of running a ballroom competition. The mass of spectators, as well as their proximity to the competition floor, should not be underestimated in assessing the performance of spectacle in ballroom. As much as competitors are cast as the objects of spectacle for the audience, the dancers cannot help but be aware of the audience, especially given the proximity of the audience to the competition surface itself. Favourable and enthusiastic audience reactions can spur competitors on, just as a lack of audience support can prove discouraging. As dance scholar and world-class ballroom coach Ruud Vermey has noted:

> The behaviour of their [ballroom dancers'] audience is significantly different from the behaviour of the theatre audience who recognizes the theatre as the artist's platform upon which something is to be 'created' and where they, as the audience, are spectators. The audience in the competition dance hall participates with as much verve as the dancers. Names of dancers are called out, flags are waved and favourites are cheered and applauded during the 'performance'. Obviously this affects the end result. (Vermey 1994: 20)

Just as importantly, however, audience members cannot help but be aware of each other as well, seeing and hearing other spectators all around the floor, as well as feeling and even smelling those close by. This extreme proximity (visible in Figure 4.4) serves as multisensory reinforcement to the spectacle at hand. Competitors, officials and audience members all then have roles to play in performing the spectacle that takes place in the competition setting. Just as clearly, all of these roles orbit around the on-the-competition-floor performances that are the conceptual centre and focus of dancesport culture.

Yet, in a twist that seemed particularly provocative early in my fieldwork, there never seemed to be a clear consensus regarding the specific nature of these on-the-competition-floor performances. Some people – coaches, judges, competitors and spectators included – told me that they considered competitive ballroom an outright sport, while others said that they considered it an outright art. Most people, however, placed it somewhere between these two poles in what seemed to be an almost unending set of permutations, such as: 'an athletic art', 'both art and sport', 'an artistic sport', 'a sportive art', 'somewhere in between', 'neither really', and 'something of each'. I do not bring this discontinuity to the forefront in order to try 'solving it', but to show how in addition to its inherent elements of spectacle, festival, celebration and performance, competitive ballroom cannot be fully understood without also examining its artistic and athletic aspects as well. This I do in Chapters 5 and 6 respectively.

Before moving on, however, a last point I want to make regarding the spectacle-like nature of ballroom competition concerns the audience experience. To the extent that a competition is a performance, an audience can appreciate it as such without understanding it. While it is true that 'the audience need not know the language of the dancers to enjoy their dancing' (Wulff 1998: 37), there can be no doubt that knowing the 'language' of the dancers can modulate evaluation and appreciation. This point not withstanding, dancing also 'speaks' for itself – needing no translation – in visual, auditory, rhythmic and kinaesthetic images. Thus, to the extent that dancing needs neither translation nor verbal cue to attract and command attention, it intermingles with – and indeed *is* – the stuff of spectacle.

5 BALLROOM AS ART

It isn't that artists are special kinds of people. It's that people are special kinds of artists.

Eric Gill

There should be no doubt that competitive ballroom is as much art as it is spectacle. The shapes, lines and movements made by dancers' bodies are far from natural; they are deliberate and trained postures that take work, effort and technique to produce. Most importantly, however, people watch ballroom dance in appreciation of its artistry. Certainly there are technical variables that are highly appreciated but people do not turn on their televisions and tune to dancing shows, go out to rent dance-based movies, or buy tickets to attend dance competitions only to partake in technical performance skills. It is the art and expression of dance that moves and inspires people, capturing attention and drawing viewers into the experience of watching dance.

Dancing is much more than just a collection of static poses and positions. It is also movement, but not just any movement. Dance is movement meant and intended to be expressive; movement meant to be more than merely functional. Dance is expressively charged and aesthetically conditioned movement of the body. Expressiveness without the aesthetics is dissemination. Aesthetics without the emotional charge is nothing more than technique. It is the marriage of aesthetics and expression that make movement artistic and meaningful. No less an expert on dance than Martha Graham has distinguished the difference between the mere *form* of dance (i.e. aesthetics/technique) and *dancing*: 'Dancers today can do anything', she notes, 'the technique is phenomenal. The passion and meaning to their movement can be another thing' (Graham 1991: 11). It is how the body is used – and to what ends – that makes movement into dance, and differentiates one genre of dance from another.

The particular qualities and conventions that make and mark dancesport what it is involve dressed and costumed uses of the body. Looking ahead, some of the considerations about aesthetic conventions introduced in this chapter are further elaborated in Chapter 9, which explicitly focuses on the costuming and visuality of competitive ballroom and unpacks the cultural encoding involved in ballroom grooming, costuming and comportment. Part IV, 'Costs, Consequences and Outcomes', builds on this, examining the images and symbols that are both evoked and invoked by competitors' conduct and comportment, including the consequences that arise from always being 'in public' among other members of the ballroom world. Within this chapter's focus on understanding the performance of dancesport as art, however, the roles played by impermanence, collectivity and convention are key.

IMPERMANENCE

Among the most compelling and captivating elements of dance is its impermanence. Dance is always brief and fleeting; so dance as art is equally brief and fleeting. An instant beyond its enactment, the art of that instant is gone forever. Memories and images of it may last as recorded images, but the art of dance is transitory; it lasts but an instant. Recorded images of dance (be they photographs or videos) are no more the art of dance than a photograph of a great painting is, itself, the art that it depicts. 'Of all the arts', notes Hammond, 'the art of movement is the most ephemeral – disappearing almost as it occurs, leaving few and inexact records of its brief glory' (2000: 138).[1] The fleeting nature of dance is central to its powers as an art form, adding significance to irretrievable instants.[2] This dynamic is further amplified by dance's bodily basis. Everyday uses of the body ranging from the mundane to the extraordinary – from brushing one's teeth to climbing Mount Everest – inform us about ourselves as embodied beings. As such, the body-as-basis of dancing resonates for non-dancers in a way that is not equally true of less bodily-based art. If it is bodily-based meanings that are tapped into and evoked in and through dance, it is the transience of dance that adds to the artistic charge of those meanings.

As an important aside, some could argue that sports are equally fleeting, but this is an erroneous conflation as both similarities and differences exist. The purpose of the sporting act remains after the fact of it in a way that is untrue of dance: after a sporting event is over, someone (player or team) has scored more points, ran or swam the fastest, jumped highest, or suchlike. What sport tries to accomplish via athletic performance remains after the event is over. Certainly ballroom competitors' placements (i.e. who came in first, second, third, and so on) remain 'after the fact' in much the same way as any other sports' statistics. But in dancesport this final outcome is far from the only purpose behind the activity. For some, of course, competition results may well be their primary purpose and goal, but this is hardly true of every ballroom competitor. The expressive nature of competing in ballroom may be of far greater importance and significance, as is the case for many dancers and in many situations. Quite a large percentage of the professional competitors I interviewed, for instance, said that they would always prefer to dance superbly, be the audience favourite and lose, rather than be placed first by the judges but dance poorly and disappoint the audience. Such assertions speak to an artistic purpose, as connecting with and 'moving' spectators trumps competitive success.[3]

For example, when asked about his experiences of winning an Amateur World Championship, Brent says that it actually turned out to be quite a let-down for them (he and his partner) because they did not feel that they had danced as well as they would have liked. By way of elaboration, Brent says that in reflecting back on everything they realized that their entire goal leading up to that World competition – including what all their training had been geared towards and what their mindset had been, up to and throughout the competition itself – was on winning and not on dancing well (as he now thinks it should have been, and wishes had been the case). A similar example comes from Charlotte Jorgensen, a past World Amateur Standard Champion and World and Blackpool Professional Standard finalist (more recently of popular TV fame in the United States as John O'Hurley's professional partner for the inaugural season of *Dancing with the Stars*).[4] Charlotte is very forthright in saying that she was never particularly fond of, nor interested in, competing. What she really loved doing were performances, and it is only because performance opportunities are so tightly linked to competition results that she really stuck with competing.

The point of these examples is that there is a difference between the impermanencies of sport and dance.[5] The measurable results of sporting acts remain after the fact; one can always see who scored the most, went the fastest, or got the most points (whatever the goals, aims and purposes of that activity). While it is equally feasible to go back and check ballroom competition results (including individual judge's marks), this ignores a major purpose of the dancing that has taken place since what matters most to many dancers, judges and spectators are items such as quality of movement, partnering and dance characterization – none of which have been captured in the recorded placements for that dancing. It is thus the ephemeral quality of dance despite its status as a competitive activity, its very impermanence, which highlights the artistic dynamics of dancesport.

ART AS COLLECTIVE

Yet however impermanent any particular enactment of dancesport may be, ballroom dancing is also incontrovertibly collective and (as such) subject to cultural conventions. All art is collective (Becker 2001: 67), and ballroom dancing is no exception: at the very least, art requires both artist and 'audience'.[6] Creativity can only exist relative to context after all; it must be creative in relation to something, otherwise it is merely random. For our purposes, then, there is no art without cultural context. Becker's (1984) notion of 'art worlds' recognizes the socially and culturally embedded nature of art, not just conceptually but in enactment as well. How many painters teach themselves how to make brushes, paints and canvases, and how to paint in a manner recognized as artistic by others, without any outside assistance? The larger point here being that 'producing art works requires elaborate modes of cooperation among specialized personnel' (Becker 2001: 71), and that 'art is social in the sense that it is created by networks of people acting together, and proposes a framework' (Becker 2001: 76).

Like any other art, ballroom dancing does not simply happen. Dancers learn from teachers and coaches in settings (typically studios) that are owned, managed, operated and maintained. These dancers dance to music that has been composed, performed, recorded, compiled, reproduced and marketed. They learn steps, patterns and techniques – whether from books, videos or teachers – that have been broken down, codified and recorded. As competitors they wear very specific and carefully constructed costuming and shoes, typically using a wide range of materials (e.g. fabrics, fringes, beading, rhinestones and suchlike), sourced from a variety of different locations and vendors, and assembled by someone else. As much as the basic substance of dance is the body, it thus remains inescapable that competitive ballroom dancing is contingent upon both 'artists' and 'support personnel' (Becker 2001: 68). Most tellingly, however, the coordination between ballroom's myriad personnel and products does not need to be created anew by each dancer. There is already a ballroom world to be navigated.

A careful look at Figure 5.1 begins to suggest the scale of the ballroom art world. Most obvious here is the one-at-a-time application of rhinestones to two ballroom dresses. But where did the dresses come from to be 'stoned'? They were made by other 'support personnel' according to the designs of yet another person. What about

5.1. Rhinestoning ballroom dresses – hand-placing rhinestones on ballroom gowns in the stoning department of Doré Designs in Cape Coral, FL, August 2007. ©2007 Jonathan S. Marion

the material from which the dresses were made? That came from elsewhere as did the sewing machines that the seamstresses used to produce these gowns. Returning to the stoning process itself, the bins visible in the background hold over 150 cuts and colours of rhinestones, all produced elsewhere, as are the glues used to secure the stones to the dress that can be seen on the work table in the front left of the frame. Add to this that the mannequin forms upon which the dresses are fitted to be stoned are purchased from yet another source, and Becker's point that art worlds depend upon 'elaborate modes of cooperation among specialized personnel' (2001: 71) begins to emerge in its true complexity – especially when we realize that the point of making ballroom dresses is not simply to make dresses, but to make dresses that competitors wear for competition (as seen in the figures throughout this book).

Just as the art world that supports the making of ballroom dresses is not started anew by each dancesport competitor, they do not start from scratch in learning their craft, nor do they learn in isolation. They do not generate their own vocabulary of movements and techniques. They do not figure out for themselves how to relate physically and interact with their partners. They do not independently select what music they will dance to or in what manner. They do not make up the gender models they think they should attempt to enact. They do not attempt to intuit what style of costuming will best match their dancing. As Becker duly notes:

> People who cooperate to produce a work of art usually do not decide things afresh. Instead, *they rely on earlier agreements now become customary, agreements that have become part of the conventional way of doing things in that art.* Artistic conventions cover all the decisions that must be made with respect to works produced in a given art world, even though a particular convention may be revised for a given work. (Becker 2001: 71, emphasis added)

In the process of becoming competitors, then, ballroom dancers learn a wide range of personal practices as well as mental models both for what constitutes good dancing and how they should go about producing it. But they also come to learn how the many different nodes of the ballroom art world are interconnected and how to access and utilize the web of ballroom-related skills, goods and knowledge.

CONVENTIONS: GOOD AND BAD

As Becker points out, 'conventions regulate the relations between artists and audience, specifying the rights and obligations of both' (2001: 72). Perhaps of greatest significance in this capacity is the sheer persistence of convention. Expanding on the point that 'conventions place strong constraints on the artist', Becker goes on to note that:

> They are particularly constraining because they do not exist in isolation, but come in complexly interdependent systems, so that making one small change often requires making changes in a variety of other activities. A system of

conventions gets embodied in equipment, materials, training, available facilities
and sites, systems of notation and the like, all of which must be changed if any
one segment is. (2001:73)

It is no more difficult to dance a Standard routine in a Latin dress than it is in a
ballroom gown. Yet there are long-standing (if evolving) conventions that differentiate
between the costuming used for Standard and Latin, and ballroom costuming from
non-ballroom clothing. Changing these conventions, say to favour Latin costuming
for Standard, is deeply implicated in a broader web of ballroom-related values and
would thus have deep and wide-ranging consequences in the dance community.

Most noticeably, any such change would transform the entire appearance of the
competition floor. Yet that would only be the very surface of the systemic repercussions involved. All of the dress vendors would have to switch their production
from Standard to Latin dresses. Latin dresses use less fabric, and typically in a smaller
variety, which would have an impact on both in-house materials production and
out-of-house materials acquisitions. Also, since the highest price tags are, as a general
rule, on Standard dresses, what steps would vendors take to compensate financially?
Maybe the price of Latin dresses would go up, or maybe staff sizes would be trimmed
down. In any case, the point remains that because 'the same people often cooperate
repeatedly, even routinely, in similar ways to produce similar works' (Becker 2001:
76), conventions of costuming and performance need to be recognized and understood as deeply interdependent elements of larger systems of practice.

Yet if the regularity of conventionalized actions is more socially and economically
efficient, it does not make unconventional actions impossible; it only makes them
more difficult and expensive (Becker 2001: 76). Actions at odds with convention are
not impossible; rather, they are improbable due to greater 'costs' in social, cultural,
political and economic capital. A dancer can, for example, dance without adhering to
any of the recognized conventions for ballroom technique or grooming – but should
then be prepared for the consequences. Far from being merely superficial then (although also not ruling it out), a judge's lower marks for an unkempt appearance
are, in part, about breaches in artistic conventions. Whatever a competitor's reasons
may be, they are in effect rejecting the very conventions that have undergirded the
careers of the current judges, a position understandably distasteful to the judges in
question.

At the same time, however, the very constraints of conventions also represent its
greatest opportunities (Becker 2001: 74), as the very stability of the norms inherent
in conventions provide the background against which dancers strive to stand out.
If stepping too far outside the box fails to produce something recognized as legitimate ballroom dancing, staying too far inside the box produces overly conventional and sterile dancing at best. Indeed, it is the personal touch, interpretation
and flair of the best dancers that establishes their position in the pantheon of ballroom greats, and not a 'perfect performance' of convention. Far from being a rigid

line of demarcation, then, artistic conventions represent a permeable zone bridging typicality and transgression.

Artistic conventions can thus be equated with the cliché of being the exception that proves the rule. If a dancer cannot show mastery of the relevant conventions they are not free to break them, just as it is the ability of the elite dancers' and coaches to venture into the inexact borders of convention – without breaching them – which sets them apart from even the most technically proficient, but fully conventional, dancers. Minor challenges to convention, especially by those who show mastery over them, represent the developmental edge of artistic innovation. As with any art form, dance evolves as minor alterations and embellishments to established conventions are made, generate interest, gain recognition, grow in appeal, begin to be copied and emerge as the new edge of conventional distinction. Significant challenges to regnant conventions are thus the most instructive and defining of cultural norms and standards, since:

> Any major change necessarily attacks some of the existing conventions of the art directly... An attack on convention does not merely mean an attack on the particular item to be changed. Every convention carries with it an aesthetic, according to which what is conventional becomes the standard by which artistic beauty and effectiveness is judged. (Becker 2001: 75)

CONVENTIONS AND CLASSIFICATIONS

Conventions are not only about production and expression of course; they also concern classification. Table 5.1 reiterates the classificatory scheme for the four main dancesport styles contested in the United States (with the ten dances of the Latin and Standard divisions being common to competitive ballroom worldwide). In the course of presenting and discussing my ballroom research at the 2005 American Anthropological Association (AAA) Annual Meeting in Washington, DC, however, I found that many non-ballroom dancers found it hard to understand how the different dances fit into the respective categories. Trying to explain the ballroom classifications proved more difficult than I had anticipated, in large measure due to my own long-standing involvement with ballroom. Yet far from being the 'obvious' groupings that I had come to recognize, ballroom classifications reflect not only historical developments but also artistic conventions of the ballroom world.

In the light of my AAA experiences then, I posted a question online at Dance-Forums.com, with a listing of the nineteen dances in Table 5.1, and explaining that I was interested in seeing how DF members would group the dances for themselves. This topic generated a number of public responses as well as a few private messages, and suggested several sets of classifications, including those based on: (1) movement and tempo; (2) ease of socially dancing them; and (3) interpersonal relationship metaphors. While I found the specifics of each suggested classifications interesting,

Table 5.1   The Rhythm, Latin, Smooth and Standard Dances

Rhythm	Latin	Smooth	Standard
Cha Cha (American)	Cha Cha (International)	Waltz (American)	Waltz (International)
Rumba (American)	Samba	Tango (American)	Tango (International)
Swing (East Coast Swing)	Rumba (International)	Foxtrot (American)	Viennese Waltz (International)
Bolero	Paso Doble	Viennese Waltz (American)	Foxtrot (International)
Mambo	Jive		Quickstep

the larger point of importance here is the range of criteria and schemes used. The lack of consensus between the different models is noteworthy, providing highly divergent combinations of movement style, dance tempo, progressive versus stationary movement, relationship metaphors and dance characterization. Most revealing, however, is that none of these schemes came even remotely close to the four dancesport categories of Rhythm, Latin, Smooth and Standard. And therein lies the point: as an art world, ballroom is not only implicated in economic and expressive conventions, but also in conventions of classification – the very conventions of cognition through which competitive ballroom is received and achieved.

For example, many new dancers ask why tango is included in the ballroom dances and not the Latin dances, whereas many experienced ballroom dancers cannot understand why someone would even think or ask this question – *despite tango's Argentinian heritage*! Conversely, few people seem to question the placement of Paso Doble within the Latin dances (also known as the *Latin American* dances) despite its European origins in Spain. The cognitive conventions of ballroom are such that, as experienced practitioners, the presence of a European-based dance (Paso Doble) in the Latin American division goes without notice just as does the presence of a Latin American dance (Tango) in the Ballroom division.

And what about the Jive, also danced as part of the Latin division, although in no way geographically Latin? This very issue came home to me when, in response to queries from prospective producers and backers for his 'Latin Fusion' show, Louis van Amstel – most widely known outside ballroom circles from seasons 1–3 of *Dancing with the Stars* in the United States – asked my help in explaining to non-ballroom people how Jive was a 'Latin' dance. The particular response I suggested to Louis at the 2003 USDSC dealt with the role of the Jive in the context of his show, but he made one comment that really jumped out for me – namely, that while it was obvious to him 'as a Latin dancer' how Jive was a Latin dance, he had been finding it excessively difficult to explain this to the non-ballroom potential backers for the show. From a purely technical standpoint, Jive can be understood as an offspring of American swing, but one that has been transformed by the application of already codified Latin dance technique. But such commonalities of technique between Jive and the other Latin dances are lost on non-ballroom dancers, whereas the long-time ballroom dancer may not even consciously realize them. As this example thus shows, artistic conventions include and work through classificatory conventions as well as economic and expressive ones, and exploration and understanding of art worlds requires attention to such classifications.

CONVENTIONS AND GLOBALIZATION

As much as the ballroom world *is* an art world, it is not disconnected from the larger world, but overlaps it. Hansen, for instance, notes that:

> Globalization in the era of hypercommunication is creating a new 'world in dress', breaking down conventional fashion boundaries. Understanding fashion as a global phenomenon is further supported by shifts in the organization of garment production across the globe as well as by the vast economic significance of garment production in world trade. (2004: 372)

True of fashion in general, this is also true of dancesport. Russian, Chinese and Korean companies produce ballroom dresses, as do Polish, Russian, English and Italian companies (to name just a few). Austrian Swarovski rhinestones are still the standard for all the best dresses, but less expensive Korean stones now represent an economic alternative. Major ballroom competitions (Blackpool first among them) serve as the ballroom industry's trade shows, with all the latest dress fashions on prominent display, both as worn by sponsored competitors and in elaborate vendor displays. Imitations and derivations of the latest styles premiering at Blackpool find their way into the circuit in short order, with the latest 'it' trends rippling outward across the ballroom art world. Indeed, dresses circumambulate the ballroom circuit even more so than dancers, with the same dresses regularly being loaned, rented and resold between dancers – across the globe.

In a related vein, citing Cohen *et al.* (1996), Hansen points out that, 'while beauty contests demonstrate the proliferation of Western styles and influences, they are also setting into motion complicated negotiations between local and global norms of beauty, gender, and sexuality' (Hansen 2004: 383), a dynamic paralleled in dancesport as the models of ballroom carriage, comportment, performance, grooming and dress codified in the West become standards that ramify onto all competitors. Irrespective of upbringing concerning bodily display and expressivity, then, the general models of dancesport remain. Scandinavian, Asian, Christian, Jewish, 'white', 'black' or any other number of such labels thus matter little to dancesport norms, yet may well serve as personally salient variables against which such norms are negotiated by individual dancers.

ART AND ASYMMETRY

Primary among dancesport's many conventions of bodily use, display and costuming are those pertaining to asymmetry – and hence to art. As Harvey notes, unlike natural selection's taste for symmetry, 'the taste for asymmetry pertains distinctly to art – and to the art of dress – and not to nature' (2007: 70), and this is well seen in the movement and dress of dancesport. To be sure, parallel side-by-side choreography (between partners) has a place in competitive ballroom, visually marking fully coordinated effort and timing. Nonetheless, the majority of ballroom is asymmetric, and in many ways. In the first place, side-by-side couples' gendered costuming marks an asymmetry integral to dancesport – in contrast, say, to some theatre dancing wherein almost identical costuming may be used across gender. Similarly, competitors' choreography is not a monotonous repetition, but is designed to display different patterns of movement and timing. Likewise, the phrase 'light and shade' is used to describe the contrasts (in height levels, speed, power, and the like) that add interest and impact to dance technique. Like dancesport movement, dancesport costumes rely on asymmetry to create art and appeal, with asymmetrical cuts, patterns, drapes, hemlines and design elements all generating added visual complexity. By design, ballroom dancing and costumes are non-monotonous, using asymmetries of movement and design to modulate and magnify the artistry of dancesport. The same dancing executed in a social setting may be equally good on technical grounds – and already artistic in its execution – but the asymmetries of dancesport costume design are all intended to showcase the art of dancesport, as seen in Figure 5.2.

WHY NOT 'ART'?

Before moving on to examining ballroom as sport, I want to introduce one final topic: namely, why is ballroom rarely given credit as *art* by other Western dance forms?[7] Vermey speculates that the reason may be 'Perhaps because it grew out of a social environment, as opposed to an artistic one, it seems to have maintained an isolation from the greater "dance as art" context' (1994: 17). Since it is sixteenth-century French court dancing that ultimately gave rise to both ballroom and ballet, this seems a somewhat strange historical oddity. Yet perhaps it is only in light of this common background that the current disconnection and distance can truly make sense, since there is little need or drive to distinguish one's self from what one obviously differs, just as there is little reason to establish one's superiority from those to whom one is obviously superior. It is only when differences are not easily seen and demarcated that making and marking such distinctions really becomes an issue.

Such speculations aside, by far and away the most common reason I have been given for ballroom's rejection as 'art' is that it is competitive. This justification is flimsy at best, as more than abundant dance contests for ballet, jazz and modern

5.2. Asymmetry and artistry – as seen in the dress and the offset pose of World and Blackpool Professional Latin Finalists Andrej Skufca and Katarina Venturini at the 2007 United States Dance Championships in Orlando, FL. ©2007 Jonathan S. Marion

dancing also exist. Far more importantly, however, competition is a deeply entrenched and fundamental component for all of these forms of staged dancing. What is the gruelling process of 'try outs' for school and troupe positions, scholarships and prominent roles, after all, if not inherently competitive? The idea that the pursuit of highly prized positions and roles far fewer in number than the ranks of those wanting them is not competitive is misleading, naive and ignorant at best, if not actually deceptive or delusional (or both). As this chapter has shown the ballroom world is an art world. Yet, as the very name 'dancesport' attests, it is simultaneously a world of physical exertion, striving and contest. More than just spectacle and art, competitive ballroom also needs to be understood as sport, the topic of the next chapter.

6 BALLROOM AS SPORT

Dancing requires a tremendous amount of physical energy. It is a path chosen by those who have a particularly strong current rushing through them, a Dionysian flow which threatens to overwhelm – 'the extraordinary potent' in full force. Those who wish to use this energy, rather then be swept away by it must build an especially strong container within themselves.

Blackmer (1989: 102–3)

Just as ballroom is often not taken seriously within the arts, this also holds true for its status as a sport despite the obvious physical effort, practice and conditioning of serious dancesport competitors. If the physical prowess of dancesport competitors is often dismissed as art by theatrical dancers who do ballet, modern and jazz, on the one hand, why is it also dismissed as sport on the other? This chapter considers these issues along three lines:

1. It considers the dichotomy between popular conceptions of sport and dancesport's subjective nature. The issue of subjectivity for sports in general and for dancesport in particular serves two complimentary purposes in these materials. First, it highlights the subjectivity of all sports, thereby undercutting the most common reason cited for dancesport's lack of fit in 'sport'. Second, it shows how expectation and focus modulate perception, including how even the same features of the same dancing can be seen quite differently.
2. The prestige, recognition and validation – including financial remuneration – of sport in modern media are held up as cultural carrots driving much of the interest in being recognized as a sport within certain dancesport circles.
3. It examines some of the intersections between sports and gender inherent in competitive ballroom dancing, topics further elaborated on in Chapter 9's focus on dancesport costuming and conduct and Chapter 10's focus on the performance of gender in dancesport.

DANCE*SPORT*: WHAT MAKES DANCE A SPORT?

In 'What Makes a Good Sport?', social psychologist Nicholas Christenfeld (1996) demonstrates that there is an optimal level of seasonal reliability – a balance between skill and chance – for fan enjoyment.[1] This model casts some interesting shadows across the arena of dancesport for several reasons. First, neither the league nor tournament models match dancesport's judging system. In dancesport half of the couples are recalled from previous rounds until a final (typically of six couples) remains when, in the final, each judge places all couples ordinally, with the couple receiving the majority of marks for each ordinal being awarded that final placement.[2] Unlike league or tournament sport models, then, the structure of dancesport competition does not provide for one-on-one[3] head-to-head competition.

The many-at-once model exhibited by track, cross-country and swimming better approximates the nature of ballroom competition as far as the structure of qualifying and preliminary heats leading up to a final event which then provides a final set of ordinally ranked results. Unlike these other sports, however, who 'wins' a ballroom competitions is often not a simple, self-evident matter. In this respect, ballroom competitions are more akin to figure skating, gymnastics, or diving, wherein 'expert' judges evaluate individual performances. Yet unlike these other athletic activities, there are no points or scores assigned in dancesport.[4] I think it is this last element, the lack of 'scoring' or 'points', that most distances dancesport from many people's everyday conceptualizations of sport.

I would suggest that unlike soccer, basketball, baseball and football, activities such as gymnastics, diving and skating are often watched for aesthetic appreciation – *aside from their competitive element* – in a way that other sports may not be. This is not to say that there is not beauty in the performance of other sports as well (oftentimes there is), only that the focus is of a different nature. How many times, for instance, have the basketball court efforts of Michael Jordan and other elite athletes been described by various sportscasters as 'poetry in motion'? But there is a difference between intentional aesthetics and instrumental aesthetics; between purposeful, deliberate beauty and visual appeal as a by-product. The performance of the diver, the dancer, the gymnast or the skater may very well be aimed at winning, but the aesthetics of the performance are tantamount to their performance and are the purpose behind their technique.[5] This is a different situation from that of the pole-vaulter, long-jumper, hurdler or basketball player who may demonstrate great beauty in action, but whose overall technique is directed to achieving an instrumental goal (be it to jump higher, or further, or make a nearly impossible basket).

The difference between intentional versus instrumental aesthetics also relates to one of the most prevalent criticisms of conceptualizing ballroom and other artistic sports – their subjectivity. Responding to a question about whether ballroom dancing should be classified as a sport or not, Travis, a highly placed dance official suggested that:

clearly dancers are athletes but, personally, I don't think dance should be a sport. I mean, if you watch how these kids prepare these days there's no denying what athletes they are, and so I guess, that it's good for them to get the recognition, but a sport is something like running, or baseball, or hockey, where you can see who ran faster, had more home runs, or scored more goals, so no, I wouldn't say that I think dancing is really a sport.

Clearly the underlying conceptualization here is that there is a more self-evident, 'objective' facet to sports than the subjective evaluations in ballroom dancing. One problem with Travis's formulation, however, lies in overlooking the oftentimes out-come determining impact of subjective judgements in most team sports. When is a foul called? What type of foul is it? When a strike, a ball, or an out? Clearly there are rules specifying the answers to such questions, but as the games are being played it is ultimately subjective human judgement that can make the difference(s) between winning or losing, advancing to the next round or ending your season, winning the championship or going home empty-handed.

SEEING THE SCENE: SUBJECTIVITY AND SCENE VERSUS SEEN

One of the issues implicit in criticisms of subjectivity is the notion that there is an objective scene against which what is subjectively seen can be assessed. While this may be the case in certain scenarios (e.g. in some cases using instant replay), human observation is inherently subjective in nature. Half a century ago, Hastorf and Cantril (1954) documented the interpretational nature of sporting events, especially those of a social nature. 'Of crucial importance', relate Hastorf and Cantril, 'is the fact that an "occurrence" on the football field or in any other social situation does not become an experiential "event" unless and until some significance is given to it: an "occurrence" only becomes an "*event*" only when the happening has significance' (1954: 132, original emphasis). And, as Hastorf and Cantril go on to note, what anyone sees in such situations are only 'a limited series of events from the total matrix of events *potentially* available to them' (1954: 132, original emphasis). This general framework explains why the same hard bump can be seen as fair (if rough) play or as an unfair and deliberate foul, and why two different judges can see entirely different things in the same person's dancing. Especially as what each individual 'sees' is filtered through their individual perspectives and orientations, and so what different individuals see *is* different. As Hastorf and Cantril summarize, 'there is no such "thing" as a "game" existing "out there" in its own right which people merely "observe"' (1954: 133). Such subjectivity in light of 'objective' goals and rules makes clear some of the discrepancies arising when individual judgements – as in dancesport – are the basis for winning and success.

As Birrell and McDonald note of sports in general, 'different accounts of incidents can serve as a point of entry into an analysis of the source itself ... why do they differ as they do?' (2000: 13). So what then are the implications of these dynamics of subjectivity to ballroom competition? As one would expect regarding the topic of subjectivity, the implications are open to various evaluations. In the first instance, different technical elements – such as ankle use, frame, line and extension – are given different evaluative weights by different observers. With different elements of performance having different significance in each person's assessment, different people may very well see the same dancing quite differently. Since what each person sees is *self*-evident to them, it is often presumed to be 'real', objective and equally self-evident to all. Different observers easily (mis)take their own assessments as objectively valid in just this way, casting those who disagree with them as either (a) less informed, or (b) obfuscating the 'truth'. Given the diversity of backgrounds (national, ethnic and otherwise) among those involved with dancesport, what is striking is not the variety of opinions but, instead, the general consensus regarding the variables in question and their overall evaluations.

Expectation and Focus   Closely related to the issue of subjectivity in ballroom competition are the elements of expectation and focus. If a couple has a reputation for clean footwork this is what is likely to be seen, with reputation serving as expectation; self-fulfilling expectation at that. In the face of unequal expectations, for instance, equivalent footwork is unlikely to be seen as equal. In this case the reputation for good footwork is likely to draw focus to itself, which effectively pulls focus away from both: (a) the footwork of others which may be equally clean; and (b) other elements of their own dancing that may be weaker in comparison. Similarly, the 'clean' couple's missteps are more likely seen as flukes, whereas equal bobbles by others are viewed as symbolic of their 'sloppier' footwork.

Let me use the somewhat more elaborated case of Lars and Jenny in order to take a more concrete look at the effects and interplay of (a) significance, (b) personal validity, (c) expectation and (d) focus. Unlike lower-level couples who might have larger gaps in their dancing, Lars and Jenny would generally be recognized as a 'good' couple, widely considered within the top twenty-four in the world. Like any couple at that level, the issue is one of relative excellence (rather than sufficiency) since such couples are generally recognized and accepted as being excellent dancers. Widely known for their speed, performance and tricks, Lars and Jenny often receive relatively low placements in the finals, placements that seem, on the surface, in direct contrast to often overwhelming audience support. In fact, many audience members view such results as politically biased against Lars and Jenny. Separate from any possible politics involved, however, Lars and Jenny's case can also be understood through the often overlapping lenses of significance, personal validity, expectation and focus.

It is easy enough to accept that observers find different elements of a couple's performance significant. Thus the same charisma and showmanship that may drive spectators to their feet can be what strikes judges as inauthentic grandstanding. Even more likely, and returning to Lars and Jenny, their charismatic performances may very well be of overwhelming appeal to the audience, whereas judges – whether by dint of expertise or simply their roles as judges – find Jenny's lack of body actions to be more significant overall. For the many audience members impressed by the charismatic nature of Lars and Jenny's performance, their viewpoint may well be felt to be the only valid assessment of Lars and Jenny's dancing. A lower placing (for Lars and Jenny) than what was just 'observed' is thus seen as 'having to be about more than just the dancing' (i.e. politics). Conversely, a judge may well understand what the audience is reacting to – and perhaps even agree – yet still find certain technical elements, such as ankle articulation, to be more significant in assessing the overall merit of Lars and Jenny's dancing. For this judge the technical element is seen as the more important criterion, and as more reflective of the true merit of the performance in question.

Such contrasting impressions regarding Lars and Jenny's dancing can also be understood via the separate but often related dynamics of expectation and focus. Audience members and judges alike expect to see speed, performance and great tricks from Lars and Jenny, expectations which, in turn, make the speed, performance and tricks of Lars and Jenny's dancing that much more visible and (oftentimes) salient. Audience members and judges alike may thus expect speed, performance and tricks from Lars and Jenny's dancing, but, where the audience may see these as validating Lars and Jenny's dominance, a judge may view these as obscuring contrast, subtlety and nuance. Audience members may expect a great performance from Lars and Jenny – *and thus see it as such* – even on an 'off' night, whereas the judge may have come to expect inconsistency and, having reservations about consistency, see Lars and Jenny's dancing *as* inconsistent even on a night when they really 'nail' all of their routines.

Different from expectation if typically directed by it, 'focus' also has explanatory value regarding Lars and Jenny's dancing. Expecting to see speed, performance and tricks from them, audience and judges alike will often focus on exactly these elements, and as a result of that focus *actually* see them. Expectation and focus work in tandem, reinforcing each other, such that Lars and Jenny are seen as faster dancers and better performers with top-notch tricks. Certainly Lars and Jenny's dancing needs to live up to these expectations, but the point remains that viewers' focus on these elements (often) magnifies these very attributes (even when really only on par with others on the floor). Since observers can only be entirely focused on one couple at a time, every extra instant focused on Lars and Jenny's speed, performance and tricks is simultaneously that much less time for these same attributes to be noted in their competitors' routines. Conversely, the same focus on Lars and Jenny's speed, performance and tricks may be at the expense of noting when they *do* slow down, turn their focus inward, or are executing more basic actions.

Overall, what is seen by different people is unlikely to be the same scene. 'The significances assumed by different happenings for different people depend in large part on the purposes and probable behaviour of other people involved' (Hastorf and

Cantril 1954: 132), and dynamics such as salience, personal validity, expectation and focus all contribute to the subjectivity of judgement and evaluation. All of these issues regarding subjectivity provide some insight into what Travis means when he says, 'clearly dancers are athletes but, personally, I don't think dance should be a sport'. The distinction that Travis makes is that 'athletics' involve physical exertion and skills whereas 'sports' provide unambiguous results. While the preceding materials highlight the subjectivity of *all* sports, Travis's comment exemplifies a fairly widely held perspective: that some such activities have objective results while others do not.

PRESTIGE, RECOGNITION AND VALIDATION

An important dynamic in any consideration of the place of dance in relation to sport (and art) concerns issues of prestige, recognition and validation. Within modern society the 'average' person – be they construction worker, janitor, school teacher, company executive or bus driver – typically has greater awareness of athletes than of artists. Certainly this is not true for all, but the average person is probably more likely to recognize, if not actually identify, more athletes than artists. And how could it be otherwise? News coverage in the mass media privileges sport in a way that it simply does not for art. Be it newspaper, radio, TV or online, daily news coverage inevitably highlights at least a sample of sporting stories and results. Given the seemingly omnipresent prestige, recognition and validation of mainstream athletes – via news coverage, endorsements and as celebrities – the appeal of gaining acceptance as a sport is quite understandable, especially considering the extensive physical exertion, effort and training typical of top dancers.

How and why modern society privileges athletics (and competition in particular) above the arts is a separate and important issue, and one deserving due consideration. For my purposes in this book, however, what is important is simply the value discrepancy between athletics and art since it offers important insight into why many dancers want ballroom to be recognized as a sport. The same efforts that constitute competitors' training and preparation – thousands of hours of practice, physical wear and tear, repetitive international travel (for the best coaching and competitions) and ongoing expenses of time, effort and money – do not garner the same perks in dancesport that they do in acknowledged 'sports'. Even the validation of simply being recognized as an athlete for their efforts typically eludes dancers.

Yet such assessments are not universal, and differences in evaluation, dependent upon national background among other related variables, show up in several ways. Given the prestige of the arts in recent 'Russian' culture, for example, being a professional dancer – and therefore 'an artist' – means something different to being a professional dancer in the United States. A quick survey of the youth couples involved with dancesport in the States reflects the different evaluations involved, with the vast majority of such youngsters being from some post-Soviet background.[6]

The cultural perception of dance in this case facilitates dance participation and involvement in a way that is not the case for many other youth where dancing is dismissed as 'just something that little girls do' – a formulation that devalues the activity via feminine association (discussed below) as being 'for girls' and making it almost forbidden to many boys whose fathers feel that their sons 'should' be playing 'real' sports such as baseball and football.

This lack of status ascribed to dancing is not, of course, limited to either the United States or to children,[7] nor is the situation as straightforward as a simple bifurcation between sport and art. As now retired professional Finnish competitor Jenne related to me, 'ballroom dancing always bounced back and forth between the ministries of culture and of sport in my country', and, 'while we always felt more at home and like we belonged in the ministry of culture, we always received greater financial support under the ministry of sport'. The exact same activity then, when viewed as sport (instead of 'culture') received greater financial backing even in a country that does help finance competitive ballroom dancing. And, while the dancers may even self-identify more as artists than as sportsmen, the (literal) value – and thus validation – of their enterprise is assessed differently when executed under the umbrella of sport as opposed to art. This is just one example of the accompanying prestige, recognition, status, respect and validation that go hand in hand with sport – rather than anything intrinsic to 'sport' itself – that seems to motivate many views and positions that support casting dance as a sport.

The impact of prestige, recognition and validation is a comprehensive dynamic that functions at both the individual and institutional levels. Jenne relates that soon after being switched into the ministry of sport (from the ministry of culture), she, along with the other competition dancers, went for performance evaluations just like any other athlete under the ministry's purview and, among other evaluations and measures taken, there was one for cardiovascular endurance. When Jenne's turn came she got hooked up, and started to run on the treadmill. Shortly thereafter the technicians told her to stop, as there was some malfunction with the apparatus. She stopped and, after they had fiddled with it for a bit, had her get hooked up and start running again. Once again she was soon asked to stop due to some malfunction. While the technicians were again going over the machine and its associated instrumentation, a non-dancer came by, also scheduled to do their cardiovascular endurance testing, who was on a tight time schedule. This athlete was soon hooked up and proceeded to complete their assessment without a hitch. Everything seeming to be back in fine working order now, Jenne was again hooked up, now for her third time, and again stated to run on the treadmill. Several moments in the technicians again asked her stop claiming that something was, again, wrong with the machine.

Somewhat exasperated at this point, Jenne asked them what was going on, especially as the other athlete had been tested without mishap whereas she had now started and been stopped three times. Rather abashedly the technicians said that they really could not explain it but that, for some reason, they just were not getting accurate read-outs for her. When Jenne asked them what was going wrong with her results, she was told that her read-outs were showing up in the zones that only elite cross-country skiers registered. 'Oh, that makes sense', she said, 'I do some cross country skiing to keep myself in shape to dance'.

To the sports technicians conducting the testing it was truly inconceivable that a competitive ballroom dancer would actually possess and exhibit the same cardio-vascular profile as an elite cross-country skier. For Jenne, on the other hand, intensive cross-country skiing was a way she helped build the endurance she felt she needed to compete at the level of ballroom competition she did. The sports technicians' confusion regarding their machine and the results being displayed clearly show that they were not trying to be disrespectful. But it is the dismissiveness inherent in their disbelief that illustrates both the degree and the persuasiveness of the lack of respect competitive dance garners as an athletic pursuit. Some of this, of course, comes from the very performance aspect of ballroom competition. Make-up, costumes, fancy shoes, rhinestones, fringes, feathers, and more, all seem to counter-indicate raw athleticism. So, too, does the very nature of performative dance, wherein effort-less execution is the image that successful competitors continuously try to evoke. Ironically, it is the same seemingly effortlessness that is both testament to the im-mense and ongoing investment in time, practice, conditioning and technique that also seems to signal non-athleticism to those less familiar with what is entailed in competitive ballroom dancing.

A similar example of the disconnection between actual and the perceived ath-leticism of competitive ballroom dancing comes from Edgar, a professional ballroom competitor and active competitive martial artist. An ankle injury sidelined Edgar from either pursuit for several months and from competition for even longer. What is interesting is that Edgar returned to competitive sparring months before he returned to ballroom competition (actually over half-a-year earlier), commenting that, 'my ankle just wouldn't be able to take that yet', as far as ballroom competition was concerned. Those present, including a mix of social and intermediate level amateur competitors, met this comment with a great deal of surprise.

Beyond personal experiences with the lack of prestige, recognition and validation for competitive ballroom dancing such as Jenne's and Edgar's, this same trend also translates across (and 'up') to the institution of competitive ballroom at large. Officially recognized as a sport by the International Olympic Committee (IOC), dancesport was prominently featured in the closing ceremonies of the 2000 Sydney Games. The lack of respect, prestige and validation for ballroom dancing was clearly demonstrated in (and by) both the lack of proportional TV coverage – only fleeting glimpses of what was in fact a prominent element of the closing ceremonies were included in the broadcast – and in the commentary, dripping with negativity, made by TV announcer Bob Costas contending that ballroom dancing was not a legitimate sport and included such flippant remarks as 'What would happen if Rita Moreno pulled a hamstring?'

While the overall lack of coverage disappointed many fans of ballroom dancing, it was Costas's comments that really drew their ire. Over the following few days, hundreds and hundreds of complaints came flooding in to DanceScape.com, the largest and most active Internet ballroom forum at the time. Some of these comments – as reported in a *Business Wire* article – included: 'The announcers were condescending and rude', 'Making a lame joke about Rita Moreno pulling a hamstring only shows their ignorance', and 'We were verbally abused and molested'. As DanceScape founder Robert Tang was quoted, the broadcast comments 'didn't just insult an individual, it insulted an entire sport' (*Business Wire*, 9 October 2000). It is this level of dismissal that underlies much of the Olympic push within the ballroom world, with sports status standing as social validations and economic opportunity.

DANCE*SPORT* AND GENDER

Although Chapter 10 is dedicated to discussing the performance of gender in dancesport, some brief comments on gender under the ballroom-as-sport umbrella are in order, especially in light of the significant interrelationships between cultural constructions, understanding and presentations of sport and gender, and how these manifest in dancesport. Although practised within a transnational arena of activity, dancesport's aesthetic foundations remain primarily Western European, which serves as the foundation to why 'femininity and athleticism are mutually exclusive concepts in American culture' (Feder-Kane 2000: 207). It should come as little surprise, then, that the 'almost hysterical assertion of gender difference' (2000: 207) Feder-Kane describes for competitive figure skating has deep parallels in competitive ballroom. As framed by Disch and Kane:

> By denying the manifest evidence that physical differences vary along a continuum and thereby perpetuating the assumption that binary opposition is inherent in nature, sport both confirms the logic of the heterosexual matrix and translates it into everyday experience. It is larger-than-life proof that sex differences are dichotomous by nature, confirmation that oppositional gender identities mimic this natural binary, and a common-sense affirmation that heterosexual orientation is normative because it is natural. (2000: 126)

The rationale underlying such dichotomous demarcations, according to Feder-Kane, is that 'when physical capabilities no longer distinguish men and women, femininity is overdetermined to keep female athletes from being labeled as masculine or lesbian' (2000: 208). Based on her work on female body-building, Bolin makes a complementary point, noting that 'to pursue athleticism is to pursue physical strength, skill and power which must be constrained so as not to impinge on the domain of masculinity' (Bolin 1998: 191). In dancesport, however, this is only one part of a larger and more complex picture. According to both Brownmiller (1984: 15) and Feder-Kane, for instance, within sport femininity is continuously constructed to assure that 'women athletes are still "just girls" underneath' (Feder-Kane 2000: 208), such that 'even as they have become embraced as stars, female skaters have often been negated as athletes' (2000: 210). But dancesport differs. Within ballroom, for instance, it is by her very accomplishments of athleticism – even as it must follow specific norms in order to be coded, and thus counted, as female – that a woman embodies femininity; a situation much closer to Bolin's description that 'professional women athletes … find themselves in a similar position where to be successful in athletic careers requires "glamour jock" look' (Bolin 1998: 206).

I am not arguing that dancesport is divorced from the essentializing model of gender represented in skating, only that the situation in ballroom is more deeply and complexly layered. Thus, where Feder-Kane's argument that an apology for a female skater's athleticism is 'actually incorporated into the competition, where costume, makeup, and gesture feminize and soften athletics prowess' (2000: 209) largely holds true for dancesport on one level, there is also a difference insofar as men's costume, make-up and gestures represent parallel apologies for ballroom's inherent sensuality. If it is widely true that 'women find their greatest popular acceptance in sports that are considered "feminine" and then are denigrated as lesser athletes' (Feder-Kane 2000: 212), this is not entirely the case with ballroom wherein women are as athletic as their partners, and indeed often more so. Insofar as it may be true that 'to suc-ceed as an athlete can be to fail as a woman, because she has, in a certain profound symbolic way, become a man' (Willis 1982: 123, cited in Feder-Kane 2000: 210), it is the converse that proves problematic for men in dance, where the more outstanding the sensuality, sensitivity and expressiveness of their movement, the more 'deviant' their presentation of masculinity. Succeeding as a sensual artist can be seen as failing as a man since, by certain Eurocentric logics, such bodily sensuality is symbolic of 'woman'.

Such cultural logics are, of course, important for understanding the roles, pres-entations, performances and aesthetics of dance. Adding another layer to this picture, however, is the reality that since ballroom culture never exists in isolation from other cultural milieus, dancesport practitioners' gender roles are always related to both ballroom and non-ballroom cultural models. Where Faller thus points out that 'the more successful a female athlete, the more she tries to embody the *culturally appropriate* gender role … a role essentially at odds with her athleticism' (1987: 154, emphasis added, cited in Feder-Kane 2000: 208), ballroom dancers always have multiples – both between different dance styles, and characterizations at the micro-level and as members of larger national and ethnic traditions at the macro-level – *of* culturally appropriate gender roles available.

Just as Appadurai (1995) recognizes that cricket in India represents a local manifestation of transnational influences, wherein the 'rules, protocols, aesthetics and style have been transformed into something that is no longer quintessentially English' (Alter 2000: 83), the same holds true for the transnational participation base of ballroom as well, and it is in exactly this way that the ballroom dance is best understood, not as a monolithic practice, but as a common form and foundation for local variation.[8] And this point is pertinent to the issue of gender norms and practices, since ballroom practitioners are not all English (or of any other single nationality for that matter), but always members of *both* ballroom *and* non-ballroom cultures and communities. In practice, then, dancesport competitors' models for 'appropriate' gender roles are always informed by shared activity-based foundations, but are always enacted in specific locations by specific people. Different ideas about bodily display, such as in Denmark and Japan, always intersect the activity-specific norms of dancesport.[9]

This is not, however, simply a one-way 'mapping-on' process, but a complex interplay between cultural models that overlap – with varying degrees of success – for individual dancers. To the extent that 'sport, as a dramatic form of emphasizing the body, functions to assist in producing a local style of social personhood' (Mentore 2000: 66), the translocality of dancesport re-enters the picture; with the 'locality' of ballroom being activity, not location, specific. Just like bodybuilding, then, dancesport is an 'an amateur and professional performance sport that is defined by its competitive element as well as its rich complexity as a sporting subculture and social identity' (Bolin 2004: 120). Thus, despite different underlying national-level cultural rubrics for appropriate use and display of the body – say between various European and Asian dancers – many of the conventions for gender that are 'in play' for figure skating also hold true for dancesport, overlaying local elaborations.

While the different styles of dancesport, the wider participation base, and the always partnered nature of dancesport creates a more complex interplay of gender roles than those of figure skating, it still makes sense that many of the conventions that have been noted and analysed in skating also play into dancesport. In the first place, the elaboration of both activities into their contemporary competitive forms occurred within the same sociocultural settings. As such, the forms, practices and performances of both sets of 'aesthetic athletes' (Schechner 2002: 26) have developed within and in relation to the same norms, values and standards. In contemporary practice as well, however, the two activities continue to overlap as ballroom coaches regularly work with competitive skaters. Perhaps even more tellingly, given the many overlaps in aesthetic and athletic traditions, several ballroom-dress vendors (including two of the larger US companies) have also become involved in costuming figure skaters. The important 'take home' message here concerns the shared cultural and historical traditions of aesthetics and athletics for dancesport and figure skating. It is no accident that the beginning levels of dancesport are widely concerned with and dedicated to working on syllabus *figures*. As such, the academic work done on figure skating needs to be given its due weight in trying to gain a better understanding of ballroom culture, even as the differences between the two performative genres should also always be kept clearly in mind.

SPECTACLE/ART/SPORT

In Part I, I have tried to show how the dancesport world is a complex hybrid of numerous cultural practices and social networks partaking of spectacle, art and sport. More importantly, while each of these categories – spectacle, art and sport – provides useful insight into the performance of dancesport, none of these labels suffices on its own. Dancesport creates its own spectacle to be sure, but of what nature? Neither art nor sport alone, dancesport's competitors are both artists and athletes, and it is at ballroom competitions that their craftsmanship and prowess are put to the test, performed and displayed. As the focal performances of dancesport, competitions are the central events of the ballroom world, functioning as festival and celebration (Chapter 7) and ritual (Chapter 8).

PART III
BALLROOM COMPETITIONS
AS EVENTS

7 COMPETITIONS AS FESTIVAL AND CELEBRATION

As important as spectacle, art and sport are to understanding the performance of dancesport, ballroom competitions are the centre of dancesport culture. The day-to-day planning, activities, practices and work of dancers, coaches, vendors and other support personnel are all ultimately oriented towards ballroom competitions. Thus, while contextually different from the carnivals discussed by Bakhtin (1984), some of his ideas – particularly those on carnival pageants as ritual spectacles – are helpful in unpacking and understanding ballroom competitions as events. Proper carnivals, writes Bakhtin, are replete with 'long and complex pageants and processions' (1984: 5), a turn of phrase that equally suits the culturally scripted progression of dancesport competitions. More importantly though, is Bakhtin's assertion that 'carnival is not a spectacle seen by people; they live in it' (1984: 7). Ballroom competitions differ from many other types of dance performances precisely in this way; most spectators are themselves participants, and 'competitions' function as culturally privileged and highlighted social gatherings.

More than just concentrations of social actors, the significance of competitions (as events) lies in their role as nexuses of cultural values. As such, while the spectacle, art and sport of competitive ballroom are inextricable and mutually constitutive elements of dancesport, they are given their most manifest shape and form in the lived events of ballroom competitions. The visual images of competitions can thus be well understood analogously to carnival images, since:

> Because of their obvious sensuous character and their strong element of play, carnival images closely resemble certain artistic forms, namely the spectacle... But the basic carnival nucleus ... is by no means a purely artistic form nor a spectacle and does not, generally speaking, belong to the sphere of art. It belongs to the borderline between art and life. In reality *it is life itself*, but shaped according to a certain pattern of play. (Bakhtin 1984: 7, emphasis added)

Spectacle, art and sport are all part of ballroom competitions, but competitions are lived events – they are social spaces where people live lives.

This chapter thus examines the role and practices of ballroom competitions as in-gatherings of 'the tribe', bringing together dancers, judges, vendors and spectators, who do not regularly see each other outside the competition setting. More specifically, the chapter highlights how competitions regularly serve as opportunities for dancers: (1) to watch and observe styles and levels of dance and dancers they are not normally exposed to; (2) to interact with dancers (and other competition-related personnel) with whom they do not otherwise regularly come into contact; and (3) to visit with those they only see in the competition setting. Each of these dynamics, in turn, contributes to and is reflected in dancers' competition dress, demeanour, and conduct.

Clearly there can be no doubt that a vast amount of ballroom life takes place away from the competition floor. Indeed, the hours put in at the studio far eclipse the amount of time spent at competitions, and many times over at that. Yet it is the competitions that competitive ballroom is all about. As much as ballroom life cannot be understood without knowing what goes on in the studios, what goes on in the studios must also be understood in the light of their relationship to the competitive circuit as well. Whatever variation in instructional pedagogy, business models and social climate there may be from studio to studio – and there are many – the fact remains that the dancers from each show up on the same competitive floor and strive to attain the same results. Thus, while the greater part of any dancer's time is spent in the studio, it is the competitions which, as epitomotic examples of ballroom culture, contextualize even local practices.

To use Goffman's terminology, ballroom competitions are 'performative' both on and off the competition floor. Beyond the publicly performed dancing, the myriad festive and celebratory dimensions of ballroom events are also performed – not as spectacle for an observing audience, but as internally self-performative where connections, commonalities and social cohesion are performed between (and for) the dancers and officials. Similarly, there are many ritual dynamics involved in the competition setting that are regularly performed on and off the ballroom floor. Rather than focusing on the activity of 'competition' then, the materials in this chapter unpack the dynamics inherent to 'competitions' as the pivotal and epitomotic cultural events that they are.

FESTIVAL AND CELEBRATION

Insofar as a ballroom competition is a thing of spectacle, which it is, it is also, in part, a thing of festival and celebration as well. At whatever scale ballroom competitions take place and are conducted, they represent in-gatherings of 'the tribe'. Studio-level competitions bring together a wider and deeper cross-sectioning of studio participants than almost any other studio-level events (with the possible exception of holiday parties which are, of course, fully fledged festivals and celebrations). And, as much as the finished grooming and costuming of competition are the stuff of spectacle, the process and conduct of dressing up and 'fancifying' oneself as competitor, official, staff, or spectator is the stuff of festival and celebration.

Beyond the most basic studio-level competition, the festival and celebration-like facets of ballroom competitions emerge even more fully in larger-scale competitions. Collegiate, franchise and local USA Dance competitions all bring together dancers who do not all come in contact with one another in the regular course of their day-to-day activities, and certainly not all at the same time. Competitions thus serve as opportunities to watch and observe competitors, styles and levels of dance one is not commonly exposed to, and to interact with other dancers and competition personnel with whom one does not regularly come in contact.

Adding to the festival and celebration-like dynamic of ballroom competitions is the fact that competitions – as a concentration of dancers – are prime markets for ballroom industry vendors. As such, the 'larger' the competition, the greater the draw for various industry vendors that sell shoes, dresses, fake tanners, costume jewellery, miscellaneous costume accessories, ballroom music, videos, and the like. Whether in the back of the ballroom, an adjoining hallway or conference room, or a nearby exhibition hall, ballroom competitions start to take on something of the feel of a 'ballroom market' as the vendors set up their booths. The presence of colourful rhinestone encrusted costumes, numerous brands and models of shoes, tiers of costume jewellery, and racks of CDs, DVDs and videos all provide constant visual (and, in the case of music, sometimes auditory) cues as to the different-from-ordinary nature of the competition setting.

'LARGER'

Although slightly impacted by prestige of various events (i.e. the average 'level' of dancers competing at the competition), overall, 'larger' competitions attract a greater number and variety of vendors, all of which feeds back into the greater festival and celebration-like dynamics of these competitions. 'Larger', however, means different things to different ballroom constituencies. What matters most to the organizer(s) of the competition is the total number of entries; the number of people factored against the number of events entered by each. Two hundred dancers dancing an average of ten heats each, for example, represent 2,000 total entries. The same 2,000 entries could, however, also come from 400 dancers dancing an average of five dances each or from 100 dancers dancing an average of twenty heats each. To the event organizer, who is paid per person per entry, these different permutations of dancers and

Table 7.1   Heat Entries: Example 1

Dancers	Average Number of Heats Entered	Total entries
400	5	2,000
200	10	2,000
100	20	2,000

entries all represent the same number of total entries and thus equivalent financial stakes, as Table 7.1 helps illustrate. To the various vendors, however, these different permutations represent quite different stakes.

While the total number of entries in each of these scenarios is the same, the number of dancers competing in each represents drastically different situations for any vendor. Four hundred dancers are, after all, a very different potential customer base to 100 dancers. Yet the numbers used in Table 7.1 represent minor fluctuations in many of the pro-am competitions contested throughout the United States, with rare students dancing as many as 300 heats or more at a single competition. Again, as far as the event organizer is concerned, 300 heat entries generate 300 heat entry fees regardless of how that total number is reached. As Table 7.2 illustrates, however, one student entered in 300 heats is still only one potential customer for the vendors whereas twenty students each entered in fifteen heats provides a potential vendor with twenty potential customers.

Table 7.2   Heat Entries: Example 2

Dancers	Average Number of Heats Entered	Total Entries
1	300	300
20	15	300

What Tables 7.1 and 7.2 make clear then is that, while the total number of entries is what counts most for competition organizers (at least from a financial perspective) in assessing the size of their event – in other words, how large their competition is – the total number of competitors in attendance is a much more important measure of competition 'size' as far as vendors are concerned. Far from tangential, understanding the differences between the total number of entries and the total number of dancers at a given competition is critical to understanding the relative status and appeal of different competitions in the eyes of most vendors and competitors alike; this, in turn, influences the degree to, and the dynamic by which, a competition is (or is not) festival and celebration-like.

Why Size Matters   'Smaller' competitions with fewer actual dancers certainly play important roles and serve significant purposes within the greater ballroom culture. They provide venues for newer dancers to test the competitive waters as it were, easing into competition without being bowled over, sometimes quite literally, by far more experienced dancers. Beyond providing a less intimidating competition environment, smaller competitions give dancers a chance to hone their floorcraft and performance skills, and a chance to assimilate the various unspoken guidelines for competitions. Smaller competitions also tend to be less expensive, hence making it more affordable for newer dancers' family and friends to attend and provide support in a way that is much less common for larger events that are likely further from home. Similarly, more students and fellow dancers from one's own studio are likely to be attending and competing at smaller more local events, so in this way too a network of familiarity and support is often built into the smaller local events.

It is as dancers attend and compete at more and more events that they develop greater familiarity and comfort with the fairly typical set up, conduct and procedures of the competitive circuit. At the same time, an informal socializing process is also at work as newcomers become familiar with an ever-expanding sphere of 'who's-who'-type knowledge, and as they informally meet and chat with more and more people at various competitions. The greater knowledge of the competition scene provides for a less daunting experience at larger-scale events, while the expanding ring of acquaintances within the circuit provide an expanding network of support on these occasions. The vast social ease with which experienced competitors move through competition venues, even in countries they have never visited before, thus has a double genesis, stemming from the long since taken-for-granted nature of ballroom competitions, on the one hand, and the supreme familiarity and comfort with the social actors surrounding them, on the other. Let me take a few steps back at this point, however, before moving on, and comment on how the different configurations of dancers and heat entries as depicted above in Tables 7.1 and 7.2 drive the cultural dynamics being discussed.

Regarding vendors, their primary expenses are the same no matter what the size of the competitions. Whether twenty dancers, 200 dancers, or 2,000 dancers show up, vendors still need to travel and transport their merchandise to and from the event, pay their vending fee,[1] and pay for their food and lodgings.[2] The number of actual dancers at an event thus becomes a critical factor for prospective vendors, as they weigh the potential revenue against the costs of doing business at any given event. Smaller events with fewer competitors may not have a sufficient number of potential customers to justify more than one or two vendors, if any, being in attendance, while, at the opposite end of the spectrum, thousands of competitors – such as at Blackpool or the German Open Championships (GOC) – justify the presence of multiple vendors of each genre – such as dresses, shoes, music, books and videos, to name some of the most common – thus adding to the festival and celebration-like atmosphere, both via the market-like feel they engender, and by providing an abundance of additional cues as to the stature of that competition as a concentration of 'ballroom culture'.

Knowing that larger events have the most dancers in attendance – and hence the highest number of potential customers – also influences the production side of vendors' business practices as well. Since more dancers equals more customers, the larger the number of dancers at an event the higher the demand for vendors' products – meaning the greater the supply necessary. Just as dancers gear up for major competitions then, so too do vendors – albeit in their own ways. The sheer quantity of product-demand represented by the numbers in attendance means that most vendors, like most dancers, orient their annual schedules around the most significant, with production quantity rising, sometimes quite drastically, in anticipation and preparation of the larger competitions.

Beyond product quantity, however, when it comes to the high-end products of ballroom dancing – namely, costuming – quality is also an issue with the larger competitions. This is not to say that the quality of the garments produced at other times is of a lower standard; instead, the pertinent point here is that the size and scope of the larger events (in terms of dancers, judges and audience) drives the demand for new and notable costuming. Larger competitions call for competitors' newest and best costumes in order to stand out among their largest competitive fields. In most cases this means that the period leading up to the larger competitions requires increased production from dress vendors; a demand further exacerbated by the dress vendors' need to also have a large supply of dresses available for sale at the event itself as well.

But, just as much as the larger spectatorship and attention of larger competitions drive competitors to show up in their best costuming, so too does this same increased visibility drive the vendors' desire to showcase their newest and best designs on their displays, ordered in advance by dancers, and especially on the vendors' sponsored couples. The largest competitions – such as the Ohio Star Ball in the United States and Blackpool in the UK – thus emerge as the events that most partake of the festival and celebration-like dynamics within the competitive circuit. Competitors show up in their newest costumes, vendors have their most extensive supply of products, and the newest styles and trends in dresses and costuming are prominently showcased.

The competitions that are of most interest and appeal to vendors are also of interest and appeal to most competitors for exactly the same reasons. Just like vendors, competitors are concerned with the total number of dancers at a competition (and, more specifically, in their particular events) and not the number of overall entries. Competitors pay the same entry fee for their events, regardless of the number of competitors they dance against and the number of rounds required to narrow this field down to a six-couple final. Smaller events often have a straight final, providing but a single opportunity for a couple to take the floor, while the largest events in the world can easily start with over 500 couples, require preliminary rounds on a preceding day, and have six rounds and up. More experienced competitors and those looking for greater tests of their dancing thus look to the larger competitions as opportunities to test themselves and to showcase their developing dance prowess. Ultimately then, the larger events are not just straightforward competitions but also festivals and celebrations of dance, occasions when the most and the best dancers and dancing are displayed and celebrated.

IT'S A VACATION

As much as competitions are regular events, par-for-the-course occasions in the lives of most competitors, they are also a break from competitors' day-to-day non-competition routines. Much of the festival and celebration-like dynamics of ballroom competitions stems from the fact that, for many competitors, their time at a competition is a break from their day-to-day routines and a chance to get together, 'catch up', and 'hang out' with friends and acquaintances whom they do not get to spend much time with outside the competition setting, as seen in Figure 7.1. For most amateur competitors (whether part of an amateur partnership or dancing pro-am), for instance, their time at a competition is usually free from their daily work and family concerns and responsibilities. As such, outside the often comparatively brief time they actually spend preparing and competing in competition, the rest of their time can be used for local sightseeing, rest and relaxation, and socializing with other dancers and competition personnel. In a relatively parallel vein, for most

7.1. It's a vacation – Banquet meal for package holders at the 2004 Seattle Star Ball, Seattle, WA. ©2004 Jonathan S. Marion

professional competitors their time at a competition is free of their regular teaching, judging and practising commitments and, like the amateurs, provides opportunities for tourism, pampering and socializing.

Asked about his favourite parts of being involved in ballroom dancing, Kent, a previous professional national champion and currently an active pro-am competitor, responded 'this', as he gestured to our surroundings in a plush hotel lobby, further elaborating with 'the travel, the nice hotels, this lifestyle'. Kent's comments suggest the leisurely perspective many competitors experience regarding their time at competitions. Trying to schedule a follow-up interview in San Diego with former world finalist and world-class coach and adjudicator Ray Rivers, for instance, was proving most difficult, when Ray asked me if I would be at the Emerald Ball in Los Angeles the following month. Confirming that I would, he suggested we do the follow-up there, commenting that he would have a much more open schedule. Although we both lived in the same city, it was only when attending an event a mere two-hour drive north that Ray and I could actually find a mutually workable time to sit down and talk. Tellingly, the scenario I describe regarding my follow-up interview with Ray is far from an isolated or unique case.

My first scheduled interview with three-times Blackpool and World Amateur Champions Franco Formica and Oksana Nikiforova, for example, did not work out in London, two weeks prior to Blackpool, as we had originally scheduled. Amid their preparation and training leading up to their first Blackpool championship they lost track of the interview, but were able to make time at Blackpool and, again, for a follow-up interview at the GOC. Similarly, four-times Blackpool Professional Latin Champions Juka Haapalainen and Sirpa Suutari were having trouble finding time to do an interview with me during my second fieldwork trip to England and, when they found out that I would be going to the GOC the following week, suggested that it would be much easier for them to find the time to sit down there, and asked if that that would be okay. As things turned out, my interview with them at the GOC ended up taking so much time that we were not able to complete it on the day we had scheduled so we completed it on the following day.

Then World and Blackpool Amateur Latin Finalists Peter Stockebroe and Kristina Juel (now World and Blackpool Professional Latin Finalists) took time to sit down for an interview at the GOC with me that same year without issues. When I was in Denmark a couple of years later, at their home studio for three weeks (after Blackpool), Peter invited me to their house for dinner but, with late developing plans post-Blackpool, never managed to find the time to actually have me there. Similarly, my interview with then nine-times undefeated US Amateur Latin Champions, and World and Blackpool Amateur Latin Finalists Eugene Katsevman and Maria Manusova took place at an IDSF competition in Palm Desert and not at their studio in New York when I was visiting for a couple of days. And, as a final example of this dynamic, my interview with five-times Blackpool and seven-times World Professional Latin Champions Bryan Watson and Carmen Vicenj did not take place on any of my four trips to their home base of London but, instead, at Blackpool.

The point of all of these examples is not, of course, simply to point out that ballroom competitions tend to allow for more available free time than the day-to-day dealings of ballroom competitors, coaches and judges. Instead, what I am trying to highlight is the break from most dancers' day-to-day structures and routines that are inherent to the competition setting and which thereby play into the festival and celebration-like dynamics of ballroom competitions. But if competitions allow for less scheduled and routinized action and activity, this is only one piece of what makes them festival and ceremony-like to members of the ballroom community. Where the vacation-like aspect of ballroom competitions contributes to competitions' festival and celebration-like facets from a structural standpoint, competitions' reunions and party-like aspects make a comparable contribution from a social standpoint.

IT'S A REUNION

It is important to realize that the festival and ceremony-like aspects of ballroom competitions are only hinted at by their 'it's a vacation' aspects. More than just structural vacations from day-to-day non-competition routines, ballroom competitions are also the consummate social scenes within the ballroom world as well. It is far from the exception, for instance, to have friends in the ballroom scene who one hardly sees, if ever, outside of competition venues. Because of the scheduling pressures typically experienced by most dancers in their day-to-day lives, the socializing dynamic allowed for by the far less restrictive competition schedules provides a social appeal, draw and outlet most reminiscent of reunions – a dynamic further entrenched because many of these friendships are among people living far apart. As Eva, a long-time ballroom acquaintance recently commented, she often forgets that one of her closest ballroom friends actually lives in Hong Kong because they see each other on such a regular basis at competitions throughout the United States.

Beyond the structural vacation from day-to-day routines, the festival and celebration-like dynamics of ballroom also arise in response to and via the compressed temporal window for socializing that is both represented and provided by the competitions themselves. Especially as dancers move their residences from place to place over time – be it in response to non-dance job pressures and opportunities for most amateurs, or teaching and partnering opportunities for professional dancers – and as they make friends within the competition venues and circuits, the ballroom competition may very well emerge as the only place that many ballroom people get to see and visit with each other (Figure 7.2). One such example comes from Robert and Borbala Bunnett (Figure 7.3), who first met at a dance camp in San Francisco, at which time he lived in Orange County, CA, and she in Philadelphia, PA. Seeing each other nearly every weekend at competitions across the United States, Robert and Borbala 'dated' from 3,000 miles apart until they became engaged – a

7.2. It's a reunion – Professional Smooth competitors Christian Clayton and Kathryn Vaughn (left), after having recently moved to Maine, catch up with fellow competitors and former studio mates Eddie Alba and Susannah Cuesta (right) from Southern California, amidst spectators walking about and other competitors warming up in the hallway just outside the ballroom at the 2004 Seattle Star Ball, Seattle, WA. ©2004 Jonathan S. Marion

situation paralleled in the international dancesport circuit, with many romantic courtships transpiring across multiple continents as competitors' paths cross within the competition circuit.

To provide a personal example of these dynamics, let me turn to two of my closest friends in the ballroom world, Jim Gray and Sunnie Page who, as a couple, were the second and third people I ever interviewed in my ballroom research. I met and interviewed Jim and Sunnie at a Brigham Young University summer ballroom camp in Provo, UT, in 2001, while they were still amateurs competing in the *Novice* division. Now professionals, we have since shared many meals, phone calls and hotel rooms, both in the United States and in England, but we have never seen each other outside a competition except for last year when, coincidentally, they happened to be in Los Angeles for coaching. On that occasion I was able to get tickets for us to watch the live broadcast of the final episode for the first US season of *Dancing with the Stars* on 6 July 2005 (and again on 5 January 2006 when we went to see the live premiere of the second season).

Numerous examples of this 'reunionesque' dynamic abound in my personal experiences within the competitive ballroom world. I met one of my closest friends, then ballroom costume designer and head of sales for Doré Designs (now owner), Dawn Smart, at the Yankee Classic in October of 2001. Despite the fact that we

7.3. Ballroom competitions as social space – a concept demonstrated by Amateur Smooth US Finalists Robert and Borbala Bunnett (here dancing at the 2007 San Diego Dancesport Championships in San Diego, CA) who dated almost weekly at competitions across the US while living 3,000 miles apart. ©2007 Jonathan S. Marion

now talk on the phone several times a week, the only times we have seen each other outside a competition setting over the past six years was in June 2002, when we were both in New York City for Louis van Amstels' *Latin Fusion* show which was being performed at Center Stage, and in August 2007 when I visited her in Florida to see the Doré shop (see Figure 4.1) while revising the manuscript for this book.

A closely related example comes from my friends Felipe and Carolina Telona, the 2007 runners-up for the US National Professional Rhythm title, and the 2004 NDCA World Mambo Champions. I stayed with Felipe and Carolina at her parents' house in Toronto for the Can-Am Dancesport Gala (24–27 April 2003) and then stayed with them again, at Felipe's parents' house in Los Angeles the very next week for the Emerald Ball (30 April–4 May 2003). I periodically talk to them on the phone, and have spent late nights talking in hotel rooms with them, but I have never seen them outside the context of a competition. Another, almost parallel, example of this nature comes from my friends FJ and Catherine Abaya, US Professional Rhythm Competitors, who hosted me in their guest room and loaned me their second car when I was in Seattle for the 2004 Seattle Star Ball – but whom I have also never otherwise seen outside the context of a competition.

A final personal example of the reunion-like dynamic of ballroom competitions concerns JT Thomas. She was living in San Diego and competing in the professional Latin division when we first met, became friendly, and I first interviewed her. Since then she has moved to New York and switched partners and styles, before going on to capture the title of US National Professional Rising Star Smooth Champion (at the Emerald Ball in 2005), become a US Professional Smooth finalist, and become the 2007 US Professional Smooth Champion. In the several years since JT moved to New York from San Diego we have seen each other many times, sitting down for meals, getting in a social salsa dance or two, just hanging out, and even sharing a hotel room, but as with both Felipe and Carolina and FJ and Catherine, only at competitions.

Before moving on to the last section of this chapter, I want to reiterate the point that these examples have been used to illustrate: that, amid the hectic routines and high-mobility common among ballroom competitors, competitions represent a nexus of many social relations (perhaps even most) between dancers and others in the ballroom community. Providing face-to-face contact between people who may otherwise only rarely see each other, competitions present opportunities for friends and acquaintances to visit and catch up with each other, re-establishing and reaffirming their social ties and bonds. Indeed, and as I quickly learned early in my fieldwork, conducting interviews at a competition in even remotely public areas guaranteed several interruptions from the various passers-by who inevitably stopped to greet and catch up with whomever I was in the midst of interviewing. An interesting twist to this came later, and further into my fieldwork, when interruptions to interviews came not only from those stopping to greet those I was interviewing, but also from those stopping to greet me as well.

IT'S A PARTY

A final facet worth noting regarding the festival and celebration-like dynamic of ballroom competitions is that of being a party. The same structural dynamics that can make competitions vacation-like provide the opportunity, the same social dynamics that can make competitions reunion-like provide the means, and the break from day-to-day pressures and routines often provide the motivation. The more invested a dancer is in the competitive side of dancing, the greater the internal pressure they often place on themselves to perform well when competing. While the psychological side of these dynamics is outside the scope of this text, I should point out that those competitors who do not find ways of dealing with this pressure are quite unlikely to remain competitors for long.

After all the rigorous preparation for a competition, including the investment of physical, mental and emotional effort that is part of competing, some competitors prefer some quiet time, perhaps merely to read a book or simply to eat a doughnut that was on the 'forbidden' list only an hour earlier. Many competitors, however, prefer to celebrate by way of partying. Also playing into the 'partying' feel, flavour and mentality for some is the simple fact that, having chosen a form of dancing that requires close and near constant contact and interaction with another person, ballroom competitors are typically of both a social and an expressive bent. Although inevitably varying from individual to individual, these characteristics provide more than sufficient grist for what is often a fairly active party mill. The nature of what constitutes an actual party within the ballroom scene varies widely, but the specifics of each individual party are not what are at issue here, only the fact that competitions often function and serve as the venues for a variety of party-like practices and engagements. From sedate wine and cheese after-parties to drinks at the bar, and from the rambunctious in-room drinking to partying out by the pool, members of the ballroom community partake in many festival and celebration-like behaviours and activities within the competition context.

The same people who are national and international champions dealing with pressures that few (but the most elite athletes) rarely face at their age, are also typical high school and college-aged young adults. The competitors who were competing in world-ranking events just hours earlier, for instance, are the same dancers who cram forty bodies into a giant outdoor hotel jacuzzi until getting kicked out by hotel security at four in the morning. But it is not only in the more coherent and organized sense that competitions provide and play into the party-like feeling and atmosphere. Especially when they are in the United States, for example, trying to find any time to sit down and catch up with some of the European competitors I am friendly with can prove exceedingly difficult as they are always being dragged off by other dancers to go to the pool, for food, or a smoke.

Overall then, there are a number of factors that both feed into and reflect the festival and celebration-like aspects of competitive ballroom. In particular this chapter has shown how alternative measures of competition 'size' matter in different ways to vendors, competitors and competition owners. At the same time, I have pointed out the use and importance of smaller events in acclimatizing competition-initiates to the competitive scene, while also highlighting how event size both drives and echoes the festival- and celebration-like facets of competitions. Larger events with more vendors and competitors are more festival- and celebration-like thus drawing more vendors and competitors, further contributing to increasing festival- and celebration-like dynamics. Most notable among these dynamics are the ways in which competitions not only resemble but also (and often) actually function as vacation, reunion and party opportunities for members of the ballroom community. 'Moments of ... change and renewal', as Bakhtin suggests, lead 'to a festive perception of the world' (1984: 9), and this dynamic is fully in play at ballroom competitions. Competitions are spaces where not only do dancers' placements rise and fall, but the ballroom community reaffirms its values and renews its sociality. It is not without reason then that the official name for the Blackpool competition – as printed on competition programmes, shirts and merchandise – reads 'Blackpool Dance Festival'.

8 COMPETITIONS AS RITUAL

INTRODUCTION

Chapters 4, 5 and 6 explored the dynamics of spectacle, art and sport as they inform and are manifested in ballroom competition. Chapter 7 focused on ballroom competitions as complex events manifesting a wide variety of dynamics of festival and celebration. Excluding any of these dimensions would ignore significant constitutive elements of ballroom culture. Yet the very fact that the ballroom insider generally knows what to expect when they step foot into a dance studio – and even more so a competition – speaks directly to the highly ritualized nature of ballroom life and to the degree of ritualization at play in many ballroom practices.

Using the work of Davis-Floyd (1996), Grimes (1996), Kertzer (1996), Myerhoff (1996) and Rappaport (1996) on ritual in general and Turner (1995) on liminality in particular, this chapter explores the rituals and practices that set ballroom competitions apart from other facets of ballroom life, unpacking the formality, invariance, symbols and rites of passage embedded in ballroom competitions. Ritual permeates the ballroom world: from the dress that dancers put on to practice, to socialize and to compete, to the way they warm up; from the way dancers train and prepare to compete to the manner in which they stand around before 'taking the floor'; and from the way couples advance through the rounds of competition to the coordination between scrutineer, MC and DJ. While dancers do engage in any number of personal rituals, this chapter uses ballroom competitions to highlight the most prominent dynamics of ritual in competitive ballroom dancing.

Obviously the 'ritual' involved in ballroom is different from the paradigmatic example of ritual: religion. This does not mean, however, that ritual is absent or lacking in dancesport; far from it. Dancesport is both ritualized and ritualistic, having many qualities of ritual, 'including being performative, having a relatively high degree of formality (inside of which creativity occurs), relating self to something larger than self, transforming persons and so on' (Steven Parish, personal communication, April 2006). As this chapter's materials demonstrate, however, understanding the hybridity between ritual and competition is fundamental to understanding competitive ballroom. Lacking religious meaning, dancesport structure and ritual still functions in accordance with, revolves around and is dependent upon its own rituals and ritual structure.[1] 'Ritual', as Blackmer notes, 'permeates the world of the dancer, whether student or performer, amateur or professional' (1989: 26), as is clearly the case with competitive ballroom.

WHAT IS RITUAL?

Like competitive ballroom itself, ritual cannot be reduced to a specific type of object or activity. I concur with Rappaport's contention then that 'no single feature of ritual is peculiar to it. It is the conjunction of its features that is unique' (Rappaport 1996: 428). In a tightly overlapping formulation Grimes makes this same point, noting that 'what we label with the single term "ritual" is a complex phenomenon requiring multiple methods to understand it' (Grimes 1996: 283). Similarly, while an in-depth analysis of what ritual 'is' (and 'is not') is beyond either the scope or the aims of this text, there are two important points to consider. First, it is important to recognize that ritual 'is not an entity to be discovered. Rather, ritual is an analytical category' (Kertzer 1996: 339). Here too Grimes makes a similar point, contending that 'ritual is not a single kind of action. Rather, it is a convergence of several kinds we normally think of as distinct. It is an "impure" genre' (Grimes 1996: 283). Second, the multiplex nature of ritual highlights the complexity of meaning and symbolism in dancesport since ritual is only one of competitive ballroom's cultural facets.

Saying that ritual is no specific *thing*, is not to say it lacks specific features; features that are at least as important for understanding ritual as for identifying it. In two closely aligned formulations, Kertzer defines ritual as 'symbolic behavior that is socially standardized and repetitive' (1996: 340), and Davis-Floyd defines a ritual as 'a patterned, repetitive and symbolic enactment of a cultural belief or value' (1996: 148). Both Kertzer's and Davis-Floyd's understandings of ritual foreground a specific set of elements, suggesting that rituals are best understood as recurring, consistent and representational socioculturally grounded practices. I think it is also important to highlight three issues here: first, in being practices, rituals are participatory; second, rituals are not only about religion, spirits or magic;[2] and third, rituals are purposive, they are meant to affect a transformation of some order. Rituals, after all, do not happen if no one participates in them, and people do not regularly participate in rituals towards no ends whatsoever.

RECURRING AND CONSISTENT

An activity must be both recurring and consistent to function as a ritual. If an activity is often repeated but happens in a different way each time then it cannot be considered a ritual. Similarly, if an activity has a set nature but only happens on an irregular and sporadic basis, it cannot be considered a ritual. 'In order to be considered a ritual', says Myerhoff, 'an action must be replicated many times, mechanically, unvaryingly, almost obsessively, with mindless attention to the smallest detail' (1974: 238–9). At the micro level of analysis, Myerhoff's position speaks to the very nature of the seemingly endless hours of rehearsal that lay behind each minute on the competition floor. It is only by exhaustive repetition – practising the same minute shifts in weight and connection – that dancers come to step out onto the floor and perform the most involved and intricate techniques without conscious thought. Indeed, conscious thought of the myriad variables involved in a dancer's movement is a hindrance, disrupting what had become second nature with intellectualization and abstraction. Myerhoff's point is equally applicable at the macro level, as all but the newest competitors can walk into almost any competition and understand the divisions, processes and procedures involved, usually without even a second thought.

Ballroom competitions provide a strong example of how 'any type of behavior may thus be said to turn into a "ritual" when it is stylized or formalized and made repetitive in that form' (Nadel 1954: 99, cited in Myerhoff 1974: 239). It is not the specific details of how ballroom competitions are run, after all, that make them into rituals. Rather, it is the specificity of roles and procedures involved in ballroom competitions – coupled with the replication of these roles and procedures – that 'ritualize' these competitions. Every competitive dancer knows which dances they will need to dance for instance, in what order and within what range of tempi. The International Standard competitor knows beyond a shadow of a doubt that the order in which they will dance their dances is waltz, tango, Viennese waltz, foxtrot and quickstep. Even if they do not know the exact numerical ranges of acceptable tempi, dancers develop an innate sense of the acceptable tempi for each of their dances.

Which dances are included, the order in which they are done and the type of music played for each are fully predictable, and if this were not so it might be much harder to say whether ballroom competitions should be classified as rituals or not. But this is the case, with the dances included in each division, the sequence in which they are danced and the accepted range of tempi for each dance all being 'givens' within the competitive ballroom circuit. The outsider (or newcomer) may only notice that everyone already seems to know where they are supposed to go and what they are supposed to do, but for the insider the configuration of dances, sequences and tempi (see Table 8.1) represent and serve as unvarying markers for culturally salient practices. As worded by Rappaport, 'at the heart of ritual – its "atom" so to speak – is the relationship of performers to their own performances of invariant sequences of acts and utterances which they did not encode' (1996: 440), and this is exactly the case with these ballroom-specific regularities.

In the few instances where there is variation from this pattern, such as the Viennese waltz being excluded at Blackpool, this is well known and easily counts as ritual in its own right. Indeed, many of the best dancers in the world say that they think they do their best dancing at Blackpool since they know exactly what to expect from year to year – versus at Worlds, which are conducted in different locations each year.[4]

Table 8.1   Sequences and Tempi by Ballroom Style (measures per minute, mpm)*

Sequence	International Standard	International Latin[3]	American Smooth	American Rhythm
First	Waltz (28–30 mpm)	Cha Cha (30–32 mpm)	Waltz (28–30 mpm)	Cha Cha (30 mpm)
Second	Tango (31–33 mpm)	Samba (50–52 mpm)	Tango (30–32 mpm)	Rumba (32–36 mpm)
Third	Viennese waltz (58–60 mpm)	Rumba (25–27 mpm)	Foxtrot (30–32 mpm)	Swing (ECS) (34–36 mpm)
Fourth	Foxtrot (28–30 mpm)	Paso Doble (60–62 mpm)	Viennese waltz (54 mpm)	Bolero (24–26 mpm)
Fifth	Quickstep (50–52 mpm)	Jive (42–44 mpm)	n/a	Mambo (47–51 mpm)

*As per the 2008–2009 USA DanceSport Rulebook.

PERFORMATIVE (AND DRAMATIC)

Without performance there is no ritual.

Roy A. Rappaport

In looking at the performative (and often dramatic) character of ritual, I am not merely reintroducing the performance-like dynamics of competitive ballroom dancing. The point here is that performance is an integral dynamic of ritual in its own right and that the ritual and ritual-like facets of competitive ballroom remain opaque if the performative and dramatic nature of ballroom-specific ritual is not addressed. Performance is as necessary to ritual as formality, being 'the second *sine qua non* of ritual, for if there is no performance there is no ritual' (Rappaport 1996: 428, original emphasis). Rituals do not happen without participation. They do not happen – indeed cannot – on their own; they are fully contingent upon being practised, that is, performed, by persons.

While some rituals may be subtle affairs, most ritual is marked, both for the self and for others, by its 'loud', obvious and self-announcing nature. As Myerhoff contends, ritual 'is a conspicuously artificial affair' (1996: 395); a point mirrored by Kertzer's observation of ritual's 'frequently dramatic character' (1996: 340). Not to belabour the point, but neither of these positions argues that ritual must be, or always is, blatant and obvious, only that there is a tendency in this direction and that rituals are always fabrications. Myerhoff's conspicuousness and Kertzer's dramaticism both connect back to the fact that rituals are neither piecemeal nor aimless; they are deliberate, intentional and meant to *do* something. Aside from predictability then, the repetition intrinsic to ritual helps mark it *as* a ritual and not just a variation of other practices, and ballroom competitions are replete with such conspicuous and dramatic markers, some of the most common being:

- the set-up of the dance floor, surrounded by various forms of seating;
- specific areas by which competitors are intended to enter and exit the floor;
- a podium, with microphone, on a raised dais from which the MC conducts the competition;
- special, often multi-hued, floor lighting;
- the rainbow of colours, fabrics, cuts, designs, rhinestones, fringing and feathers of competitors' costumes (or the traditional tail suit of the gentlemen in Standard);
- the men's meticulous grooming and the women's elaborate coifs, false eyelashes and false fingernails;
- most competitors' fake tan and stage-like make-up;
- judges standing along the edges of the competition floor – with their backs to the audience, obstructing spectators' view of the floor – with clipboards and scoring sheets in hand.[5]

All of these items listed, especially when taken together (which is how they are performed), both draw attention to the ritual activity itself and, even more importantly, serve as conspicuous markers that something of significance is going on.

This marking of significance via ritualized elements is important in a number of ways. First, the non-ballroom passer-by who might stop to watch a couple practising in the hallway, or to watch a moment or two of a televised competition, still easily recognizes that there is clearly 'something going on' when they wander by a competition. Of far greater significance, however, these same markers serve notice to the dancers, officials and spectators alike that what is happening is culturally substantive and of impact. Indeed, it is these markers – including their overall repetition and consistency across time and place – that cast competitions at the centre of the ballroom universe. Competitions are where champions rise and fall, where new trends in dance and costume fashion emerge or fail and where the models of what constitute good dancers and good dancing are established, reinforced and displayed.

Also pertinent here is Myerhoff's point that 'in societies without writing, official statements about a person's status and skill are often given in dramatic, ceremonial form' (1974: 46). Clearly the dancesport community has writing and websites, newspapers, magazines, newsletters, email, text messaging, international cell phones and website-based forums have all played a role in the relationships, interactions, development, recording and dissemination of dancesport. At the same time, however, what matters most – what sets the context within which dancesport life unfolds – is still what happens in relation to the competition floor. Sitting or standing around the floor, standing on the edge of the floor itself and marking the dancing, or dancing on the floor not only provides incontrovertible evidence but also defines persons as a spectator, judge, or competitor for a given event.

More specifically speaking, who is it – which actual person – that walks out onto the floor when the judges are called and then stands on the edge of the ballroom floor, with a judge's clipboard in hand and proceeds to mark the couples as they dance? The answers to these questions are unmistakable; and such evaluations are not open to interpretation. A person either walked out onto the floor when the judges were called or they did not. They stood on the edge of the floor or they did not. They had a judge's clipboard whereon they marked the event or they did not. There is no grey zone of the 'well, they weren't really holding their clipboard up high enough to be a real judge' variety. There is thus no doubt regarding the status of someone who meets this 'dramatic, ceremonial form' as a judge – including all the ramifications of that status within the full sociocultural context of competitive ballroom dancing.

The marking and differentiation of status seems even more blatant among the ranks of active competitors. Dancing on the competition floor provides a plethora or Myerhoff's 'dramatic, ceremonial forms', each providing and in fact constituting, 'official statements about a person's status and skill' (1974: 46). The nature of their costuming is probably enough, on its own, to quickly classify someone as a Standard, Smooth, or Latin/Rhythm competitor.[6] Which dances they compete in, to which music and at what tempi, makes any such classification automatic; as would the movement styles, techniques and choreography they utilize. It is blatantly obvious, for example, which couples step out onto the floor in each round of competition, making the quarter-final, semi-final and final. Then, in the final, the couples' results are embodied in the final line-up, with the winners standing nearest those conferring the awards,[7] the runners-up next, and so on down through the last place finalist (typically sixth). While there may thus be any number of disagreements as to whether competition results were 'fair', 'correct', or the way they 'should' have been, there can be no doubt as to the 'official statements about a person's status and skill' which have been 'given in dramatic, ceremonial form' (Myerhoff 1974: 46). As Leach asserted over a half a century ago, ritual 'serves to express the individual's status in the structural system in which he finds himself for the time being' (1954: 11, cited in Rappaport 1996: 429).

REPRESENTATIONAL

It is important to realize, however, that the performative and dramatic aspects of ritual are not for entertainment alone; they are also both representational and transformational. It is each dynamic of ritual (in sequence) that generates the efficaciousness of ritual, being both what rituals actually 'do' and how they do 'it'. Put differently, rituals cannot be effective if those that they are meant for do not understand them or what they are about. As Davis-Floyd points out, for example, rituals work 'by sending messages in the form of symbols to those who perform and those who receive and observe it' (1996: 149). Clearly then, rituals cannot work in the absence of shared symbolic content. Messages cannot help but fail when what is represented in unknown or not understood. So what are some of the more prominent representations – and the messages they convey – in the ballroom world?

JUDGES AS ELDERS/SHAMANS

Within the world of dancesport, the symbolism of the line-up communicates the relative aptitude of the ballroom dancing skill, ability and performance that was produced and displayed by each couple (in accordance with the appropriate rules and procedures) at that competition. Yet as straight forward as this may seem, this depends on certain symbolic understandings that are easily taken for granted. To start with, an absolute outsider, unfamiliar with any of the symbols involved (including language), might well have no way of knowing that they were watching a competition. Perhaps the 'judges' are simply ballroom elders making sure that the ritual dances are performed correctly?

Far from being far-fetched, this is, among other things, exactly what the judges *are* doing! Except, of course, that the status of these 'elders' is not contingent upon age, but upon other, achievable, qualifications. Having made her competitive mark and retired quite young, for example, Charlotte Jorgensen is far younger than many of the competitors she now regularly coaches and judges. Yet the point remains, even in cases such as Charlotte's, insofar as ballroom judges *are* repositories of dance knowledge, ballroom lore and historical anecdotes, the judge as elder analogy certainly holds up. Yet judges are more than just resources for ballroom-related wisdom and learning; they are also the coaches who effect change – both in the general structural landscape of ballroom and in competitors' very ways of moving. As coaches, judges are guides to the cultural values and practices of ballroom, providing insight and advice regarding social and political structures of ballroom dancing and competition. As both arbiters of ballroom status(es) and conduits of personal change, thinking of judges as ballroom shamans also strikes me as an apt analogy. Just as more and more powerful shamans are sought out for increasingly particular insight and advice, or in order to effect more penetrating insights or changes, so too do ballroom competitors seek out the counsel and guidance of the most proficient coaches.

But what if our hypothetical outsider did not have conceptual categories of ritual elders or of shamans as lenses through which the ballroom competition could be viewed? Perhaps they would 'see' a ritual performance after which the performers are called forward and presented to the rest of the congregants by rank of seniority or 'tribal' status? Each couple is clearly dressed differently from the others, so perhaps certain sumptuary laws are in effect which, if our outsider knew how to 'read' them, would reveal each couples' status? Or maybe our outsider does not see a ritual; maybe they merely see a performance? And, whether ritual or performance, perhaps they only think it a costume contest of sorts that all of the dancers perform (be it a ritual or not) and are then ranked according to each couple's costuming? And how does our outsider know that it is the last-place couple that is called first and the winning couple that is called last?[8] Given such contingencies, if our outsider somehow manages to guess or deduce that it is the dancing which is being judged, how will they know how to interpret the line-up? Without knowledge of what the line-up is meant to represent, might they not very well think that the results are the exact opposite of what is actually the case – in other words, that the couples are announced from winner on down and not the commonplace practice of last to first?[9] The point of all of this hypothesizing is not of course to posit what an outsider might actually think but, rather, to highlight the role and importance of symbols and symbolism in transmitting and communicating the meanings and significance of what is being represented via ritual.

SYMBOLS AND SYMBOLISM

Rappaport follows up on his contention that 'no single feature of ritual is peculiar to it' (1996: 428) by asserting that 'ritual is that frill of decoration that communicates something about the performance or the performer' (1996: 429). Such communicative frills are, of course, the symbols and symbolism embedded in ritual. Unlike decorative embellishments, ritual's symbolism informs, recruits, evokes and modulates culturally salient models and meanings. To provide one example, the costumes worn by ballroom competitors are certainly meant to draw the eye and attention to the dancers and to embellish their movements. But these same costumes are also culturally loaded objects, physical elements of systems of meaning and significance. 'Most simply', as Davis-Floyd notes, a symbol 'is an object, idea, or action that is loaded with cultural meaning' (1996: 149), and that is exactly the case with the ballroom costumes in question. The costume is part of the dancing; communicating information about the nature of the dancing, the dancers, bodies and gender (among other things). As such a large topic and one deserving consideration in its own right, costuming is focused on more explicitly in Chapter 9. For the moment, however, it should be clear enough that the short revealing dress worn in Latin has, and conveys, very different models and meanings of femininity than does the elegant ballroom gown of the standard competitor – both to the dancer and to others.

To provide another example, take the case of the judges' clipboards: really nothing more than thin pieces of wood or plastic with integrated clips at one end that hold some sheets of paper to the surface. Clearly there is nothing intrinsically meaningful about these objects, especially as academic students may use them to take notes, artists to sketch and draw, teachers to take roll, contractors to mark construction progress and parameters. Many families may even have such a contraption attached to their refrigerator door, with a list of items that expands up until their next grocery outing. What is key here is that holding a clipboard clearly does not make a person into a student, an artist, a teacher, or a contractor, any more than it means that anything written on it must be a grocery list. Likewise, holding a clipboard in no way makes someone a ballroom judge or imbues them with the background, knowledge or skills that would entail. Yet within the context of a competition, the significance of the judge's clipboard far exceeds its properties as a physical object. Within this context the clipboard signifies the judges' qualifications and credentials to serve as judges, their authority to do so and also their obligation to do so.

In the same way that not just anyone can hold a clipboard and say they are thus a judge, neither can any judge simply decide to contribute their assessments to any competition simply by choice; they need to be eligible, selected and hired to do so. Conversely, the judge adjudicating a particular event – with clipboard in hand – cannot make a decision to not mark an event. At the same time that the clipboard itself has no significance then, within the appropriate ritual circumstances (i.e. used by the appropriate practitioners, in the appropriate setting), this simple object not only signifies who is a judge but simultaneously invests them with the power and obligates them with responsibility to judge that event. I think Myerhoff's formulation that 'one may view symbols and the rituals in which they are embedded as providing order, meaning and moral coherence and at the same time providing regulation and restraint' (Myerhoff 1974: 233), thus well fits and explains the symbolism of the judge's clipboard. It is only within the competition context that the clipboard simultaneously signifies, authorizes and obligates. 'Symbols', as Myerhoff also notes, 'convey meanings which are activated. They are *experienced* rather than merely *thought about* when used in rituals' (1974: 231; original emphasis).

Certainly judges, dancers and audience members may all think about who is judging an event (versus who is not) including such things as judges' own dance backgrounds, results and judging histories. But, with clipboard in hand, these judges are actually *experienced* by everyone as judges as well; they *are* the ones who will judge that event. Others, with identical qualifications, backgrounds and skills may assess the exact same performances, as may competitors and audience members – indeed few people watch a competition without making at least some choices between which couples they prefer – but those with the clipboards are the ones whose marks are counted in determining which placements are ultimately announced and thus count as the results. And, perhaps most importantly, this signification, authorization and obligation is mutually perceived, experienced and understood by all parties alike – by the judges themselves, competitors and spectators (Figure 8.1).

It seems easy enough to say that the meanings of the judges' clipboards or of the competitors' costumes do not inhere in the items themselves. A judge is a judge with or without a clipboard, just as a dancer is still a dancer whether in or out of costume. A group of dancers can all dance their routines, following all the regular rules and

8.1. The ever-present judge's clipboard – Victor Kanevsky judging at the 2004 Yankee Classing Dancesport Championships in Boston, MA (left); Michael Barr judging at the 2007 British Open Dancesport Championships, Blackpool, England (right). ©2004 & 2007 Jonathan S. Marion

regulations – while a group of judges could mark who they thought best – and the opinions of these judges might be of interest or significance to these couples. Yet even if danced in the same facility, this event would not 'count' in the same way, lacking, as it does, the repetition of significant markers. If one of the most prevalent features of ritual is repetition, if our no-costume-and-no-clipboard contest happened regularly – that is, with competitors and judges repeating their dancing and evaluation over and over and over – these events might very well start to matter; their symbolic force, and hence cultural significance, would start to rise. As things stand, however, competitions take place in certain venues, under certain circumstances, with certain key personnel and are publicly accessible (if expensive) events,[10] and the repetition of this pattern provides a conceptual map for what happens – and how – under these circumstances.

Over time and through association, the trappings of competition start to count as culturally communicative symbols; as Rappaport's 'rituals frill of decoration'. Their communicative efficacy of is of a particular nature, however, since the majority of items that persons handle daily are rarely considered as having ritually symbolic significance. As the examples of the judges' clipboards and competitors' costumes exemplify, 'symbols are conceptions made concrete and tangible, often (but not always) in the form of an object', but as Myerhoff goes on to point out, 'These conceptions are of a special kind – highly emotional' (1974: 237). Like any other cultural value, the emotional charge of a judge's clipboard or of a competitor's costume are highly variable; these symbols do have significance for judges and competitors. Why such items are significant is a different issue though. Not a question of symbolism, per se, but of symbolic significance, what is significant about symbols (within ritual contexts) is their ability to effect transformation. Far from being a *type* of meaning, symbolism is a *mode* of meaning.

TRANSFORMATIONAL

'Social rituals', as Mary Douglas has pointed out, '*create a reality* which would be nothing without them' (cited in Kertzer 1996: 342, emphasis added). This meaning-generating view of ritual closely parallels Myerhoff's contentions that 'symbols are basically sources of information, "models-of" as well as "models-for" reality; that is, they do not merely *reflect* but actually *shape* other aspects of life' (Myerhoff 1974: 230; original emphasis) and that 'ritual is a form by which culture presents itself to itself. In ritual, not only are particular messages delivered, but the ritual also *creates a world* in which culture can appear' (Myerhoff 1996: 397; emphasis added). The point of these formulations is that ritual-reality is no less 'real' for being constructed. Far from only being *about* reality, rituals generate and are part of it too. Perhaps even more accurately stated: since rituals are real, so too is ritual reality.

'The performance of ritual', posits Rappaport, 'establishes the existence of conventions and accepts them simultaneously and inextricably' (1996: 433). Those performing a ritual know that they have done so. Even if they are unconvinced of a ritual's efficacy, participants cannot ignore their own participation or the reality of that ritual. Performing ritual provides both tacit acknowledgement and participatory testimony to that ritual (including all its trappings) and it is in this manner that we can say that 'all rituals are efficacious to some degree merely by their taking place' (Myerhoff 1996: 407). But we mean more than this when talking about ritual as generative of reality. Despite claims such as Myerhoff's that rituals 'are not purposive and instrumental, but expressive, communicative and rhetorical acts' (1996: 407), I think Rappaport has it right when he argues that 'ritual not only communicates something but is taken by those performing it to be "doing something" as well' (Rappaport 1996: 429).

Why would rituals exist and be performed if people did not think they did anything (in at least some manner, shape or form)? Far from being rare and esoteric rites, performed by only select groups of people, ritual, in all its forms, is the stuff of everyday life. Certainly some places, settings and groups have more or less, just as some people find rituals more compelling than do others. In all cases, people participate in ritual, however, and 'through ritual the individual's subjective experience interacts with and is molded by social forces. Most often, people participate in ritual forms that they had nothing to do with creating' (Kertzer 1996: 340). If religious rituals are the most commonly recognized, it may be only because the subjectivity inherent in religious precepts is widely recognized (at least by those outside the religion and, quite often, by those inside it as well).

Insofar as people often look to religion for meaning(s), I would suggest that various religions can best be viewed and understood as *deliberate meaning systems*. People regularly turn to religion not only knowing that religion has meanings to offer, but actively looking for those meanings. I would suggest that other activities, however, when pursued with sufficient conviction, are best thought of and should be considered to be *unintentional meaning systems*. What I mean by 'unintentional meaning systems' is not that the activities are unintended, but that one does not participate in them intending to redefine one's systems and structures of meaning. Few dancers, if any, start their dancing with the expectation, let alone intention, that their dancing will come to reframe their personal meaning systems. Yet it is not without reason that Blackmer makes his observation: 'it seems to me that professional dancers ... are members of a vestigial religious order' (1989: 109). As one of the first dancers I interviewed related, she used to love to go snowboarding, motorcycle riding and even went skydiving. As she became more interested and involved with ballroom dancing, however, she began to cut back and eventually stopped these other activities because of what a possible injury to her ankle, knee or leg would mean for her dancing. It is exactly this type of orientational slippage that I have in mind then in describing dance as an unintentional meaning system.[11]

Just as Myerhoff says that symbols are a 'highly emotional' type of conceptualization (1974: 237), so too are rituals emotion-laden conceptual models. 'In the performance of ritual an exchange takes place', argues Kertzer 'and the emotions aroused in ritual infuse the cognitive view fostered by the rite, rendering it compelling' (1996: 347). As such, the greater one's exposure to and performance of ritual, the more that the emotions aroused in (and by) that ritual get linked with, melded into and infuse the models from which that ritual has grown and of which it is a part. Note, this is a very different – and much larger – proposition than saying that exposure breeds acceptance. Far from arguing that one merely becomes accustomed to the content of ritual (although this is inevitably the case as well), the point here is that ritual participation informs evaluations and conceptualizations that are external to the ritual itself. Attending and participating in more and more dance competitions, for example, does much more than merely acclimate one to what can be expected at ballroom competitions for example (although it certainly does that as well).

As I have been pointing out, rituals generate reality as much as they reflect it (e.g. Kertzer 1996: 342; Myerhoff 1974: 230 and 1996: 397; Rappaport 1996: 433). The same competition that displays dancing is also the very ritual by which the dancing is recognized; wherein the same results that recognize the best dancing are the very placements by which what is 'best' is established as such. As much as the competitions thus reflect the practices and values of the larger dancesport milieu, they are simultaneously the very 'sites' where what counts as the best dancing is established for the wider ballroom world. 'Rituals', as Kertzer so aptly points out, 'do not simply excite, they also instruct' (1996: 347). Far from reflecting static norms then, competitions are the very places where evolving styles and standards are measured against one another and from which new models and expectations are (variably) dispersed and assimilated.

Liminality   Ultimately the efficacy of rituals may reside in their ability to effect transformation. The transformative nature of ritual, however, is based on their ability to propagate liminality. These threshold states, most tightly linked to rites of passage, are intrinsic to the structure and conduct of ballroom competitions, especially in relation to dancers' results and advancement through the competitive rounds. The vast conceptual and experiential distance between day-to-day perspectives of the ballroom studio and the time-out-of-time quality experienced at competitions derives, I would argue, from the liminal nature and qualities inherent in dancesport as both ephemeral art and competitive dance.

While competing, the status of ballroom competitors is well described by Turner's classic formulation that 'liminal entities are neither here nor there; they are betwixt and between the positions assigned and arrayed by law, custom, convention and ceremonial' (1995: 95). While on the floor competing, in front of both judges and spectators, no placements have yet been made; no couple has yet won. Almost undoubtedly some couples will be dancing better than others, but as the dancers are in the process of actually dancing, the results do not yet exist. Stepping out onto the competition floor effects a liminal state – and status – for the dancers. They do not yet know how they will dance; they do not yet know how the audience will respond; and they do not yet know how the judges will mark them. Everything is 'on hold' while the hyper-now of the competition unfolds – everything but the dancing itself that is.

Defining exactly such states of transition, transformation and indeterminacy, Turner describes liminality as:

> 'A moment in and out of time,' and in and out of secular social structure, which reveals, however fleetingly, some recognition (in symbol if not always in language) of a generalized social bond that has ceased to be and has simultaneously yet to be fragmented into a multiplicity of structural ties. (Turner 1995: 96)

This matches and illustrates the lived experience of ballroom competitors. Away from their day-to-day schedules, routines and responsibilities, these dancers are also away from their day-to-day social roles, statuses and interactions. Despite any social distinctions and differences that exist off the floor, all competitors take the floor as an undifferentiated group, albeit with the purpose of differentiating between the very statuses that are (predominantly) absent in the on-the-floor competitive interactions.

'Liminality', as Turner notes, 'implies that the high could not be high unless the low existed' (Turner 1995: 97), and here too ballroom competitions well match this description (and provides excellent examples). 'Making it' to the quarter, semi, or final does not really matter if everyone does; indeed, it is only insofar as some people do not make it into higher rounds that 'making it' takes on value. Thus, while all couples may step onto the floor as (structurally) equal competitors, none can advance (within this setting) if others do not. No one can place first without others failing to do so. To use Turner's words then, the time spent on the floor by competitors is nothing if not *communitas* during a time of liminality, with world champions having no more rights on the floor than the least skilled newcomers competing alongside them. Dancers' time on the floor *is* time-out-of-time and separate from the day-to-day social structure of the ballroom world; with dancers regularly competing against their friends and even in the same events as their own teachers and coaches.

Just as Bakhtin contends for carnivals, ballroom competitions mark 'the suspension of all hierarchical rank, privileges, norms and prohibitions', being 'hostile to all that was immortalized and completed' (1984: 10). Not in all ways of course, but just as 'during carnival there is a temporary suspension of all hierarchic distinctions and barriers … and of certain norms and prohibitions of usual life' (Bakhtin 1984: 15), so too for ballroom competitions. Unlike carnival, some hierarchical distinctions do remain, such as between competitors and judges. Yet dancers of highly different ranks dance the same dances, at the same time and to the same music regardless of outside 'ranking', and each judges' scores counts the same as every other, despite any issues of individual expertise, prestige, or seniority.

These generalizing moments of activity, of time-out-of-time – wherein and whereby all the dancers equally count as and, in fact, equally *are* competitors – is all in the service of setting social positions and status for the day-to-day, time-in-time conduct and structure of the ballroom world. Competitors' results are the very stock by which their prestige and status rise, their own expertise is assessed and their appeal as instructors, performers and competitors grows in cultural capital. The quintessence of such preliminal–liminal–post-liminal shift – the transition from structure to communitas back to structure – can be seen in the finals of the most prestigious competitions: Blackpool, Worlds and, to a slightly lesser extent, the International and the UK. The best dancers enter these competitions with known rankings, but those rankings have no structural meaning once the competitors step out onto the competition floor. Neither dancers, nor audience, nor judges know what the final outcome will be, as it is precisely at these pivotal events that champions are both crowned and fall.

Even when results among a regular set of finalists seem consistent, this is only at certain moments. New challengers arrive, old ones retire, existing partnerships dissolve and new partnerships are formed. For the dancers as much as for the audience, who the dancers are in a structural sense is in flux; and, indeed, nothing symbolizes this more than the moment before the final results are announced

(Figure 8.2). Dancers and audience alike only know who danced in the final, not what their placements will be and social structure remains suspended for a timeless instant (Figure 8.3), until the results are announced and, in their announcing, either reaffirm or reconfigure the social structure and restart social time (Figure 8.4).

8.2. After the dancing – The 2004 World Professional Latin Finalists all congratulate each other after completing their last dance. They will then leave the floor and, at the end of the night, be called back onto the floor for a line-up (see Figure 8.4) as their placements are announced. ©2004 Jonathan S. Marion

8.3. Finalist line-up – Amateur Standard finalists awaiting their results at the 2004 Yankee Classic Dancesport Championships in Boston, MA. ©2004 Jonathan S. Marion

8.4. 2004 World Professional Latin results – Repeating World Professional Latin Champions, Bryan Watson hoists the winner's trophy high overhead as Carmen looks on, bouquet of flowers in hand, at the culmination of the 2004 WD&DSC World Latin Championships, held at the 2004 USDSC, Hollywood Beach, FL. ©2004 Jonathan S. Marion

PART IV
COSTS, CONSEQUENCES
AND OUTCOMES

9 COSTUMES AND CONDUCT

Dress is clearly neither culturally nor politically neutral. It is loaded with significance. Clothes are stuff that 'speaks volumes.' But what they say is never entirely clear. We must interpret the language of dress in any given situation.

Keenan (2001b: 181)

In Part II, 'Performing Dancesport', I considered competitive ballroom as a meta-genre of spectacle, art and sport, while in Part III, 'Ballroom Competitions as Events', I examined ballroom competitions as socially structuring events that are both festival/celebration and ritual. In Part IV, I revisit these topics, but through the concrete examples of ballroom costumes, conduct, gender and, ultimately, what it is like to live a dancesport life. Working from ideas about dress and fashion from Barnes and Eicher (1997), Eicher and Roach-Higgins (1997), Goodrum (2001), Keenan (2001a,b) and Wilson-Kovacs (2001), as well as Bourdieu's ideas regarding bodily practice and habit (e.g. Bourdieu 1977), this chapter uses the norms and standards for ballroom costuming and comportment as a jumping-off point to explore the aesthetic standards and values of dancesport and how these values and commitments get played out in the ongoing dress and behaviour of the ballroom world.

Much of ballroom's spectacle comes from the costuming involved; the same dancing done in day-to-day street clothes lacks the impact created when executed by fully costumed and coifed competitors. Ballroom costuming is designed and intended to maximize and facilitate the artistic and expressive impact of ballroom, enhancing the artistic images being produced by ballroom dancers while simultaneously standing up to the physical rigours and stresses involved in the tremendous movement and motion competitors produce. There are also significant differences in the costuming worn by dancers in the different divisions and styles – on both aesthetic and functional grounds – as well as in the costumes that the same couples wear for different competitions. There can also be no doubt that ballroom costuming simultaneously responds to and constructs the visual images and impressions that lie at the centre of competitive ballroom.

COSTUMES DON'T DANCE ON HANGERS (AND COSTUMES DON'T JUST HANG ON DANCERS)

Just as Castro (1991) and Savigliano (1995, 1998) have pointed out for Argentine Tango, and Mitchell (1994) has pointed out for Flamenco, the institutionalized practices of ballroom establish a conceptual framework for movement and meaning. These movements and meanings are more than intellectual abstractions, they are about real bodies in real life. This chapter thus focuses on the visible use, adornment and presentation of those bodies – including the meanings that are thus being enacted, encoded, reinforced, challenged, presented and performed within the context of competitive ballroom dancing.

'Clothes', as fashion theorist and cultural geographer Alison Goodrum points out, 'are activated by wearing them, just as bodies are actualized by the clothes they wear' (2001: 92). This is an important starting point: clothing is never only about itself – functional or communicative, dress is always more than simply self-referential. What makes cloth into *clothes*, after all, is that it is cut and designed for and worn by bodies, not simply folded and put in a drawer, hung on the wall, thrown on a bed, or put on a hanger in the wardrobe. Sociologist William Keenan makes a parallel argument in defining 'bodies, as the elemental canvas of the dress arts', which, as he goes on to point out, 'are imprinted with potent social and cultural identities through the medium of clothing' (2001a: 22). There is no doubt that 'the relationship between our bodies, their clothes and the manifestations of identities is a complex matrix of exchanges and interchanges within the social world' (Goodrum 2001: 87–8). At the same time, however, some of these relationships are more prominent than others in any given situation. Within ballroom there are two such dominant relationships – one common to most cultural settings and one that is ballroom-dance specific – and it is only in their intersection that ballroom costuming can really be understood. In ballroom, as in any social setting, 'dress is both an indicator and a producer of gender' (Barnes and Eicher 1997: 7). Yet while ballroom costuming can only be understood in relation to gender, gender alone does not explain ballroom costuming.

A distinction more significant than anything but gender, and unique to ballroom, is the specific style of dance. Here 'style' does not mean a dancer's personal way of moving (although that too can be important), but the larger, structurally central issue of what division of dancesport a dancer trains and competes in. Internationally this distinction is between Standard and Latin, with the two American-style divisions of Smooth and Rhythm being added into the mix in the United States.[1] While the International and American dance styles do differ, there are strong aesthetic similarities between each pairing, with Smooth being the American-style counterpart to International Standard, and Rhythm being the American-style counterpart to International Latin. What this means for costuming, at the grossest

Table 9.1   Basic Costuming Trends, by Ballroom Style and Gender

Style	Female	Male
Standard/Smooth	Ball gown	Tails/Tuxedo
Latin/Rhythm	Tight short dress	Tight shirt and trousers (pants)

level of description, is illustrated in Table 9.1. The point of this depiction is not, however, to suggest that ballroom costuming is in any way this straightforward. Rather, this general categorization helps to depict the framework within which ballroom costuming is culturally conceived, achieved and perceived.

Far from being abstract categories, the intersection of dancesport style and gender dictates costume choices; choices which, in turn, reflect and reveal dancers' sociocultural group memberships. 'Dress serves as a sign that the individual belongs to a certain group', as Barnes and Eicher note, 'but simultaneously differentiates the same individual from all others: it includes and it excludes' (1997:1). Thus, the brief descriptions provided in Table 9.1 suffice to allow the reader to determine (generally) at a glance which style is being danced in any of this book's Photographs on the basis of costuming alone.

As Figure 9.1 thus illustrates, the same dress that marks its wearer as a woman also marks her as a Latin dancer – but, at the same time, just as surely marks her

9.1. Latin costuming – as worn by World and Blackpool Professional Latin Finalists Michael Malitowski and Joanna Luenis at the 2005 Embassy Ball Dancesport Championships in Irvine, CA. ©2005 Jonathan S. Marion

as 'not man' and 'not Standard dancer'. As Eicher and Roach-Higgins have aptly pointed out, and as Figure 9.1 makes equally clear, 'we can expect dress to precede verbal communication in establishing an individual's gendered identity as well as expectations for other types of behavior (social roles) based on this identity' (1997: 17). Gender and dance style are communicated not only at the same time, but via the very same symbols. Before delving into this topic more deeply, however, I want to refine the intersecting fields of gender and costuming style. The groupings used in Table 9.1 can be subdivided between American and International styles and expanded to include footwear and hair styling, as per Table 9.2.

I want to examine this expanded set of intersections between costuming and gender in the light of two important points. First, as Keenan delineates, 'clothes are society's way of showing where we belong in the order of things, our role and position in the social pageantry' (2001a: 4) and it is in exactly this way that the

Table 9.2   Elaborated Costuming Trends, by Ballroom Style and Gender

Style	Female	Male
Standard	Ball gown with floats; Solid-piece shoe, either 'nude' or matching dress with approx. 2.5 in. heel; Hair up, black or blonde	Black tail suit; white bow tie; 1 in. standard heel in either black leather or patent; Short hair; no facial hair
Smooth	Ball gown with no floats (may have some open cut-outs); Closed-toe shoe, either 'nude' or matching dress with approx. 2.5 in. heel; Hair semi-up; black, blonde, or red	Long-sleeved shirt with waistcoat or dinner jacket; tie either black or matching partner's dress. 1 in. standard heel, either black or matching trousers; Short hair, no facial hair
Rhythm	Short dress, often w/fringe, feathers and beading; Open-toe shoe, typically 'nude' or matching dress with approx. 3 in. heel; Hair up or down; black, blonde, or red	Tight trousers and shirt; 1.5–2 in. Cuban heel, either black or matching trousers; Short or long hair; little facial hair
Latin	Shortest dress, often with fringe, feathers and beading; Open-toe shoe, typically 'nude' or matching dress with approx. 3 in. heel; Hair up or down; black, blonde, or red	Tight trousers and shirt; 1.5–2 in. Cuban heel, either black or matching trousers; Short or long hair; no facial hair

stylistic variations, listed in Table 9.1 – while always enacted through the lenses of individual tastes and preferences – situate dancers within the social field of ballroom dancing. Citing Butler (1990), Goodrum makes the second point I want to consider here – namely, that 'gender is encoded via the repeated stylization of the body and of action within a rigid frame' (2001: 91). Far from merely providing classificatory criteria, then, the costuming variables noted in Table 9.2 provides dancers with tightly scripted modalities for culturally enacting gender.

Imagine two couples. The first couple consists of a woman dressed in a full-length ball gown, with a heavily rhinestoned bodice, full sleeves, a full satin skirt and with full floats running between the back of the dress and her wrists. She is wearing close-toed satin court shoes with a 2.5 in. heel that have been dyed to match her dress and her hair is pinned up in an elaborate upswept style (using fifty or more hair grips) to which at least half a can of hairspray has been added. Her partner is dressed in a custom-made black dancesport tail suit, offset by a bright white shirt, collar, bow tie and cuffs. His shoes are shiny black patent leather, with suede soles and a low 1 in. (normally shaped) heel. He is clean-shaven and his short hair is shiny and immobilized thanks to the generous use of professional-grade gel and pomade.

Now consider a second couple standing alongside. This couple consists of a woman dressed in a short, slinky dress that clings tightly to her body, with a plunging neckline and that leaves her arms and back entirely bare. Her legs are also bare and on her feet she wears strappy, open-toed dance shoes in a nude satin with a 3 in. heel; her short, brightly coloured hair hangs freely, but is neatly groomed. Her partner is dressed in tight, high-waisted trousers and his long-sleeved black shirt clings tightly to his torso. He wears black leather shoes with a 1.5 in. Cuban heel and his hair may very well be pulled back into a short ponytail. While both couples will seem tanned, the Latin competitors will probably be more so, and while both women will have fake eyelashes and heavy make-up – necessary to be seen under the bright lighting and from across the competition floor – the Latin woman's make-up may be stronger and a bit edgier, with her fake eyelashes possibly even displaying small rhinestones and her fake nails likely to be noticeably longer and more vibrantly coloured.

So what comparisons can be made between these four dancers? What similarities are there? What contrasts? While there are clear differences that separate along gender lines, such as dresses for the women versus trousers for the men, there are also differences that mark by style, including the tighter fit of the Latin competitors' clothing, their deeper tans, higher heels and looser hair styling. But so what? Certainly it is important not to over-generalize what is being communicated by these costumes since, as Goodrum warns, 'fashion has no absolute or essential meaning' (2001: 101). That being said, however, an unmistakably 'important sociocultural aspect of dress' is 'that it is imbued with meaning understood by wearer and viewer' (Eicher and Roach-Higgins 1997: 15). While, to the complete outsider, our four dancers might appear as simply two women and two men, the ballroom insider is more likely to see a Standard couple and a Latin couple.

The point here is not that the ballroom insider is not fully aware of the genders of the dancers but that the more salient difference for predicting where these dancers each fit into the sociocultural ballroom milieu is based on dance style, not gender. It is in exactly this way that gender, even as the more hegemonic discourse – more easily taken for granted as a category for classification – may not be the more salient variable between Standard/Latin and Female/Male in this scenario. More accurately, however, gender and dance category are mutually informative dynamics of role, place and identity within the ballroom world. A dancer is not male *or* a Latin dancer, female *or* a Standard dancer. Each dancer is either female or male *and* dances a particular style; and, as noted above, each of these intersections corresponds to particular codes of costuming. Men cannot only be said to dress and dance differently from women any more than Latin dancers can only be said to dress and dance differently from Standard dancers. From one perspective then, every dancesport woman dresses and dances as a female Latin dancer (or Rhythm, Smooth or Standard) and every ballroom man dresses and dances as a male Latin dancer (or Rhythm, Smooth or Standard). Or, conversely, every Latin dancer (or Rhythm, Smooth or Standard) also dances as a female or male. Ballroom costuming, as Keenan says of clothes in general, thus serves to 'unite and divide us at one and the same moment, making us members of this group but not that one, conferring upon us this sort of identity but not that one, indicating affiliations of this kind but not that kind' (2001a: 32). While every dancer may thus be dressing according to powerfully gendered models, it is inescapably true that different images of 'femaleness' and femininity are implicated and invoked by the different types of women's costumes, just as different images of 'maleness' and masculinity are implicated and invoked by the different types of men's costumes.

SEEING AND BEING

'Our clothes', notes Keenan, 'mark us out in social and cultural terms. To "look the part" is to fit into a definable social niche' (2001a: 31) and this is exactly what we see with dancesport competitors' costuming. But this is only half the picture; clothing is not only how one represents one's self to others, but also to one's self. If 'dress is generally indicative of behaviour and belonging, social placement and taste culture membership' (Keenan 2001a: 26), and is also 'the best available prelude to action and reaction ... it tells us, by and large, where bodies and selves belong in sociological terms' (Keenan 2001: 27) – it does so as much for one's self as for others. And it is in this way that costuming serves as a nexus of intercontextualization for an array of social, cultural and psychological processes and dynamics.

The same costuming that identifies a dancer's social position as a female Standard competitor, for example, is equally informative of this structural positioning to the dancer herself as it is to other dancers. 'Dress', as Keenan says, 'is key to the social construction of ... our self-image' (2001a: 32). But this only scratches the surface of the implications for her costuming. Beyond situating herself socially, this dancer's costuming also informs cultural expectations – again both for herself and others – regarding a wide array of values and behaviours. Additionally, and perhaps even more importantly, however, there is also a self-reflexive dynamic at play in both the social and cultural positioning informed by this dancer's costuming. She not only knows the social and cultural implications of her costuming, but also that others know those implications as well. Dress thus functions not only as a self-defining and self-constructing device and process – although certainly functioning in this way as well – but also as a cultural field of interpersonal interaction. Viewing costuming in this way, as a cultural field of interpersonal interaction, helps unpack several concomitant processes.

Complementing the presentational and situating dynamics of costuming, sociologist David Martin notes that 'dress mediates how we see ourselves and how others see us' (2001: xv). But Martin continues this argument by pointing out that 'if we want to pass muster we had better make the right choice' (Martin 2001). The second half of Martin's postulation is as significant as the first. How people dress – especially amidst the variety of options readily available in the industrialized West – is a far cry from being some gigantic sociocultural painting-by-numbers. If culture provides an array of options and parameters for social positioning and expectations for dress, persons are still agents with their own perspectives, values and agendas. It is thus that our dancer does not step into her ball gown merely because she is a Standard dancer, but also because she wants to be seen as one – and seen as one doing what it is that a Standard dancer is supposed to do.[2]

While I think Goodrum suggests an overly agentic view of fashion when she points out – citing Bourdieu (1986), Craik (1994) and Mauss (1973) – that 'fashion is purpose-built to secure certain effects – techniques of fashioning the body are a visible form of *acculturation* in which identities are created, constructed and presented through the habitus of clothing' (Goodrum 2001: 87, emphasis added) – she still makes an apt point. People do not merely act within a cultural field of interpersonal interaction; they act to achieve certain aims. After all, our dancer does not merely want to dress like a Standard dancer, but to be *seen* as one. As already noted, however, such wanting is in fact a duality: dressing as a Standard dancer – in order to be seen as a Standard dancer – presents our dancer as a Standard dancer both to herself and others after all; and it is in this way that dress can be said to '(re-)present us to ourselves and to the world' and that 'body-selves are made up to "look the part"' (Keenan 2001b: 181).

Insofar as being seen *as* a Standard dancer is important to our dancer, all of the trappings implicated in being seen as a Standard dancer take on value for her as well. Yet, as I have been pointing out throughout this chapter, our dancer is not only a Standard dancer, but a female Standard dancer – a multiplex role with its own codes of conduct and costuming. It is thus that, at the same time as our dancer wants to be seen as a Standard dancer, she is doing so through a cultural lens that has gendered implications and it is in exactly this way that ballroom costuming both responds to and creates its own cultural value. What this means in practice, is:

> Acquiring knowledge about gender-appropriate dress for various social situations extends to learning rights and responsibilities to act 'as one looks'. Accordingly, gendered dress encourages each individual to internalize as gendered roles a complex set of social expectations for behavior. These roles, when linked with roles of others, represent part of social structure. (Eicher and Roach-Higgins 1997: 19)

Wanting to be seen as a Standard dancer, then, our dancer learns how to dress like one but, at one and the same time, she is also internalizing gendered value structures. In learning, trying and then enacting her role as a Standard dancer, our dancer comes not only to identify within this gendered-value structure, but to interact with other ballroom persons accordingly, which only reinforces the selfsame value structure.

Looking at these dynamics from a slightly different angle, sociologist Dana Wilson-Kovacs contends that 'the cultural practices that define the body influence its representations and contemporary ideas of femininity and masculinity. These ideas are reflected, in turn, by bodily display and conveyed through our choice of dress' (2001: 159). In line with this formulation, we can say that the ballroom world offers different sets of cultural practices – of which being a female Standard dancer is but one – and that each of these cultural models are not only personified via costuming, but also influence the ideas of the individuals enacting these models. The crux of this interaction lies in the fact that in following certain models of dress one does not only learn to see one's self, but to be one's self, through this model.

CLOTHES EQUAL COSTUMES

Despite the tremendously visual spectacle of ballroom competitions and costuming, it is important to recognize that *all* clothing is costuming. Off the competition floor as much as on it, 'dress behaviours and bodily adornments most assuredly typify and represent the quintessential "routines of social life"' (Keenan 2001a: 36). As such, it is not only competitors' competition costumes that instruct and inform dancers' social interactions but, in fact, their entire repertoire and manner of dress within the ballroom world. Which of the dancers depicted in Figure 9.2 for instance, seems more likely to be a Latin dancer: Toni Redpath, on the left, or Katarzyna Kozak, on the right?

The answer is Katarzyna, on the right. And this answer seems to be an easy one to arrive at, even for non-dancers, after having been shown only a few sample photographs of both Latin/Rhythm dancers and of Standard/Smooth dancers competing. Indeed, the only times when any non-dancers have chosen Toni, it turns out that they thought I was asking a trick question while, in fact, their initial

9.2. Standard/Smooth or Latin/Rhythm? – Toni Redpath (left) and Katarzyna Kozak (right) as spectators at the 2004 USDSC, Hollywood Beach, FL. ©2004 Jonathan S. Marion

impression and gut instinct had actually favoured Katarzyna. So why is it so easy for people – who do not know that Toni retired as undefeated US Professional Smooth Champion and that Katarzyna is a past US Professional Latin finalist and Blackpool Professional Latin Rising Star Champion – to select Katarzyna as the Latin dancer? Even more importantly, why is this association so robust that even people who do not know anything about ballroom dancing can make this assessment correctly after having just seen a couple of contrasting illustrations of entirely different Standard/ Smooth and Latin/Rhythm dancers in competition (in the appropriate costuming for each)?

The underlying point here is that who dancers are as competitors is inseparable from who they are 'in the round'. As such, what counts as appropriate competition costuming for various dance competitors is not – and cannot be – isolated from their identities as ballroom dancers. If, as argued above, being seen as a particular type of dancer informs being a particular type of dancer, this is still the case off the competition floor. The ballroom world is one that most serious competitors live in, albeit not exclusively so. What this means is that the communicative field of dress is no less subject to cultural conventions off the floor than on it, and that the same style-specific gender models implicated in competitive costuming ramify onto clothing in general. It is dress that 'constitutes one of the most basic methods through which we are able to place ourselves and others in the social world' after all, and that serves to 'socialize the body into a cultural being' (Goodrum 2001: 86–7).

It is not only on the ballroom floor, then, that the Standard/Smooth dancer is expected to be the proper and distinguished ballroom gentleman or lady, or that the Latin/Rhythm dancer is allowed – or even expected – to be more 'fiery' and overtly sexualized. A particularly telling example of the different gender models and expectations that I have noted before (Marion 2006: 11–12) comes from Charlotte Jorgensen who, as a very highly placed amateur Standard dancer, came to *watch* a competition while 'wearing a skirt with slits all the way up both sides and thigh high leather boots'. Going on to describe people's reactions, Charlotte recounts that 'It shocked people. They said to me "You can't wear that!"' The point, of course, is not what Charlotte was actually wearing, but that this outfit violated the norms and conventions she was subject to as a Standard dancer. The underlying point to Charlotte's scenario is that, 'within ballroom, one's appearance as a dancer is typically culturally glossed as one's character as a dancer and, as such, is subject to different evaluative frames for Ballroom and Latin dancers' (Marion 2006: 12).

With all of this now in mind, I briefly want to revisit Figure 9.2. The definition of dress given by Eicher and Roach-Higgins as 'an assemblage of body modifications and/or supplements displayed by a person in communicating with other human beings' (1997: 15), highlights the socializing and communicative functions of clothing, even as the nature of such socialization and communication remain culturally variable. Given this premise though, it becomes much easier to see how even the non-dancer can make the correct selection for who is a Latin dancer when looking at the photograph of Toni and Katarzyna. Even without knowing about ballroom costuming, or having additional information about the gender models implicated, the non-dancer can extrapolate from competition photographs and can *see* the closer association and relationship between Latin/Rhythm costumes with Katarzyna's outfit and Standard/Smooth costumes with Toni's.

Part of what makes dress such an efficacious medium of communication is that 'some of the information that is transmitted from person to person by dress is not easily translatable into words' (Eicher and Roach-Higgins 1997: 15) and thereby bypasses linguistic filtering. The ease with which non-dancers can select Katarzyna as the Latin dancer with only a couple of dancesport pictures upon which to base their selection strongly evinces this exact point. Putting this and the reaction to Charlotte's outfit together thus highlights the significance of costuming – by which I mean all clothing – within the ballroom world and makes it clear that:

> The femininity of the ballroom lady in her elegant full-length ball gown ... is clearly not the femininity of the Latin lady in her short, skimpy Latin dress ...

and it was exactly this type of norm that Charlotte had violated... As such, it is not only that the ballroom and Latin competitors put on different costumes and perform different roles – which they obviously do – but that what it means to dance as a male or a female and by implication to be a male or a female, evokes different images, connotations and elements. (Marion 2006: 12)

NOT ONLY COMPETITORS WEAR 'COSTUMES'

If competitors' everyday clothing is costuming as much as their competitive costumes (albeit far from as spectacularly), it is also important to recognize that it is not only competitors' who are wearing 'costumes' in the ballroom world. All clothing is communicative and socializing – all dress serves to situate socially according to cultural values. Eicher and Roach-Higgins appropriately note that 'the dressed person is a *gestalt* that includes body, all direct modifications of the body itself and all three-dimensional supplements added to it' (Eicher and Roach-Higgins 1997:13, original emphasis) – not only certain categories of dressed persons. While the competitors' costuming may thus be the most evident and most culturally elaborated costuming in the ballroom world – and their competitive costumes in particular – this is far from the only costuming that is involved or that matters.

How are spectators dressed? Are they wearing jeans and T-shirts, tuxedos and cocktail gowns, or something in between, with each wardrobe style contributing to very different competition atmospheres. Whether explicitly recognized or not, how an audience is dressed is itself a significant and constitutive element of the context through which the dancers, officials and spectators all experience a competition. The difference between spectators in school T-shirts and sweatshirts versus tuxedos, Armani suits and silk ties should not be underestimated as a fundamentally constitutive component of the differences that set a collegiate competition apart from Blackpool. Albeit on a smaller scale, this same dynamic, is also part of what sets the afternoon and evening sessions apart at most US pro-am-based competitions, lending greater prestige to the evening sessions.[3] Simply stated, the fact that spectators dress in a certain fashion is of great significance in setting the tone and mood of a competition, with more formal attire helping to frame more socioculturally substantive results.

A variant of this audience dynamic is also in play for the competition officials since, while far fewer in number, the relative visibility of each official is far greater. If competitors and audience members perceive cues from the dress of competition spectators, this is just that much more the case for judges and other visible officials. It is a different experience to pick up one's registration materials or purchase a competition programme from a staff member in casual versus professional attire. Similarly, seeing judges arrayed around the floor in slacks and blouses, versus jeans and tee-shirts, changes how these judges – even as the exact same people, with the exact same credentials and qualifications – are perceived and experienced. Listening to the MC announce the competition results from the dais *is* different if she or he is wearing casual dress rather than a suit.

The question that begs to be asked here is why? Why should what a judge or an MC is wearing have the impact it does? Competitors, even when off the floor, are members of the category being evaluated and judged in the ballroom world, so it seems easier to understand why their appearance matters to the extent that it does. Ultimately, however, three factors need to be figured into this picture. First, dance is never detached from other social and cultural norms and standards – a topic to which I will shortly return. Second, and as previously noted, the communicative functions of dress are experienced universally (even as the particulars of such communication remain culturally variable) so are applicable to everyone. Finally, because competitive ballroom dance is driven by the engine of visual aesthetics, participants in the ballroom world are primed to be hyper-aware of visual cues and communication.

In saying that competitive ballroom dance is driven by the engine of visual aesthetics, I do not mean that other, non-visual aesthetics do not play important and even pivotal roles, in competitive ballroom dancing. Indeed, the dancing itself – its execution in action – is far more dependent on the aesthetics of touch and kinaesthetics. Yet as a competitive activity, judges make their determinations and audiences choose their favourites based on what they see. In theory could not a judge dance with each dancer to evaluate them instead of watching? All fourteen judging criteria suggested by Dan Radler (as discussed in Chapter 3) are judged visually – posture, timing, line, hold, poise, togetherness, musicality and expression, presentation, power, foot and leg action, shape, lead and follow, floorcraft and intangibles – but it is important to note how many are primarily visual in nature to begin with. Overall then, those who watch and are involved in dancesport learn to key into and interpret visual cues and, as such, are culturally primed to take notice of – and meaning from – the visual symbolism and communication of clothing.

Before moving on to look at the connections and relationships of dance to non-dance, I want to call attention to one other form of dress that is of tremendous significance within the context of ballroom competitions. As Eicher and Roach-Higgins point out, 'some types of *political dress* are neither body-hiding enclosures nor uniforms. Instead, they are *small* attached, inserted, *hand-held*, suspended, or *rigid preshaped objects*' (1997: 21, emphasis added). What are the judges' clipboards (as introduced in Chapter 8) if not exactly this type of political dress in both form and function? Certain qualifications are needed to be a judge, but it is the clipboard in hand that not only confers the authority and responsibility to judge, but that visibly signifies this political authority.

Further compounding the significance of the judges' clipboard is its extreme visibility. As depicted in Figure 9.3, it is impossible not to see the judges while watching the dancers since the judges are standing on the competition floor itself. Depending on where a spectator is seated and a judge's position on the floor, the judge

9.3. Clipboards as political dress – Jim Gray and Sunnie Page dancing Professional International Standard at the 2005 Embassy Ball Dancesport Championships in Irvine, CA (left); and Donald Johnson judging at the 2005 Desert Classic Dancesport Festival in Palm Desert, CA (right). ©2005 Jonathan S. Marion

may be front and centre in the spectators' view. Especially given the audiences' seated position and the judges' standing position, the actual marking on the clipboard is also thus at eye level for the spectators. The right frame in Figure 9.3 shows past US Professional Latin finalist and Blackpool Professional Latin Rising Star Champion Donald Johnson in the foreground and past Russian Professional Latin Champions and World and Blackpool Professional Latin finalists Sergey Ryupin and Elena Khvorova in the background. This particular event, the Desert Classic, was one of only two competitions that Sergey and Elena competed at in the United States in 2005 (the other one being the 2005 USDSC).

The point here is that it would be impossible to take advantage of the opportunity to watch Sergey and Elena without being blatantly aware of Donald, on the floor, as a judge, with his clipboard in hand. Finally, it helps to illustrate how it is not only audience members who are always faced with the judges' clipboards. Yet, as the position of the clipboard in the lower right of the left frame also suggests, as much as competitors may not be able to avoid seeing these elements of political dress, it is the evaluative gaze enabled and empowered by the clipboard that establishes the evaluative gaze – the very perspective that gets internalized in the process of developing as a ballroom competitor.

DANCE AND NON-DANCE

All dance worlds – of which ballroom is only one – have their own styles of movement and dress, yet 'style is an aspect of dance that separates it from the non-dance world, but the inherent meaning refers back to the non-dance world' (Brinson 1985: 209). As previously noted, for example, audiences and judges wearing more formal attire convey greater prestige and social gravity to a competition. I would suggest that this is because this convention mirrors the meanings of such clothing in the non-dance world. If the ballroom world is a cultural world unto itself – as I generally take to be the case – this does not mean that the ballroom world exists in a different sociocultural universe with its own set of laws and forces. If different stellar bodies display different characteristics, this is because the same forces of gravity, magnetism, stellar fusion, electrical bonding and so forth are acting on different configurations of space and matter and not because the forces are different. It is in exactly this way that the ballroom world should be understood as unique, yet only explicable within a context larger then its own parameters. International forces of economics, politics and globalization manifest and are felt within the ballroom world in unique ways, for instance, yet cannot be understood within the context of ballroom alone. Ballroom competition and costuming exist as unique *configurations* of aesthetics, values and practices, not *as* unique aesthetics and values.

IT'S IN THE DETAILS

In concluding this chapter on costuming and conduct I want to suggest that, in many ways, the internalization of cultural content takes place at the level of – and through – details. Members of the ballroom community live through cultural values via the specific acts and practices that demarcate and define ballroom life – as numbers get pinned to a competitor's back, as fake tans are sprayed on, as cuff links are fastened and as dresses are zipped and hooked. 'Dress', as Barnes and Eicher point out, 'is not only visual; it may also include touch, smell and sound. It has an impact on the viewer, but also on the wearer' (1997: 3). The smell of fake tanner, the feel of fake eyelashes and nails, the weight of rhinestone-encrusted dresses and the sound of a dress's beaded fringe are the minutiae of experience which dancers wrap around themselves in constructing and living their cultural lives.

A new but enthusiastic college ballroom team member offers the following example of the fine-scale details that a dancer may absorb as they pursue their dancing. In an online discussion (on the Dance Forums website) of ballroom shoes, Daisy writes that:

> I always know what colors, heels, widths, fabrics, etc. they have in certain styles
> … for instance, when I went to the Ohio Star Ball, I was trying on a pair of
> Tina's to get the right fit and the guy handed me the box and I sat down to

9.4. Competition make-up – US Professional Rhythm finalist Kristina Pchenitchnykh,[4] assists the then new Rhythm professional Julie Goldman apply her make-up at the 2004 Seattle Star Ball, Seattle, WA. ©2004 Jonathan S. Marion

> try them on and without looking at what heel height was on the box, I walked back to him, holding up the shoe and I said 'You accidentally gave me 2" heels … I wanted the 2.5" to try on' and he said 'those ARE 2.5" in heels' and I said 'Impossible … the 2.5" heel doesn't come in tan leather, it comes in tan satin … and these are leather!" The man was astounded, but shook his head, laughed, told me I was right and went back to get me a pair of 2.5" heels. (www.dance-forums.com)

Even more experientially than this, however, it is in learning practices such as how to put on competition make-up – i.e. in learning how to achieve a look that will show up to good effect under stage lighting and to audience members and judges from 50 feet away across the ballroom floor – one concomitantly learns to see and thus experience, through ballroom eyes. It is exactly this that Figure 9.4, the final photograph in this chapter, depicts.

10 PERFORMING GENDER

Despite the designation of 'gender studies', which seems to indicate attention to
how men and women are constructed socially and culturally, often in relation
to each other, studies on gender have focused on women. This has also been the
case in studies on dance and gender.

Wulff (1998: 109–110)[1]

Working from Hanna (1988) regarding gender, dance, culture and the body, and
based on the different uses and presentations of the body and dress entailed in the
different divisions of ballroom dance, this chapter examines the gendered practices
and cultural implications of the different uses of the body between the Standard,
Smooth, Latin and Rhythm ballroom styles. Also considered in this chapter are
the heteronormativity of dancesport gender roles, the gender-based division of
partnering responsibilities, biology as experiential filter and how the performance of
dancesport gender extends off the ballroom floor.

(EN)GENDERING IDENTITY

Since dance can only be realized through bodily enactment, it emerges as a particularly efficacious medium for the transmission of meanings that – because of their
intrinsic embodiment – often pertain to sexed identities. While dance inherently
implicates the embodied 'self' of the dancer, 'more often it calls attention to one
of the two types of human bodies – male or female' (Hanna 1988: xiv) and it is
this dynamic that undergirds 'the potential of dance to convey sexual imagery that
confirms or challenges attitudes about being a man or a woman' (Hanna 1988: xiv).[2]
As an often emotion-laden and hypocognized activity[3] dance is deeply intertwined
with gender. 'Who performs what and how in dance', Hanna points out, 'tells us
many things' (1988: 148). Messages are thus conveyed about artistry and athleticism
– what counts as artistic for a man and what for a woman? What counts as skill, or
ability, or talent for each? Are there differences and if so, what are they, why are they
there and what do they mean within their larger cultural surround? 'Movements', as
Hanna has said, 'carry the inner feelings and cultural overlays of sexuality and sex-
role identities' (1988: 134). 'Whether a ritual, social event, or theater art', she notes,
'dance has important yet little-recognized potential to move and persuade us about

what it is to be male or female' (1988: 3). The motions of dance are part of larger complexes of culture and communication (Brinson 1985: 214).

Hopefully a brief personal anecdote will serve to highlight the (unfortunately) conceptual transparency of the inter-implications between dance and gender. In 2001 I went to a movie with a fellow anthropology graduate student. As we were waiting in line we were discussing our research projects and I was truly startled when my colleague expressed surprise that I considered gender an important part of my research. Her surprise struck me as particularly significant for two reasons: first, she had on previous occasions voiced her dislike of any form of dancing where she, as a woman, must 'follow'; and second, she had also expressed dissatisfaction with the convention in competitive ballroom of a couple being designated by the number on the *man's* back. These are both phenomena wherein dance and gender serve as intercontextualizing frames of reference for each other, so how was it that she thought my project would not involve gender? In the case of competition numbers, for instance, the placement of the couple's number on the man's back is predicated on costuming (Figure 10.1). Whereas a man's costume is likely to be an

10.1. Competition numbers – as seen on Blackpool Professional Latin Finalists Peter Stokkebroe and Kristin Juel-Stokkebroe (left) and World and Blackpool Professional Standard Champions Mirko Gozzoli and Alessia Betti (right) at the 2007 British Open Dancesport Championships, Blackpool, England ©2007 Jonathan S. Marion

unembellished solid-coloured shirt or jacket, with a 'blank' back, a woman's costume may be backless, have elaborate floats, or be heavily detailed, patterned and stoned. As such, placing the number on the woman's back proves far more disruptive.[4]

Gender is never an autonomous system, unconnected from other social, cultural and personal facets of human life. Definitions and understandings of self – within which gender is highly implicated – are, of course, integrally linked to cultural discourses. Even more importantly perhaps, bodily practices and discourses often involve at least some degree of transmission and enactment below the level of conscious processing.[5] This is especially significant since, while most learning is conscious, that which transpires out of conscious awareness often involves emotional conditioning (D'Andrade 2000: 64, based on LeDoux 1996); which is why embodied discourses – such as those implicated by dance – often emerge as particularly stable patterns of and for cultural behaviour. Indeed, since the majority of daily operations are organized outside of awareness, this leads to the activation of goals and procedures which are themselves outside of awareness (D'Andrade 2000: 67, based on Mandler 1984). It is by way of such dynamics that dance – as an often emotion-laden and hypocognized activity – is most implicated in gender.[6]

Values (gender-related or otherwise) do not, of course, manifest themselves directly but, rather, matter via their instantiation through action systems. By looking at concrete activities the values associated with such action-systems (here dance) emerge as rich material for social analysis. Many indigenous societies have both men's dances and women's dances, for instance, yet as several feminist scholars have warned (e.g. Nicholson 1986; Rosaldo 1980), rather then assuming the significance of such a distinction, what is called for is an analysis of the significance of this bifurcation within its own context. Why the divisions? What is the content/purpose/subject of women's dances? Of men's? What cultural collateral do these contents/purposes/subjects hold within that society? When are the women's dances performed? When the men's? What is the significance of this timing? All of these are questions (amongst many others) must be asked since such practices always 'operate within … a matrix of … practices that inform women's and men's actions and behaviors' (Blackwood 2000: 17).

As I have argued elsewhere, individual lives are about the meanings that are constructed through personal experiences (Marion 2000). In serving as a locus of factors necessary for 'salienation' (Marion 2000), dance emerges as a particularly efficacious medium for the transmission of meanings which, because of their intrinsic embodiment, often pertain to sexual identities. Whether sociological, political, psychological or anthropological, research that casts dancing as a (purely) social phenomenon fails to address the level at which such sociocultural practices are actively engaged in by persons. Even the intersectional themes of more contemporary research approaches often overlook the individualized meanings – including conceptions of gender – that dancing has for individual dancers. Undoubtedly dancing is social, but not *just* social.

As Peter Brinson points out, 'dance derives from and maintains, strong continuing links with surrounding circumstances of life' (1985: 209); more than just movement, dance should be understood as 'a part of human culture and human communication' (1985: 214). As such, dance often plays a role in many functions of social processes – such as, commercial, political and propagandist (e.g. Strathern 1985) – all of which also have implications for gender (e.g. Heng and Devan 1992). Nor can dance be separated (necessarily) from music and language (e.g. Brinson 1985, regarding the case by Blacking 1981; Kaeppler 1985).[7] While the intersection of language and gender seems widely accepted within the academy, the idea that dance, like language, serves as a means of cultural communication receives short shrift.[8] As Hanna has pointed out, however, part of the 'immediate wallop' that dance can have in 'commenting on sexuality and in modelling gender', stems from its 'attention-attracting motion, language-like qualities, replete multilayered meanings, multisensory assault, composite of variables that change attitudes and opinions and accessibility and humanity' (Hanna 1988: 22). This important conceptualization underlies the role of dance in both exemplifying and constructing gender,[9] and helps to explain how and why dance can continue to matter long after 'native' historical bases have passed.

Unlike many other leisure pursuits (e.g. mountaineering), women have always been involved in 'ballroom' and the institutionalization of gendered rights and duties is well demonstrated by the lead/follow division – and concomitant expectations – that are part and parcel of this dance style. The man not only has the right to lead, he is obligated to do so. If the man does not lead, the woman cannot follow, and if the woman does not follow the man cannot lead. A naturally progressing outcome of this is that even when learning a given dance, say the cha cha, what it is that a man and a woman learn is not identical.[10] This is not to say that this role differentiation is equally accepted or practised by all dancers but, rather, that any variances take place within – and are influenced by – these institutionalized standards. More importantly, however, a man's and a woman's bodily experiences of learning to dance and of dancing, are different as well, inevitably giving rise to different identities as dancers.

BIOLOGICAL SEX AS EXPERIENTIAL FILTER

By providing different experiential filters for males and females, biological sex predisposes the sexes to different experiences.[11] 'Our bodies', as Downey points out, 'structure what we perceive' (2005: 31). This position is not as overly-deterministic as it may appear, since what is being asserted is not that sex is the cause of different identities in and of itself, but that *as a filter* biological sex leads to different experiences which, in turn, provide the building blocks for different identities.[12] Men and women have different anatomies after all, meaning that dancing in a closed frame – chest to chest and with thighs passing between each other – is a different experience for men and women. Pointing out that biology predisposes different experiences is not only about sex of course; a tall dancer has a different experience of dance to that of a short dancer, while a naturally slim person's experience of dance differs from that of a larger person, and so on. Given the strict sex-based division of roles in dancesport, however, sex represents an inescapable biological filter on dancers' experience of dance.

The notion that biological sex represents a primary experiential filter does not, of course, divorce sex from the cultural scripts of gender that get mapped onto it. For example, males and females have different centres of gravity which provide for different embodied experiences of the same bodily actions – but which bodily actions are seen as manly or womanly in the first place remain cultural elaborations. Recognizing that physical aesthetics are socially prescribed does not make them any less salient however – no more feasible to reject or refuse within their sphere of application. By way of illustration, any dancer may thus recognize and even reject the larger social and cultural models of male and female attractiveness that are celebrated and perpetuated in Western media. At the same time, however, their very participation as a ballroom dancer places them in the middle of an aesthetic system that largely overlaps with these same mental models. The point here is that just because one recognizes conceptualizations of attractiveness as constructed does not mitigate the pervasiveness or significance of these models.

GENDER, DANCESPORT AND HEGEMONY

Because the gender norms of dancesport are inseparable from the activity itself, they are functionally inescapable. Thus the same dancer who consciously rejects dancesport's models of grooming, costuming and conduct is still subject to these standards insofar as they participate in the larger dancesport system. In other words, one's appearance matters in a system where appearance matters. Standards of grooming, appearance, dress and attractiveness – as socially and culturally defined and appreciated within dancesport – thus become part of many dancers' self-definitional 'vocabularies'. Because these models and conceptualizations are linked to dancers' own bodies, they become deeply intertwined with dancers' identities. The pervasiveness of such ideas about body-image can be profound, co-opting personal frames or reference (in this case for dancers) for self-image and self-definition (e.g. Bartky 1979; Chernin 1981; Wolf 1991; Lin 1996). It is precisely by defining the topics and terms of negotiation that hegemonic norms and values have sway,[13] and it is the intrinsic insidiousness of such co-optation that Parish is describing when noting that:

> Cultural images of self and society that achieve hegemony – that stand as powerful and pervasive self-images and societal images from which people take meanings that integrate them into social practices – may animate behavior and attitudes long after a deliberate, conscious ideology has been exhausted and abandoned. (Parish 1996: 229)

Thus, since the gender models of ballroom are so deeply entrenched in the dancing itself, they now function as bi-directional filters on perceptions and conceptualizations (of male/female, man/woman and masculinity/femininity); pervasively shading past experiences while also setting the hues of new ones as they are constructed.

Because gender models (including their associated aesthetic schemata and coding) are so intrinsic to the bodily practice of ballroom – and since bodily experience and change is so powerfully charged regarding identity – the gender models embedded and embodied in ballroom are felt and lived; even if/when/as they are consciously questioned. As Parish points out, 'hegemony takes form in the feelings that *suffuse practice*, not just in terms of those conscious values that are codified as "official" beliefs' (1996: 228, emphasis added). Further reinforcing the hegemony of gendered norms in ballroom is the reality that 'in relationships of power, the dominant often has something to offer and sometimes a great deal… The subordinate thus has many grounds for ambivalence about resisting the relationship' (Ortner 1995: 175). A female dancer is not going to be thrown off the dance floor for refusing to wear make-up, earrings, or false lashes. Yet such violations of prescribed aesthetic standards will factor into judges' marks. To the extent that this woman has any interest in competing, she not only has incentive to follow the gender models in question, but also – through her chosen commitment (as per Stromberg 1986) to dance – is personally invested in following them as well.

HETERONORMATIVITY IN DANCESPORT

Intrinsic to the gender models in ballroom is deeply embedded heteronormativity, pairing male (leader) and female (follower). The heteronormativity in question, however, is an interesting one, focusing, as it does, primarily on gender roles and relations and remaining largely unattached to issues of sexuality. At the same time as the pairing of male and female is cast as the overwhelming norm for partnering – and as the only acceptable standard of partnership for all dancesport competition sanctioned by the international membership organizations of the IDSF and WDC – this seems to be driven (at least primarily) by aesthetics of gender and not sexuality. This distinction between gender role (under the rubric of aesthetics) and sexuality lies in the fact that the norm for partnering is that *all* men are cast as leaders and all women as followers regardless of sexuality. When I first started my fieldwork, half the men then in the World and Blackpool Professional Latin finals were homosexual, well illustrating the difference and separation between the performance of dancesport's gender(ed) roles and personal sexuality. While this ratio is not representative of the general distribution of Latin competitors, it is noteworthy that almost all of the out gay men in dancesport are represented in the Latin ranks (a topic I shall return to shortly).

The overwhelmingly dominant aesthetic of partner dancing (and especially ballroom), then, is the pairing of male and female – and many, many hours of ballroom coaching go into trying to choreographically and stylistically design and depict the 'male/female relationship' between partners. With the single major exception of Rudd Vermey – who feels that a man and a woman dancing together are already 'man' and 'woman' – the gendering of a couple's on-the-floor relationship and interaction is an important element, emphasized by almost all the elite coaches worldwide (heterosexual or otherwise). The heteronormativity in ballroom is a complex one, however, and not without its own conflicts as well. In general, sexuality is not part of the norms in question, yet the most traditional and oldest of the codified competitive styles, Standard, has proven the most resistant to accepting gay men as viable examples of the 'properly gentlemanly' character of a ballroom champion. This is in contrast to the wider acceptance of gay men as Latin champions.[14]

While a commonly voiced belief among some dancers suggests that the greater flamboyance characteristic of Latin better suits gay men, this essentializing stereotype overlooks (or ignores) reality: the majority of men dancing Latin are not gay. What seems closer to the truth is that the more overt sexuality of Latin (versus Standard) allows for sexualized identity (of any nature) in a manner that the more 'refined' identity-image of Standard does not. As such, the stereotyped hypersexuality of homosexuality finds a better fit in Latin dancing. Or, alternatively, one could argue that participating in the publicly heteronormative sexuality of Latin dancing can be viewed as a cultural compensation for private non-heterosexuality. Inevitably this varies on an individual basis, though, as none of these scenarios actually speak to real numbers, but only to those whose sexuality is known within the community. Given the tight knit and continuously overlapping nature of the ballroom community, however, as well as the 'lived-in-public' nature of most of ballroom life, few secrets (if any) remain secrets for long. What seems the most compelling argument is simply that homosexuality is more accepted by the judging establishment within Latin dancing[15] – for whatever variety of reasons this is the case – thereby making Latin a more likely dance-path for those who, in their personal lives, do not act out the same heteronormative pairing that they do on the dance floor.

WHY MORE GAY MEN?

Under the larger rubric of sexuality relating to heteronormative gender roles and patterns, a compelling question remains concerning the discrepancy between the visibility of homosexual males among the ranks of elite Latin dancers and the almost complete absence of 'out' homosexual females among this same population (with only one widely known exception). Given this lack of 'known' non-heterosexual females among the ranks of highly accomplished competitors I was unable to pursue this topic in any substantive manner but, in speaking with many dancers – including several of the elite competitive gay males in question – a basic model still emerged for trying to understand the apparent discrepancy between non-heterosexual male and female interest and participation in dancesport. The underlying and differentiating dynamic seemed to be one of aesthetics, as homosexual male dancers commented on appreciating the appearance and shapes of both male and female bodies and of the interaction between male and female bodies on the dance floor – a position contrasted with one where non-heterosexual females were not equally appreciative of male bodies.

While only an anecdotal model for the time being, within Western frames heterosexual women and homosexual men seem to express a far greater non-sexualized aesthetic appreciation for the beauty of women's bodies in general, than heterosexual men and homosexual women do for men's bodies. Applied to the apparent discrepancy between homosexual male and female ballroom competitors, then, it seems that homosexual men are more likely to appreciate the aesthetic possibilities, creations, interaction and performance of partnership with a woman than homosexual women would be to have parallel aesthetic interests and appreciation for a man. While further work is needed to flesh out this model more fully, it comes from and fits the data I have to date and 'seems right' to the competitors I have suggested it to, including several homosexual elite male dancers (i.e. Blackpool and World professional finalists) among them. Returning to the larger gender-role implications of heteronormativity, however, I want to focus on different understandings of equality in looking at the roles of men and women roles in ballroom.

BALLROOM'S 'EQUALITY OF EQUIVALENCE'

Simply taking the traditionally male and female roles (of lead and follow respectively) as sexist anachronisms makes the mistake of confusing kind with value. A leader cannot do any more actual ballroom dancing without a follower than a follower can without a leader. While to the ballroom-outsider 'following' may, perhaps, be seen as 'lesser' within the context of current dancesport 'leading' and 'following', the dominant model stresses the mutual necessity, responsibilities and aptitudes of these as complimentary skill sets. Both roles are indispensable to ballroom dancing. Certainly men and women are cast as having different roles in partnered dancing, including different norms of physical expression, appearance and aesthetics. On its own, however, this should not be automatically seen as unequal or chauvinistic since difference is not, a priori, asymmetrical (e.g. Nicholson 1986: 92, 103; Rosaldo 1980). What seems closer to the case for partner dancing is what Spiro (1979) recognizes as an 'equality of equivalence' instead of an 'equality of identity'. Men and women in ballroom are different from each other: they dance different parts, with different roles and responsibilities and in response to different gender models. Yet both male and female are valued and the female member of a partnership may be the more famous or the one elevating the status of a new partnership.

Yet while difference in role should not be conflated with difference in value, as a rule males are still socioculturally dominant within dancesport. Indeed, while the complementarity of men's and woman's roles within the dancing relationship are regularly espoused, several common practices and factors illustrate (and propel) the gender discrepancies often in evidence in dancesport. Perhaps the most regular testimony to embedded gender disparities lies in the common practice of discussing partners' placements and results using only the man's name. This pattern surfaces in informal conversations and online postings, such as 'do you think Slavik should have been placed ahead of Michael?', but is also manifested in the headlines of dance newspapers wherein major competition results are announced solely under the men's last names, such as 'Watson and Hawkins Win!'. The problem inherent to such comments is that even *if* the male is the stronger member of any given partnership, it is still the couple who has danced and been judged; partnering – and one's partner – matter. This same male chauvinism commonly carries over into teaching when couples offer workshops together: the man typically leads the overall lesson, with the woman supplementing.

Still, at the same time as this overall tendency is evidence of enduring structural sexism, there are equally respected and successful partnerships where the woman takes the guiding role in group teaching situations – testimony to the variability and permeability of this very norm. And variability there is – in abundance. One woman, a professional US finalist, argues against the very terms 'lead' and 'follow' – asserting that you lead a horse or a dog, not a woman – while another woman, also a professional US finalist, talks about how long a 'leash' the lead should provide through the tensions and elasticity of arm and body. Similarly, one man, a professional Blackpool champion, talks about how his partner is a woman and not merely 'a piece of dance apparatus', and another man, also a professional Blackpool champion, speaks about how he uses his technique and energy to dominate his partner on the floor – albeit specifying that he means emotionally dominate, not physically.

So what sense can be made of these divergent viewpoints? As with any ideas, cultural sharing is never total, uniform or complete. Rather, underlying themes get incorporated by persons who – no matter how culturally contextualized – are always acting agents with their own perceptions, experiences and agendas. Within dancesport it is the practice that is activity-driven, not the dancers' personal meanings or motivations. Just as one dancer can be motivated by the desire to win, another by the desire to perform and entertain and yet another by the desire to create – all within the context of dancesport – so too with understandings of gender roles, as different models of male/female and lead/follow are equally viable in creating competitive ballroom dancing. Just as motivation to win, perform and create must all be channelled within a framework of activity-based cultural standards, however, so too with gender roles and how they are performed. Variations and divergent conceptualizations can exist, but only within a range congruent with a male-lead/female-follow heteronormativity.

So what then of the different views of lead/follow? Are some partnerships between equals and others not and if not, is the male always the partner with more power? Here again Spiro's equivalence model of equality is useful, as neither male nor female can excel in dancesport save in relation to their counterpart. Since there is no such thing as a great leader who cannot lead or a great follower who cannot follow, and since these roles are gendered male and female (at least within the dominant heteronormative arena of dancesport), these roles – and hence genders – are interdependent; a dynamic exacerbated by the dyadic nature of competition. If males and females play complementary functional roles in all societies, within dancesport it is each male and each female who must function complementarily to succeed. No one – male or female – ever wins a ballroom competition sans partner. While each couple negotiates its own specific balance, each pairing must function interdependently to succeed. As such, the conscious understandings of lead and follow may vary greatly – ranging from rejecting these very terms to casual use of the term 'leash' – but two constants remain: (1) partnering itself and (2) the shared responsibilities of partnering.

PARTNERING ITSELF ... AND ITS SHARED RESPONSIBILITIES

Partnering itself is not just the sharing of a conceptual framework, of course, but also a physically functional endeavour. This curtails the viable variation of lead–follow in practice, even if not in concept. As such, which bodily signals count as what messages for each partner are more consistent than the models used to frame these body-signals. This means that within the context of competitive partnering the performance of gender is less variable than the meanings and understandings that dancers may have about dancing, even their own. This standardization of performed-gender conveys a more unified impression than is actually the case though. Since it is the performance that is culturally encoded as most important, this is what gets seen as dancers' gendered roles. In other words, relatively standardized gender roles get performed by dancers – both on and off the ballroom floor – separate from (if not independent of) personal understandings of those very roles. Especially given many competitive dancers' wide-ranging backgrounds (regarding nationality, education and more), dancers' ideas about gender and gender roles can hardly be reflected by the highly circumscribed roles valued and hence rewarded within the competitive milieu.

While consciously enacted by some (at least in some situations), it would be a mistake to think of the gender roles thus being performed merely as acted. Indeed the performed roles typically resonate for those who enact them, even if in different manner and measure for different dancers. Those who take greatest issue with the gender roles of competitive ballroom dance are extremely unlikely to be interested in or willing to make the enormous investments of time, money and effort that are required. As such, some degree of personal resonance may already exist and, where not, there is at least unlikely to be too high a degree of disagreeability. An interesting example and one that re-emphasizes that the gender roles performed in dancesport cannot be simply dichotomized into male/female, concerns dancers' choices of competitive style, i.e. Standard, Latin, Smooth, or Rhythm.

Asked why they compete in the style they do, competitors provided a wide range of responses ranging from preferences in music, favourite dances, available partners, natural aptitudes, easiest success, to 'that was the style the only available teacher taught'. Woven throughout all the responses I received were other threads, however, including those of costuming and personal presentation. Here, the image of the 'princess' was perhaps the most widely mentioned and women citing this image as part of their initial interest in ballroom rarely ended up being Latin or Rhythm competitors. This same dynamic also showed up, albeit in reverse, in the words of dancers who chose Standard because 'there was no way I was going to be seen wearing one of those skimpy little Latin costumes!' Whether personal images, such as that of the princess, or personal comfort with bodily display, dancers' choices of ballroom style often correspond to, and are built upon, ideas about gender congruent with those of their chosen style. Neither the woman who wants to dance like a 'princess', nor the woman highly uncomfortable with skimpy attire, is likely to *want* to be a Latin competitor – and thus she finds herself performing a gender role more in line with her own predilections.

Revisiting equality-of-equivalence versus of equality-of-identity, the examples above help to demonstrate that however constrained by heteronormative standards, the gender roles available to and performed by dancesport competitors include options. There is not just one model for each masculine and feminine behaviour and neither the Standard-lady nor the Latin-woman can be said to be dancing or performing the more 'female' role. In other words, there are, at the very least, 'equivalence' models of appropriate gender available within the larger ballroom world in other words, not only a Standard-woman counts as female. Certainly the gender roles thus allowed remain tightly scripted and constrained, but that is true in many cultural settings. What this helps to highlight, then, is the plurality of models for gender valued and accepted within dancesport. While it may not look like it to the ballroom outsider – who may only notice the tightly scripted and performed gender roles in play – the choice of dance style provides very different models for performing gender; models that dancers often choose based on their own predispositions towards (or at least not at drastically at odds with) one of the gender models privileged in dancesport.

Yet no matter how important and foundational personal preferences may be, they are only part of the picture. Feeding back into these aredancers' ongoing efforts and investment in their own dancing. The more dancers work on their dancing – as a complex of understanding, skill and performance – the more they are investing their own energies and efforts in perfecting certain models of gender. Most important in this respect is that dancers care deeply about their dancing, want to be good at it and find it meaningful. As such, the gender roles practised as part and parcel of their dancing are not merely performed as if by actors, but are enacted daily as part of personally salient practices. The gender roles that dancers perform are thus internalized within the context of day-to-day practices and strivings: they are roles that dancers are continually surrounded by (whether consciously recognized or not) and (often consciously) want to fulfil.

'Elegant', 'sensual', 'powerful' and 'fierce' are all words I have regularly heard being used to compliment women's dancing. Equally divergent male counterparts exist, including 'attentive', 'commanding', 'self-contained' and 'dominant'. Even within one ballroom dance style then, say Latin, there are multiple accepted performances of gender; and dancers' bodies and costumes – as the mediums of their own performance – can be used, and are, in different ways. All of this ultimately ties back into the issue of partnering itself, however, since the skills and practices of partnering, while predicated upon the complementary activity between partners, is concomitantly grounded in each partner's performance of specific models of gender. Yet since there is both personal and dance-style variability to the gender roles performed, the shared responsibilities of partnering include interpersonal negotiation – that is, shared conceptual mapping – of each partner's role. Part of what emerges, then, is that there are multiple viable performances of gender within ballroom. At the same time, however, these gender roles are performed relative to one's partner and his or her performance of gender.

This negotiated performance most clearly shows up among the elite competitors, those whose technical proficiency allows for greater freedom of performance and expression. At the extreme are the distinctly different characterizations of the same dances performed by World and Blackpool finalists; differences that may be harder to recognize among less proficient dancers. Even at this level, however, dancers dance with a partner and part of partnering involves discovering and crafting (a) who a couple are as partners and (b) who one is as a dancer within that partnership. It is here that any dancer who is uncomfortable with the terms 'lead and follow' is highly unlikely to partner another dancer who discusses the appropriate amount of 'leash' without a second thought.

It is here, too, where 'equivalence' best explains the dynamics of partners' gender roles, as different understandings of how to dance *as a couple* are crafted within the couple. One couple may thus see the man as the clearly dominant member of the partnership, while another couple may see the man in the supporting role, and yet another couple yet may see the two roles as evenly split between them.[16] While always framed within the male-lead/female-follow framework, in practice there is always a negotiation of specifics – often in words and always in action – within each partnership. The roles performed by each partner follow tightly scripted gender-norms, but cannot be dismissed as unequal simply because they are different. This is not to say that inequalities do not exist (as indeed they do), but rather to emphasize that the blatantly different performances of gender – of which male and female costuming are the most blatant marks – are not unequal in and of themselves.

PERFORMING GENDER OFF THE DANCE FLOOR

Like everything else in ballroom, gender is performed both on and off the dance floor. In truth, it is the off-the-competition-floor performances of gender that are, in many ways, the most significant and telling. On the floor performances – of which gender is primary – can, if considered independently, be mistaken merely as acted roles. No doubt there is an element of acting involved and no doubt the exact roles played on the floor are not carried off unaltered. None the less, the seeming effortlessness with which accomplished dancers perform is the result of tremendous investments in time, effort and practice. Indeed the entire purpose of practice is to automate valued bodily postures and movements, and to routinize them in such a manner that they do not require conscious effort or attention. It is this process of bodily training and habituation that lies at the heart of ideas about muscle memory, 'enskillment' (Ingold 2000), 'bodily capital' (Wacquant 2004) and 'sweat equity' (see Marion, forthcoming). The same trained automation that is the purpose of practice – that removes the means of movement and action from requiring deliberate conscious enactment – is what transforms dancers' performed identities into more than acted roles. A dancer's attention, training, effort and practice are all channelled into being, and being seen as, a certain type of dancer and person – whether dressing in a style-appropriate manner to practice (e.g. he in a button-down shirt and tie for Standard, she in a short skirt for Latin), or how one conducts oneself while practising at the studio, or how one carries oneself when an audience member. All of these factors play into the topic of the next chapter, which is what it is, and means, to live a dancesport life.

11 LIVING THE DANCESPORT LIFE

Working off Bourdieu's (1977, 1979, 1980) concepts of sociocultural practice and habit – *praxis* and *habitus* – this chapter continues to examine the social and cultural consequences of the aesthetic and cultural dynamics discussed in Parts II and III. Where Chapters 8 and 9 primarily focused on the aesthetics of costuming and gender performance, this chapter provides wider insight into the consequences and outcomes of living a dancesport life. How do competitors' commitments to the practices and values of dancesport feed back into and reshape their lifestyles, career trajectories and overall frames of perception, assessment and evaluation? How does being a competitor shift a dancer's relationship with their coaches, dance partners, romantic partners, other dancers, friends and family? What interactions between their dancing world and their non-dancing world(s) are most salient to ballroom competitors and why? Exploring these questions sheds light on what it is like for competitors to live their lives within the context of competitive ballroom dancing.

Ballroom dancers and those involved in the competitive ballroom circuit understand what is meant by terms such as 'ballroom', 'Latin', 'Standard', 'American', 'International', 'Rhythm' and 'Smooth' not as abstract or arbitrary labels, but as everyday experiential categories. International Style Foxtrot, for instance, is not just the competitively codified form of a dance first performed by Harry Fox. Widely considered 'the dancers' dance' of Standard – meaning that it is the most exacting – it is also a foundational component of every Standard competitor's ongoing learning, training and development. Indeed competitors' legacies have been cemented by their renditions of a dance (be it the foxtrot, tango, or quickstep), serving as a basis for comparison, discussion and accomplishment long after they have taken their last step on the competition floor.[1]

As work such as that done by Downey on Capoeira (2005), Wacquant on boxing (2004), Jackson on clubbing (2004) and Wulff on ballet (1998) all demonstrate, physical enterprises – of which dancesport is clearly an example – are far more than just physical practices. Indeed such 'techniques of the body' (Mauss 1973) are deeply embedded in matrixes of interrelated social, cultural and political logics and cannot be understood at any real depth save in reference to these experiential frames. Where competitions thus highlight activity-specific standards, norms and values, it is in dancers' daily activity and interactions that these values are rehearsed, practised and enacted. Whether at a competition or in the studio, dancers' actions and practices are not simply elements of some abstract competitive ballroom culture or community, they are part of living dancesport lives – lives that are lived on and off the dancesport floor.

THE DANCESPORT STAGE

Part I of this book set the stage for the materials that followed, defining and laying out the structure of competitive ballroom dance in Chapter 1, providing a brief history in Chapter 2 and explaining the judging that is at the heart of ballroom competition in Chapter 3. What I want to make clear in this final chapter is that while useful as analytical orientations and frames, the materials in this book should not be mistaken for the lived experiences of ballroom competitors and others in the dancesport community. Ballroom competitors do not think of 'Latin' as being from Latin America, for instance, whereas the average television viewer very well might and those from Latin America might well question (with due cause) how the dances being shown are in any way Latin American dances. Yet while McMains's (2007) criticisms of the aesthetic appropriation, colonization and imperialism of the 'ballroom industry' has some teeth as far as what gets presented to the wider public *as* Latin dancing, those *within* dancesport conceptualize 'Latin' as how these dances as practised within the sphere of 'ballroom' dancing.[2] In fact the very idea that the ballroom category 'Latin' could be thought of meaning 'as done in Latin America' came as a shock to many of the more experienced ballroom competitors I spoke with when I pointed out how the current presentation of 'Latin' dancing on television shows such as *Dancing with the Stars* and *Strictly Come Dancing* could be taken in just this way by those unfamiliar with the genre.

In practice this failure to differentiate ballroom versions of various dances from their non-ballroom inspiration, influences and counterparts is also perpetuated by the commercial engine of dance teaching. As my own initial forays into a ballroom studio well demonstrate, many studios and teachers will claim 'expertise' which the beginner is ill-equipped to recognize that they actually lack. Some of this is an understandable response to market pressures, especially since those who are less proficient are unlikely to draw a strong and regular clientele from one specific style. As such, they face economic pressures to teach as broadly as possible despite being less qualified to do so. Since they draw sufficient business from within their sphere of specialization, for instance, world champions rarely teach outside their area of specialty. In contrast, relatively green instructors (with far less experience and expertise) are more often expected to teach dances across several styles. In this same vein, many non-ballroom dances – such as salsa, meringue, hustle, west coast swing and Argentine tango – get taught by ballroom instructors *as ballroom dances* in many ballroom studios.[3]

Needless to say, this greatly complicates the task of the ballroom newcomer in sorting out what is (and is not) considered part of the ballroom cannon. But, at the same time, the 'instructors' providing this information may be comparatively new to ballroom themselves, not yet know any differently and merely be parroting back what they have been trained to say. What is significant here is simply that such dynamics are far from transparent and that even legitimate criticisms of the ballroom industry should not be mistaken as describing the understandings or perspectives of individual dancers.

In this same way, any account of the history of ballroom dance that can be placed on paper, such as that provided in Chapter 2, should never be mistaken for the lived reality it describes. The meetings, organizations and persons involved all have individual perspectives, aims, goals and agendas to be sure, but so too do the far more numerous others not recorded in any particular account. Some dancers are highly involved with some of the organizations mentioned – as officers, officials, volunteers, or employees – yet far more are not. Some dancers will know many of the different people, accounts and organizations I have described, yet few (if any) will know them all. The point being that while important as background, and framing is for any systematic level of understanding, no such history describes the personal-scale enculturation of individual dancers who learn specific 'bits and pieces' in a piecemeal manner and as specific elements enter their personal matrix of involvements.

This same distinction between overview versus experience applies to ballroom judging as well. As experienced as any judge or coach may be, they do not take all the variables discussed in Chapter 3 into account simultaneously, and certainly not in uniform measure to each of their peers. While the variables discussed frame and represent the criteria involved in judging dancesport, they do not capture or describe the evaluative stance of any particular judge, nor account for what weight each variable contributes to a specific judge's assessments. In counterpoint to this, no coach prioritizes every component in equal measure, just as no dancer can simultaneously work on or practices each of these dynamics. In everyday practice different coaches and judges value different combinations of dancesport criteria, just as each dancer may choose to prioritize and work on any specific element. Prior to such choices, however, competitors learn about what is judged.

Lacking *an* official rule book, ballroom competitors come to learn about and understand the various components of judged aesthetics through their own involvement with ballroom dancing as both spectator and dancer. Standing on the 'edge' of one's foot may mean nothing to someone the first time they set foot in a studio, while months later they easily recognize this flaw in other newcomers. Many a beginner cannot differentiate technique from choreography, whereas the more experienced eye can assert what was superior dancing regardless of any disqualification (for being out of category). Far from being a mere kinaesthetic paint-by-numbers activity, then, assessing and evaluating dancesport is experientially nuanced and complex. There are no set recipes of 'percentages' that constitute good dancing, just as there is no universal sequence of dance elements. While certain criteria – such as timing and posture – are significant from the outset, the progression thereafter is highly variable and it is only via time, experience and exposure that dancers come to understand various dance-components as bodily-expressions rather than abstract ideas.

THE PERFORMANCE OF DANCESPORT

Paraphrasing Goffman (1976: 89), Ruby aptly points out that 'the purpose of performance is to both maintain and perpetuate the social worlds of the performers and their audiences' (2000: 253) – a dynamic clearly in evidence both on and off the floor within the dancesport community. Wherever the grand spectacle of a ballroom competition takes place – be it in a luxury US hotel, the largely black-tie affair of the British Open Championships in the Empress Ballroom at Blackpool's Winter Gardens, the artistic expression of television demonstrations or at the invitation only World Superstars event in Japan, the athletic competitive efforts on display in college gyms, at the Olympic training facility in Århus, Denmark or the Crystal Palace Sport Centre in London – the performance of ballroom dancing is always communicative to both to practitioners and spectators. In the practices of learning, training and competing, competitors not only participate but tacitly endorse the very frame of their participation. The disenchanted may complain, the pragmatic may recognize the status quo as the cost of participation and the optimistic may think that things can change, yet whether enthusiastically given or not, in each case participation constitutes a performed endorsement of the extant social order.

In taking lessons one thus learns more than dancing alone, and advancing up the competitive ladder can also be seen as sanctioning the accepted order. Taking lessons from whom one is 'supposed to' can certainly be seen as a micro-political manoeuvre (that is, advantageous to one's competitive aspirations), but it simultaneously signals acceptance – via adherence – to the macro-political order. The same teacher that it may be fine to work with 'on the sly', for instance, may raise a red flag to the established order if consulted in public. In a related vein, the same attempts to gain different perspectives on one's dancing from a variety of coaches can also be seen as a lack of trust and loyalty. By way of illustration, let me provide two examples, one from Glen and Dorothy and one from Kent and Tessa.

Competing in the professional American rhythm division, Glen and Dorothy had been considering revamping their mambo to incorporate some contemporary salsa club influences. Knowing that I am a salsa club regular, Glen and Dorothy asked me if I had any ideas, especially in the form of some short sequences that they might be able to incorporate into re-choreographing their mambo routine. After confirming that they were still interested the next time we were at a competition together, I suggested that we meet at the practice room to have some floor space. Within less than a minute Glen was quite tired and wanted to know if we could just do it in their hotel room. But, as this gave insufficient space, Glen reluctantly consented to walking down the hallway to the elevator landing on their floor. At the time this struck me as a slightly odd interaction but, in retrospect, it makes perfect sense. Whereas Glen and Dorothy may acknowledge my familiarity with salsa, within the broader ballroom world I am most widely recognized as a photographer first, 'the guy doing the research', co-owner of dance-forums.com and as a low-level amateur competitor by some. As such, for Glen and Dorothy – as professional competitors – to be seen in the practice room 'consulting' with me, a lower-level amateur competitor, would be to perform an inversion and hence rejection, of the accepted and expected social order.

In counterpoint to Glen and Dorothy, mid-level amateur competitors Kent and Tessa regularly asked for my impressions and observations between rounds of competition. While Kent and Tessa certainly knew more about dancing (especially in their style), my general impressions provided feedback and perspective that Kent and Tessa appreciated being able to take into account before their next round. This difference between Glen and Dorothy and Kent and Tessa cannot simply be reduced to that of professional versus amateur competitors, however, as the most highly accomplished competitors can consult whomever they wish, just as can the relative newcomers. Yet most competitors fall somewhere between these two poles and for them such considerations – as performed in public – can be quite significant, both serving as and representing social perpetuation through participation.

CROSS-COACHING ... OR NOT!

By way of example, Tessa relates that as far as she knows, she and Kent are one of only a handful of couples and perhaps even the only one, to have worked with both Keith and Hank, each of whom is widely recognized on the world stage as a top-tier competitor and coach. This is interesting and significant because chance alone does not account for this situation. Instead, it is the natural outcome of dancesport's social, cultural and political systems, with Keith and Hank being products of and representing different 'schools' of dance – and hence different philosophies of movement, performance and execution. These differences make working with both somewhat counterproductive, yet there is more at issue and at stake than diminished practicability alone. Differences between coaches' philosophy and focus is a dancesport 'given' and which coaches' approaches are compatible with each others' is generally well known and recognized information amongst competitors. Crossing the boundaries between different 'camps' (taking 'a lesson or two' from a visiting coach excepted) thus generates conflicting utility, but also signals rejection of the ultimate validity of the one's coaches' philosophies. While the reality may simply be wanting a different perspective, or merely wishing to work on a specific element admired from another coach, crossing certain unspoken lines is seen as and is thus performative of, a rejection of the supremacy of their own coach's approach. Crossing such lines 'reads' as a rejection of the established order, representing – and thus counting as – a 'second guessing' in action.

PARTICIPATION AS PERFORMED PERPETUATION

Ultimately this same dynamic – the maintenance and perpetuation of the performers' and observers' social worlds (Ruby 2000: 253) – underlies everyday studio conduct as well, since 'both dramatic *and nondramatic performances* share the purpose of maintaining society and assisting its members through the recurring and unusual crises that constitute a part of all human experience' (2000: 264, emphasis added). Expectations for off-the-floor conduct thus emerge as equally significant in marking one's acceptance of and adherence to the social order, as does one's on-the-floor comportment. It is not therefore merely a matter of competitors wearing appropriate competitive costuming, but also how competitors dress off the floor as well that signifies their participation in – as well as their tacit acceptance via perpetuation of – the social world of dancesport.

Showing up at the studio in 'appropriate' attire, be it for practice or lessons, serves as a similar performance of acceptance and belonging. The gentleman's button-down shirt and tie and the woman's long flowing skirt for Standard visually demonstrate acquiescence to gender and style specific norms while simultaneously providing visual cues and models of exactly those standards, both to the dancers themselves and to anyone else who may see them. As Myerhoff notes of ritual in general, 'doing is believing and we become what we display' (1986: 268), and it is in exactly this way that the routinization of dress and activity in the studios and at competitions emerges not merely as acting the part but as performing and thus becoming it. Showing up in designer jeans before changing into specially made practice wear signals and perpetuates attention to grooming and presentation that are part of the intended self-image of ballroom dance.

A final point to be made here is that performances are never divorced from outside influences. I take it as true that any performance like 'any particular ritual dramatizes certain issues and mutes others' (Geertz 1983: 40, cited in Stewart 1986: 312), but the issues thus modulated come from outside the frame of the specific performance (or ritual) in question. What marks and thus makes any event a performance is that it is framed as such: and whatever is framed is always meant to convey something. The communicability of performance thus rests on always having its genesis outside its own framing. In other words, both the substantive content of performance and the framing that marks performance are contextualized (i.e. framed) by their larger cultural milieu. More than just culturally framed then, performances are culturally framed frames. As such, performances are neither static in their performance nor in their culturally framed framing. Just as the enactment of a given performance is never fixed, so too is its cultural contextualization continuously, albeit not infinitely, variable. Indeed, as soon as content is invariably fixed it is no longer performed.

It is important to recognize that performance is culturally framed; highlighting both the always contextualized nature of performance acts and their reception and the ever-present connections between performances and their sociocultural surround. This is a salient understanding for dancesport, since studio and competition experiences can never be wholly disconnected from or unaffected by larger ballroom and non-ballroom happenings. If it seems only common sense to point out that all performance is subject to broader sociocultural influences, I still find it crucial to point out that the aesthetic images and fantasies ballroom portrays do not separate it from these same considerations. If pregnancies, births, illnesses and deaths are not the everyday experience of ballroom dance, this does not mean that they are absent from the lives of ballroom dancers. More than just personal-scale events, such considerations may ramify across wide swathes of the competitive community as different dancers, partnerships and coaches enter and exit the competitive scene.

This same dynamic also plays out in reaction to much larger world events as well. It makes no sense to try understanding the Diamond Dancesport Classic (in Orlando) on 9/11 or the Yankee Classic Dancesport Championships (in Boston) a few weeks later, for instance, without recognizing the larger non-ballroom frames to these competitions. Similarly, both the 2003 Can-Am Dancesport Gala (in Toronto) and Blackpool competitions need to be looked at in light of that year's SARS outbreaks and scare. Finally, and in a similar vein, the economic considerations of teachers, coaches, competition organizers, vendors and competitors are all interconnected with broader non-ballroom economic forces and pressures. While more could be said about any one of these scenarios, such considerations are beyond the scope of this book, save in recognizing and emphasizing that the cultural performances of ballroom life are never separate from and are always contingent upon larger contextualizations. With this key caveat in mind, I now want to address dancesport competitions as concomitantly sociocultural events and lived experiences.

DANCESPORT COMPETITIONS

As discussed in Part III, ballroom competitions are far more than just competitive events. I explored competitions as festivals and celebrations in Chapter 7 and as ritual in Chapter 8. While this was useful for analytic purposes, it is important to recognize that these two perspectives are neither experientially differentiated nor comprehensive. In other words, the experience of ballroom competitions is: (a) not lived via categorical distinctions; and (b) exceeds the totality of such categorical straitjacketing. Prime exemplars of what Myerhoff defines as a 'definitional ceremony' (e.g. Myeroff 1986: 262), dancesport competitions are experientially intense cauldrons of personal and collective social, cultural and political interactions and performances. Competitions are events where the ballroom community not only shows itself – both to itself and others – but reaffirms, renews and revitalizes itself. More than performed demonstrations of ballroom culture, ballroom competitions are lived enactments wherein and whereby 'more than merely self-recognition, *self-definition* is made possible by means of such showings' (Myerhoff 1986: 261–2, emphasis added). While officially about the dancing, as in-gatherings and embodied concentrations of ballroom society and culture, ballroom competitions are social sites of cultural evaluation and perpetuation. The social structure, order and statuses of community members are not only re-established by being displayed at competitions, but are established anew via their display.

The definitional nature of ballroom competitions functions along both official and unofficial vectors and neither of these dynamics is lost on the most serious competitors. Officially, who wins what – including at which competitions and against who – establishes what counts as good dancing and, from a personal perspective, who count as the best dancers. From local studio competitions up through the World Championships and Blackpool, different trends rise and fall, but always with consequences for the dancers involved as their own investments (including time, effort, money and dedication) are affirmed or found lacking, either of which can redirect the life-course of those involved. Unofficially, how one conducts oneself under the social spotlight of competitions 'speaks' volumes. Where a successful pro-am instructor may gravitate towards the centre of the social interactions in the hotel bar each night, the same dancer cannot be seen as a 'party person' if they wish to be taken seriously in climbing the ranks as part of a professional partnership.[4]

Interrelated but distinct from competitive considerations, the social networks of the ballroom community are most visible and are actively woven at competitions. In many ways this only makes sense, as competitions are where more dancers come into contact with each other than at any other time, and the bigger the competition the bigger the spheres of interaction. While competitions represent occasions to interact with others sharing one's interests and values, the reality of ballroom life is also that dancers, teachers, vendors, coaches and judges each have their own agendas and interests for attendance and involvement as well. Just as Stewart describes Trinidadian Carnival fêtes, then, ballroom competitions too 'are social events at which the experience of friendship is enacted; they are events at which friendship may be initiated or vitalized. But they are also events at which pseudo-friendships may be instrumented on behalf of some practical need' (1986:298). Thus, while ballroom competitions are incredibly social affairs, they can (rather ironically) simultaneously be tremendously lonely events as well, as one can never being entirely sure of the sociality versus instrumentality undergirding the social enactments of others. Ballroom competitions thus have double lives: one that is tremendously gregarious, celebratory, festive and social, but another that involves constant social evaluation, assessment and vigilance. While this is actually true of all ballroom living – at the studio as well as the competition – it is most prominent and most telling in the competition setting given the greater number of dancesport personnel present and the interdependent reinforcements of their social world.

Such mutual attention and awareness along shared lines of distinction at times plays out in another interesting manner as well: the dynamic described by Stewart, wherein 'one's presence at a fête, while a satisfying experience in itself, may also produce an aggrandized awareness of oneself and one's value to others' (1986: 298), is equally applicable to ballroom competitions. Certainly not true of everyone or all of the time, but spending a significant portion of one's time at competitions certainly provides experiential fodder for the self-aggrandizement noted by Stewart – Drake, the studio owner who is shocked that the name of their studio is not known by every judge in the country, providing just one small-scale example. Compounding this with the general dancesport aesthetic and importance of 'being seen', a sometimes comical narcissism can develop, such as when the 2007 Michigan Dance Challenge coincided with a World Wrestling Entertainment event, with the same hotel serving as home base for both events. How the professional dancers and coaches interacted with one another in the hotel bar is telling. While many of the dancers asked to be photographed with the wrestlers, most interesting are some of the group shots where the wrestlers have been shunted to the back of a pack of dancers and you would need to know they were there to even pick them out in the photograph. This should not be misread as an unfortunate accident amidst the jostling of a crowded group photograph. A similar and even more telling example comes from a small group of 'ballroom guys' who were having their pictures taken when one of the wrestler's girlfriends, a porn star, tried to join in the photograph – only to be almost literally pushed out of the frame with a rather confused look evident on her face. Typically used to being a centre of photographic attention, this woman's cultural models did not account for the 'look at me' and 'I'm here, and hence important' elements of dancesport amplified to their height at ballroom competitions.

Also significant is that, as experienced, ballroom competitions are never just one 'thing'. The same competition is often a very different event for amateur competitors, pro-am competitors, professional competitors, spectators, coaches, vendors, officials and judges. Certainly the experience of a competition, like any other experience, is an individual one and will vary from person to person, but one's institutionally pre-scribed role and status serve as social linchpins for one's means of participation and belonging as well. Many serious lower-level pro-am competitors in the United States will not see the finals of the professional events or the professional shows intended to be the highlight of many competitions. Why not? Because the lower-level pro-am events are typically scheduled in the early morning while the professional events last late into the night. Thus, the pro-am competitor who may need to get up as early as 3 a.m. to make a start on her hair and make-up can ill-afford to be watching events that may not end until 1 a.m. or later. Ostensibly attendees and participants at the same competition, this woman's experience of the event may share little, if any, overlap with that of a fellow student – even from the same studio and trained by the same teacher – who is competing in an amateur partnership.

Typically billed as a 'pro party' on the last night and commencing after the completion of many US competitions, members of amateur partnerships are not infrequent participants at these informal gatherings, whereas all but a few of the most widely travelled and accomplished amateur pro-am competitors seldom are. Given that these parties typically happen after the completion of the entire competition, any differences in what times these dancers may need to compete the next day cannot account for this difference. When trying to understand the patterning of this discrepancy, the picture that quickly emerges is one of socio-structural maintenance. Amateur partnerships function as structural equivalents to professional partnerships – with both partners being peers within the partnership and having a non-peer teacher outside the partnership – whereas pro-am partnerships intertwine the dynamics of partner and teacher. As such, the presence of pro-am students at the 'pro' parties threatens to collapse the distinction between teacher and student further, potentially complicating the boundaries of teacher–student interactions and requiring teachers' 'student-present professionalism' at a time when they are supposed to be able to interact more (although certainly not entirely) freely.

COMPLICATING GENDER

If, as noted in earlier chapters, the performed fantasy and images of ballroom dancing are meant and intended to represent a seamless complementarity between male and female, unfortunately this level of cooperation is sometimes more fiction than reality. I am not saying that such interdependence is always an act or false, as indeed many couples truly are teams on and off the floor, with each partner thinking of themselves as 'we' in many situations rather than 'me'. I am also not saying that the heteronormative stance of the official ballroom industry is not unproblematic, but, rather, trying to tease out how that stance ramifies onto and through the experiences of ballroom living. Aside from general social pressures to conform to the specific models of gendered dress and behaviour interlaced throughout this book, the significance of how gender is constructed in ballroom also plays out both overtly and more insidiously between partners.

At the most overtly problematic level are instances of male scarcity driving female acquiescence. Put more bluntly, I find it problematic when a female dancer can go to her coach to complain that her partner is being abusive – both physically and emotionally – and be told by that coach that she should consider herself lucky to have a partner at all. I have heard similar accounts from dancers across the United States and Europe (and beyond) and in each variation the comparative dearth of male to female dancers gets factored in as a reason why the female should leave well alone. I am not suggesting that such abuse is rampant in ballroom or even commonplace, as I lack the qualitative data to even hazard a guess at the actual frequencies, but it certainly happens.

More than the fact that such abuse does happen within ballroom – and in contradiction to the idealized on-the-floor image of seamless cooperation – what I find most noteworthy here is the reasoning and rationale provided for not leaving the partnership in each of the cases I have heard about. Male or female, in each situation the argument made was that the female dancer was 'lucky' to have a partner and should therefore refrain from rocking the proverbial boat despite the disagreeableness of her partner's conduct. Again, I am not suggesting anything about the frequency of such activity and indeed I assume that many (if not most) such scenarios are the end of such partnerships. I do think it noteworthy, however, that where such partnerships remain in place the argument provided always finds purchase in the conceptual space between ballroom's heteronormative stance on the one side and the discrepant numbers of male and female dance competitors on the other. Regardless of any comments or conclusions that could thus be made (or not made, as is the case here) regarding the ballroom community, such stories – of which I have heard several, both from those involved and from those overhearing a coach's comments – speak to problematic outcomes of various ballroom values.

Far more common than such overt comments, however, are the pressures that these same dynamics consistently exert on dancers. Perhaps the most telling example of the insidiousness of this value system and structure comes from Jacqueline, who recounts how when she was sixteen she first had sex with her then 18-year-old partner. Specifying the parameters of this event, Jacqueline comments that he *was* a good dance partner and, not wanting to risk losing him as a partner, she felt pressured into a sexual encounter he initiated. Jacqueline is very clear that her partner was not aggressive with his sexual advances, nor did he ever threaten a dissolution of the partnership were he to be rebuffed. Nonetheless, his significance to Jacqueline as a dance partner is predicated on his value within a sociocultural matrix that mandates heteronormative partnering and hence privileges males (due to their comparative scarcity). This systematic positioning does not speak to intent and indeed Jacqueline's partner – like many others – may have had no awareness of these dynamics or how they played into this scenario. Yet this particular incident remains telling at both the personal and the social levels.

At the personal level, Jacqueline's account illustrates how larger social and cultural dynamics can play into personal-scale experiences in unintended manners. I do not think this suggests that the overarching ballroom system is in *any way* intended to provide coercive sexual pressure on a legal minor for fear of losing a dance partner, for instance, yet this is exactly how things played out in this particular situation. It is therefore important not only to differentiate between the social forces at work here but also to look at how these play out in, and as, the intentions and experiences of the parties involved. In this particular case, while nothing indicates deliberate coercion from Jacqueline's partner – or even any awareness of the coercive position from which he was acting within their shared social matrix – personal-romantic and personal-dance-partner relationships show up as being complexly intertwined with activity-based cultural values and gender ratios that privilege male competitors. As such and to whatever extent, 'the main task of the social sciences' remains the study, understanding and analysis, of 'the unintended social repercussions of intentional human actions' (Popper 1966: 95), how social values and aesthetics ramify onto individually lived lives must remain at the forefront of social analysis, and this is where briefly flipping our attention to Jacqueline's partner helps to provide insight into the larger dancesport world.

As previously noted, I have no reason to think Jacqueline's then partner intended his sexual advances to be perceived as anything but his own natural feelings towards her. I base this assertion on: (a) Jacqueline's own account; (b) my many interactions and discussions with her partner, even though none dealt with this particular incident;[5] and (c) the fact that two years' later they were still a romantic couple. If my reading of this is wrong, then Jacqueline's partner recruited the social dynamics and his cultural capital therein in a deliberately manipulative and self-serving manner. While I do not believe this to be so, there are certainly circumstances where this happens, such as when the significantly better dancer partners a much lower-level competitor in exchange for all the training, travel and competition expenses being paid by the lower-level dancer. As such a trade-off between money and skill demonstrates, however, this is not to say that there is not something gained by both parties and certainly money is valued within ballroom – as a means to many ends if not as an end in its own right.[6]

Returning to Jacqueline's partner, however, I think a far more valuable lesson can be learned in recognizing that he was unaware of the social dynamics that weighed in Jacqueline's choice to allow his sexual advances to come to fruition: namely, the power inherent in his positioning within the webs of values, statuses and norms that constitute dancesport culture. This is most telling in that it highlights broader anthropological understanding of how those who are socioculturally privileged are often unaware of the coerciveness of their structural dominance. Grounded on heteronormative partnering, Jacqueline is the one who faces a scarcity of possible partners and finds this structural threat a compelling reason for not risking the disruption of her partnership (recall that her partner never even hinted at any such course of action). This is not to suggest unlimited male control, as there are many ballroom women who leave their dance partnerships for any number of reasons, yet the reality remains that males enjoy a certain structural power within the ballroom frame, one reinforced by non-dance-based life trajectories after one stops competing.

DANCE ISN'T EVERYTHING

Even the most ardent competitors typically realize that dance is far from everything. Indeed, the effort and toil involved in reaching the pinnacles of dancesport success are typically sufficient evidence of this reality since, if nothing else, the physical wear and tear on a dancer's body already suggests mortality – of their competitive career at the least, if not of their body overall. Whether choosing to retire from competition to have a family or waiting until retiring to try having a family, the majority of active competitors consider child rearing a 'second act' that follows their competitive careers. It should come as little surprise, then, that it is women who largely disappear (or at the least, retreat) from the active ballroom scene once children arrive. This is not to say that doting parents do not bring their babies to competitions or that these newcomers to the ballroom world are not fussed over by an inordinate number of enthusiasts. Indeed, the fact that many competitors have put off starting their own families while still actively competing provides an emotional charge for great interest and vicarious enjoyment of those babies who are brought 'for a visit'.

While the centre of much personal attention, it comes to these returning women in their role of 'mother' and not as 'dancer', 'coach' or 'judge'. On the personal level this may be entirely satisfying and acceptable, but at the structural level this does remove women from the functional-network disproportionately to men. The rough gender balance between active competitors mandated by heteronormative stand-ards is thus structurally disrupted, with far more men continuing their careers as coaches and judges and thereby continuing to accrue sociocultural status and capital whereas their one-time peers largely disappear from the active scene. Note, how-ever, that this is by no means a hard-and-fast rule and that the women who remain active as coaches enjoy the same status and prestige as their male counterparts, with names such as Shirley Ballas, Lorraine, Tone Nyhagen and Vibeke Toft ranking among many active competitors' lists of the top coaches. While the dancesport-based ethic of shared value thus plays out as equal validation for men and women as coaches, the non-dance-based practices of women as primary caregivers removes disproportionately more women than men from the active dance circuit – as both coaches and judges – thereby reinforcing the structural dominance of men within the competitive circuit.

A telling exception to this pattern concerns professional competitors' retiring in the United States, with the active pro-am system causing something of an inversion in immediate post-competitor status. Given the far higher demand for male pro-am teachers than female ones, upon retiring as a couple many women find themselves judging competitions where their dance partners, as pro-am teachers, remain active competitors. On the one hand, this boosts the woman's clout as judge-hence-coach, but, on the other hand, it raises the man's clout as a linchpin connecting the competition organizers to the economic lifeblood of dancesport in the United States, namely, the pro-am students' money. While the ranks of the recently retired thus funnel more women than men into judging in the short term (separate from the issue of having children just discussed), the men dancing as pro-am teachers at one competition can still judge at others and thus come to exhibit and wield both official sanction and economic muscle in building their post-professional-competition careers, as driven by the drastically greater demand for male pro-am teachers. Again, there is no functional prohibition or cultural proscription against women filling these same roles and, when they do, they are fully accepted. At the structural level, however, the nature of the market forces parallels and feeds into the family dynamics that take more women than men away from the ballroom floor once they have stepped off it as active professional competitors.

THIRD PARTIES TO PRIVACY

Another point of interest regarding the interplay between structural positioning and personal experience concerns third parties to privacy in the ballroom world – namely, not those that private matters pertain to, but those structurally positioned as 'needing to know' or, at the least, to be easily told. Those positioned in the 'need to know' category typically include a couple's main coach and potentially their costume designer. When Jacqueline and her partner became a couple romantically, for instance, their primary coach knew far in advance of anyone else, including their friends, fellow dancers, and lastly their parents. Concerning the decision to tell their coach, Jacqueline says 'she was going to see that something was different between us anyway, besides which, if we told her she might be able to use that to help teaching us'.

There are two parallel lines of reasoning revealed in Jacqueline's comment; the first pertaining to perception, the second to presentation. On the perception side, Jacqueline's statement speaks to the emotionally near space in which dancers work with each other and their coaches. Certainly a coach with whom one consults per-haps only periodically, or even on a frequent and ongoing basis, might not be told personal relationship-level items (although they might), but one's primary coach is, in many ways, part of 'the team' and is likely to be working with their dancers on a regular basis and over extended periods of time. As such, a dancer's main coach is positioned to be the most likely to see any change in how the partners relate to each other. On its own, however, this side of the picture really only amounts to a 'she would have found out anyway', which leads back to the second part of this picture: presentation. As further elaborations by Jacqueline and her partner made clear, they felt that each and every bit of information that their coach had about them and their relationship had the potential to provide the coach with more avenues for information to be presented and explained to them. Using the rumba as an example, Jacqueline points out how their coach knowing that they were romantically involved opened up new avenues for discussing dance characterization and interpersonal nuances. (It is not without reason that many coaches describe part of their job as being that of a marriage or relationship counsellor.)

If coaches may be third parties to privacy due to often emotionally and always physically close working conditions, there are times when the same can be said of a couple's dress designer. World and Blackpool Amateur Standard finalists Warren and Kristi Boyce now talk openly about how when Kristi was pregnant the only person they told was their dress designer, since: (a) she would have to make adjustments to Kristi's usual measurements; and (b) the Boyce's wanted to enlist her aid in producing a design that would camouflage Kristi's pregnancy during the next upcoming major competition. In this case, then, a dress designer is structurally cast as being a member of the couple's 'team' and thus 'needing to know' in order to be able to best assist them. Separate from but related to such direct 'need-to-know' persons are those who may structurally be situated in place to know. Here again dress vendors provide a key example, with dress customers typically discussing even the most personal of details while being assisted in trying on dresses. The conceptual model seems to be that if one is physically naked the lack of bodily privacy gets socially mirrored; the lack of physical secrets allowing for and suggesting an equally intimate interpersonal social distance.[7]

BALLROOM'S PUBLIC NATURE: VISIBILITY BITES BACK

A final topic not be underestimated concerns the 'public' nature of ballroom life. In many ways similar to the way that privacy exists only by social convention in small traditional social groups, the same is often the case within the ballroom community – especially at competitions. Whether in the sports hall of most European competitions or the hotel settings of most North American ones, privacy exists, if at all, only by social convention. Hallways, changing rooms, restrooms, local restaurants and cafés, nearby stores and shopping centres, and the surrounding streets and pavements are not 'away' from the scene, as other dancers, judges and vendors also and inevitably, frequent these same locations. As such, ballroom's inescapable social surround plays itself out in myriad ways and with equally wide-ranging implications at both the individual and collective levels.

One interesting question – especially given both the high visibility and the possible consequences – is why some competitors continue to exhibit what many consider to be such questionable behaviour. One of the more far-reaching facets of ballroom life that comes to the fore here, is exactly how much of ballroom life is publicly lived. Coaching, teaching and practice all typically take place on the studio floor and only very rarely happen in private,[8] which means that any and all behavioural miscues are therefore quite likely to be subjected to observation. Add in the fact that both lessons and practices are activities that lend themselves to inevitable, and at times great, frustrations. The studio setting, then, is one that can be rife with vexations amidst often quite competitive individuals and passionate personalities. Inevitably, this mix gives rise to less than idyllic reactions and behaviour (at least at times) which, taken in conjunction with the public nature of the studio, account for any number of occurrences.

Yet beyond the immediate public of the ballroom studio is the extended public of the larger ballroom scene. Everyone who was present at the time of any given occurrence is inevitably connected to other individuals involved within the scene. And, *because gossip has to do with being part of the network*, it is rare indeed that any such information does not quickly start to travel.[9] This set of dynamics alone, however, does not account for the full range of interactions in question, for while it may relate to 99 per cent of ballroom life, it does not address its most public face – competitions. So the question remains, why do some competitors continue to exhibit what many consider to be questionable behaviour, especially given the possible repercussions, in the high visibility arena of ballroom performances and competitions?

Even more than the studio, ballroom competitions highlight exactly how much – and to what extent – ballroom life is publicly lived. Even if no one can really know everyone else (although it can certainly feel and seem as though they do at times), everyone does at least know someone else. The interconnectedness of the immediate and extended public of dancesport is not only still at play at competitions, but all the more concentrated via both physical and temporal proximity. You no longer have to wait to phone or email a friend about what you 'just' saw, you can now tell them in your room, in the changing room, in the ballroom, in the bathroom, over a meal, or just in passing down the hallway. More specifically, the built-in proximity of ballroom competitions contributes through two mutually facilitating mechanisms: simple opportunity and immediacy of re/action. With the concentration of individuals present at a competition, there is simply more opportunity both to see something and to have someone report it. Layered on top of this is also an immediacy factor. With time, all but the most shocking or otherwise memorable of events recede in one's awareness. The general proximity characteristic of ballroom competitions, however, provides not only possible material for comment, but the geographic, temporal and social opportunity to do so as well.

BEING ALONE IN PUBLIC

A large number of the competitive ballroom dancers I have interviewed and spoken with have mentioned a strange inversion of the 'always-in-public' nature of ballroom living: that of an almost constant feeling, in one dancer's words, of always 'being alone in a crowd'. What does this mean, however, and why does it seem to be such a widely distributed and shared sentiment? As the comments and explanations of many competitors indicate, this dynamic is the result of one simple fact, namely, that they are participating in a competitive genre of activity. As such and despite the regrets voiced by several competitors, there is a lack of forthrightness built into the social interactions of the ballroom community, and a dancer (or a couple) can never really quite trust others within their competitive arena. Is 'Fred's' advice really his honest opinion or is it misinformation? If you confide in 'Jane' regarding problems you are having with your partner, does she jump on that apparent weakness and then come out 'all guns blazing at you' on the competition floor?

One of the consequences of this dynamic is that the friendships that do form with one's real competition are exceedingly rare at best. A Rhythm couple and a Latin couple can easily be friends then, as they do not go head to head on the ballroom floor. And the same applies to a Standard couple and a Latin couple (unless, of course, either compete in 10 Dance), or a Smooth couple and a Rhythm couple and so forth. But dancers can also easily be friends within their same division, just so long as there is some type of barrier to any 'real' competition between the two. Let me turn to Greg and Russell to provide a concrete example of exactly this type of within-style friendship. Russell had just broken into the semi-final at Blackpool for the first time when Greg was winning the same event. To the non-ballroom initiate the difference between a semi-finalist and a finalist – even the winner – might not seem so great. Within the ballroom ranks, however, such a difference amongst adult competitors is typically quite sizable and significant. Indeed, the vast majority of Blackpool semi-finalists never even makes the final, let alone wins what is the most prestigious and coveted ballroom title in the world. Due to the results gap between them, then, the fact that they competed in the same event all the way up through the semi-final was not an impediment to Greg and Russell's close friendship.

Yet Greg and Russell are the exception, especially as the dancers one has the most consistent contact with are specifically those who *are* one's closest competitors. No competition attracts competitors of every level equally and the larger events often have different divisions and styles dancing on different days. What this means is that the dancers most likely to have overlapping schedules for travel, training and competitions are others in a similar structural position – one's closest competitors. This, then, is the underlying dynamic of why so many competitors make such comments as feeling 'they are alone in a crowd': the same structural positionings that produce the most congruence in shared schedules and experiences between dancers and couples are the exact same criteria which call into question the intentions and sincerity between them.

As this chapter illustrates, the analytical frames presented in each of the previous chapters are each but facets of a far more complex picture. The materials in each chapter have sketched in the prominent perspectives of the dancesport world, yet as this chapter highlights, all of the factors involved merely serve as background when compared to the human dynamic and the complexities of really living the dancesport life.

12 CONCLUSION

In this book I have used dancesport to explore issues of aesthetics, bodies and behaviour as both cultural sources and products. Far from being ballroom-specific, however, these materials address the role of culture in mediating the relationship between aesthetic values and bodily practices, including how cultures work through both mind and body and how cultural practices give rise to both intended and unintended consequences alike. Responding to the need for ethnographers not to be absent from their ethnographies, the extended introduction uses my experiences – first, as a fledgling ballroom dancer, then as a ballroom dance anthropologist, and finally as a professional ballroom photographer – to sketch out how I first became interested in this topic, involved with this cultural world, and how the research for this book came about. Providing insight into how one may enter the ballroom world, these materials also provide an informed frame of reference for assessing and analysing the claims and arguments made in this book.

In Part I (Setting the Stage), I set up the remaining sections by introducing competitive ballroom dancing, the history and background behind contemporary performances and practices and the judging criteria of dancesport. Chapter 1 provided an overview of dancesport as it is practised today, including the major divisions and categories of competitive ballroom dancing and the specific dances contested in each division, as well as issues concerning the significance of translocal fieldwork. Next, Chapter 2 provided a brief history and overview of ballroom dancing, including its ancestry in the French Court Dances of the sixteenth century, the British Blackpool dance festival and the major dance organizations salient to contemporary dancesport. Chapter 3 complemented these more general orientations by describing the actual practices and qualities assessed in dancesport, revealing the judging criteria of competitive ballroom dancing.

In Part II (Performing Dancesport), I explored the performing of dancesport as an activity involving elements of spectacle, art and sport. Chapter 4 focused on the performed-for-an-audience dynamic of competitive ballroom dance and culture, including the smaller-scale spectacle of dancers' day-to-day, personal-level conduct, practices and interactions, highlighting how this all plays into the dance, dress and demeanour of dancers both on and off the floor. Chapter 5 then addressed the artistic and art-making dynamics intrinsic to competitive ballroom dance, foregrounding the issues and roles of impermanence, collective production and artistic conventions implicated. Finally, Chapter 6 focused on the physical demands and skills of dance-sport, as well as its competitive nature. Beyond a simple nod to the dancers' athleticism, however, this chapter analysed the interrelated dynamics of competition and subjectivity implicit to dancesport.

In Part III (Ballroom Competitions as Events), I focused on ballroom competitions both as festivals and celebrations and as rituals. Chapter 7 examined the role and practices of ballroom competitions as in-gatherings of 'the tribe', bringing together dancers, judges and vendors. More specifically, this chapter highlighted how competitions regularly serve as opportunities for dancers – to watch and observe styles and levels of dance and dancers they are not commonly exposed to; to interact with dancers with whom they do not regularly come into contact; and to visit with those only seen in the competition setting. Chapter 8 then explored the rituals and practices that set ballroom competitions apart from other facets of ballroom life, unpacking the formality, invariance, symbols and rites of passage embedded in ballroom competitions.

Finally, in Part IV (Costs, Consequences and Outcomes), I examined the effects of the values and practices of the competitive scene, highlighting the general costs, consequences and outcomes of ballroom costuming and conduct, gender performance and living the dancesport life. Chapter 9 used the norms and standards for ballroom costuming and comportment to assess the aesthetic standards and values of dancesport, including how these values and commitments get played out in the ongoing dress and behaviour of the ballroom world and how ballroom costuming and dress simultaneously responds to and constructs the visual images and impressions that lie at the centre of competitive ballroom. Chapter 10 then examined the gendered practices and cultural implications of the different uses of the body between the Standard, Smooth, Latin and Rhythm ballroom styles, including how the differences in costuming – both between styles, and within each style by gender – evoke, present and enact very different gender models within ballroom. Finally, whereas Chapters 9 and 10 focused on the aesthetics of costuming and gender performance, Chapter 11 examined the wider social and cultural consequences and outcomes of living the dancesport life, including how competitors' commitments to the practices and values of dancesport feedback into and reshape some of their lifestyles, career trajectories and overall frames of perception, assessment and evaluation.

There is, of course, much about competitive ballroom dancing not covered in this book. The social and political systems are far more complex that I have briefly touched on here. Interesting issues such as personal motivation and psychological satisfaction fall outside the scope of this text, as do larger issues of the marketing, selling and economics of the ballroom industry and the teaching, training and transmission of expert knowledge, aesthetic values and bodily skills. Similarly, there are important issues regarding nationality, class, race and ballroom's participation-base that fall outside this book's purview.[1] Likewise, the different experiences and considerations between the various ballroom subcultures – ranging from beginning amateur competitors to professional world champions, vendors, coaches and judges, DJs and MCs, scrutineers and deck captains – remains a separate and more elaborate task. What this book has done is to provide an overview of the cultural arena within which dancesport lives are lived. It describes the practices, values, commitments and relationships that comprise competitive ballroom dance, serving as the cultural umbrella under which ballroom lives unfold. Some of the key considerations called into the foreground concern the complex intersections of spectacle, art, sport, festival, celebration, ritual, performance, costuming and gender within competitive ballroom. Most obvious in the costumed competition of dancesport, the intersections of dress, body and culture are about much more than ballroom alone.

BALLROOM AS DRESS, BODY AND CULTURE

Ballroom competitors, judges and spectators regularly talk about ballroom costuming,, yet this book addresses the larger topic of ballroom dress, including all of the grooming, clothing and accoutrements utilized both while competing and at other times. Ballroom dancers compete under their own names and never as 'a swan', 'a soldier', 'a tree', or an unidentified chorus member. Because ballroom competitors' always compete as themselves, their competitive garb differs from the costuming of theatrical dance forms. To the extent that 'dress ordinarily communicates aspects of a person's identity' (Eicher 2004: 271), then, this is equally true for dancesport competitors both on and off the actual ballroom floor, suggesting that the classifications of 'costume' as 'put on identity', and 'dress' as 'personal identity', can best be understood as a continuum. Far from dressing by happenstance, dancers, judges, spectators and officials always dress within a matrix of expectations; expectations that that both reflect and inform ballroom living and values.

As Klepp and Storm-Mathisen note, for instance, 'when clothes are used in accordance with conventions and norms, they are not noticed much. However when clothes are used in a way that differs from the norm, this can attract attention and provoke reactions' (Klepp and Storm-Mathisen 2005: 324). The basic matrix of ballroom costuming between gender and dance style (discussed in Chapter 9) is not therefore so much noted within its enactment, but in its absence. The same high-heeled shoes commented on by almost all ballroom neophytes are taken for granted, and only really noticed when missing, such as when a competitor quickly pulls on a shoe when they should already be on the floor. Because dress is always about bodies, however, such conventions are always about larger issues. Indeed, 'because it both touches the body and faces outward towards others, dress has a dual quality … this two-sided quality invites us to explore both the individual and collective identities that the dressed body enables' (Hansen 2004: 372). As both what is worn and what is seen worn by others, then, dress informs and displays ideas about identity – perhaps most widely apparent with gender. 'The genders', as Harvey asserts, 'never have dressed in isolation' (2007: 83) and 'the complimentarity of gendered dress shows especially when men and women meet to dance' (2007: 84).

Historically speaking, for instance, Harvey points out that (prior to the twentieth century), 'the signature of male dress has been the offer to open layers of clothing while still never uncovering more than face and hands' (2007: 77); a description perfectly mirrored in men's Smooth and Standard style costuming. Harvey also notes that even as 'the expectation that men will be *more* covered than women is deeply engrained in Western culture' (2007: 82, original emphasis), historically *shape* has been shown more by men (2007: 73) – a situation clearly mirrored in men's form-fitting trousers, shirts and coats versus women's dresses and gowns. As an index of both gender *and* dance style, however, ballroom costuming well illustrates that 'gender is made visible not by showing or hiding the body as such, but by showing or hiding more or less of it' (Harvey 2007: 82). The Standard woman wearing a long-sleeved ankle-length ball gown with copious floats concealing her back clearly covers far more than the Latin man wearing form-fitting trousers and an equally tight shirt open to below his sternum. Yet at one and the same time this same female dancer is less covered than her male Standard counterpart, just as the male Latin dancer is more covered than his female Latin counterpart.

The point here is that if, 'at all times, unavoidably, dress reflects the tensions of "gender politics"' (Harvey 2007: 72), then, like gender, gendered dress is often far more complex than first impressions might suggest. For example, given that 'the body that claims more authority and power is likely ... to be more covered' (Harvey 2007: 82), what sense is to be made of a Standard woman who is more covered than a Latin male? Historical developments, notwithstanding, this costuming example can be read as indicating both gender status *and* Standard's widely recognized status as the most prestigious style. Also interesting in this light is that the same Standard ball gown that may visually signal a soft, ladylike femininity may weigh as much as 15 pounds or more (depending on the number of rhinestones and the type and amount of cloth involved), literally leaving its wearer with a heavier burden to carry than her partner as they dance together. As this scenario helps to exemplify then, 'dress, in short, is like a punning language, expert in double meanings and part of its work is to manage the contradictions surrounding the body' (Harvey 2007: 66). Ultimately, however, things are more complex yet, since, as Strathern points out (citing Connerton 1989: 33), 'clothing not only conveys messages that can be decoded; it also helps to actually mold character by influencing the body's move-ments' (Strathern 1997: 29).

More than just reflecting ideas about bodies, dress modulates these same ideas. Thus competitor's costuming not only marks specific gender models, but provides a specific experience of gender as well. As such, the costuming of Smooth and Rhythm dancers – similar to those of Standard and Latin dancers – not only signals different models of masculinity and femininity, but is directly implicated in different bodily experiences and expressions of these roles (as seen in Figure 12.1).

12.1. Costumes as signs and sources of gendered bodies – as seen in the dancing of US Professional Smooth Champions Tomas Mielnicki and JT Thomas at the 2007 United States Dance Championships in Orlando, FL (left); and US Professional Rhythm Vice Champions Felipe Telona Jr. and Carolina Orlovsky-Telona at the 2007 San Diego Dancesport Championships in San Diego, CA (right). ©2007 Jonathan S. Marion

More than just enacting gender in their costuming and dancing, competitors create that which they inhabit. As Banet-Weiser points out, 'the enacting of gender produces gender' (1999: 90, based on Butler 1990). If this is most obvious in ballroom costuming, it is the hours upon hours that dancers' spend training and practising certain ways of moving – wherein (and whereby) dancers' bodies serve as both 'template and tool' (Comaroff and Comaroff 1992: 87) – that prove the most enduring.

That dancers' uses of their bodies produce the most enduring models for their identities is not surprising, since the 'self that acts on the world necessarily does so through the medium of the body' (Reischer and Koo 2004: 307). Certainly 'the bodies we cultivate are ultimately indexes and expressions of the social world they inhabit' (Reischer and Koo 2004: 299); but this is only part of the picture. Thus while dancesport privileges certain ways of bodily being, such bodily enactments feed back into ballroom understandings and practices of the body. In defining 'somatic modes of attention', as 'culturally elaborated ways of attending to and with one's body in surroundings that include the embodied presence of others', Csordas (1993: 138) aptly draws attention to the body as both filter of experience and tool of social engagement – and wherein the body is implicated in the making of its own meanings.

The feedback between body and identity is complicated. In the first place, and as noted by Bourdieu (1977: 218; cited in Strathern 1997: 29), 'every group entrusts to bodily automatisms those principles most basic to it and most inseparable to its conservation'. Just as different conventions of ballroom costuming disappear from conscious awareness, so too then with dancers' perceptions, views and understandings surrounding the body. Travelling back to San Diego from the 2007 United States Dance Championships in Orlando, FL, for instance, I was struck by the difference between the bodies I had been surrounded by at the competition versus those around me while waiting to board the airplane. The same bodies that constituted a 'normal' group of air travellers stood out to me as abnormal relative to the hundreds of dancers with whom I had just spent five days. In a similar vein, Melinda, a professional US finalist, relates that on visits back 'home' (where she grew up), she is always surprised at the discrepancy between what the 'average' woman in her mid-to-late thirties looks like – meaning body shape and tone – and how much this contrasts with Melinda's day-to-day experiences within the ballroom world. Such anecdotes are more than interesting side notes, however, pointing (as they do) to the 'the body beautiful as an icon of social values and, less benignly, as a mechanism of social power and control' (Reisher and Koo 2004: 299) as Marx and Foucault both recognized.

Insofar as 'developing and displaying an ideal body type thus signals one's co-operative participation in a culturally meaningful system of values' (Reisher and Koo 2004: 300), dancers' bodies serve as an index of cultural accord. As such, the 'overweight' dancer may not only be seen as carrying a few extra pounds, but as not taking their dancing seriously (since they would be in 'correct' shape if they did). Add to this the fact that within Western contexts bodily messages are typically understood as being about the self (Reisher and Koo 2004: 300), the overweight dancer may well not be taken seriously as a dancer. Such issues are not abstract considerations within the ballroom world. These are common concerns, with many competitors – who would be considered extremely fit and attractive in almost any other setting – being envious of the bodies of other dancers. A personal anecdote related to these considerations concerns Louis van Amstel's *Latin Fusion* Broadway show at City Center in New York City. As an observer to the final three days of cast rehearsals, I was a guest at the opening-night premiere and had back-stage access to the following day's matinee, after which the cast were all invited to a dancer's house for an informal after-party and to use the hot tub. As much as I appreciated the invitation to go along with the cast – both personally and from a research standpoint – I was also relieved to have had previous plans to meet my sister and brother-in-law for lunch while I was in town, thereby avoiding comparisons (even by myself) between my physique and those of the serious competitors comprising the cast.[2]

Expanding on Butler's argument that 'the various acts of gender create the idea of gender and without those acts, there would be no gender at all' (1990: 140), Reisher and Koo point out that 'if gender is a series of repeated performances, then the distinctions of gender are dependent on the quality of its enactment by the body' (2004: 310). The prominence of gender within dancesport does not therefore simply reflect ballroom values, but is in fact created through the regular practices of dancesport dancing and costuming. Furthermore, ever-increasing quality of bodily enactment *is* the purpose of dance training and practice. As such and as materials throughout this book illustrate, dancesport exemplifies 'the extraordinary capacity of the body not only to symbolize the social world, but also to participate actively in the creation of that world' (Reisher and Koo 2004: 315). Bodily enactments do not simply reflect cultural conventions and understandings, after all, but perpetuate these models as they are constantly recreated anew in practice, and it is in this way that dancesport's constructions of gender gain salience through participation and practice.

Salience is not the same thing as acceptance, however, so just as Wachs says of women's participation in co-ed softball, participation in dancesport represents a 'complicated situation in which belief systems surrounding ideologies of gender difference are often simultaneously challenged and reinvigorated' (2005: 527). In her analysis of beauty pageants, Banet-Weiser (1999) makes a parallel case, pointing out that where the swimsuit and evening gown events are spectacles of homogeneity, the talent and interview events are performances of heterogeneity. In Banet-Weiser's words, on the one hand, 'the swimsuit and evening gown events are clear spectacles: the display of standardized feminine bodies parading before a panel of judges is evidence not only of self-discipline, but also of the conformity that is produced by such surveillance' (1999: 88); while, on the other hand, 'within the talent and interview competitions, contestants constitute themselves as active, self-possessed and most of all, deeply embodied' (Banet-Weiser 1999). Yet dancesport is even more complex, with the spectacle of often swimsuit-like Latin dresses and evening-gown-like Standard dresses only fully presented and on display within the context of dancers' demonstrations of skill and talent. Perhaps even more importantly, the heteronormative standard for dancesport partnerships depends on (and demands) both men and women as mutually cooperating participants.

While this book has focused on the culture of competitive ballroom dance, a final piece of the dancesport puzzle – and a tremendously telling one at that – concerns the process of competitors' enculturation. After all, saying that 'all aesthetics are socially grounded' (MacClancy 1997: 2) is not the same thing as saying that all aes-thetics share common social grounding, and so how dancers come to learn about and participate in dancesport matters. While one can come to competitive dance at almost any age, the most elite competitors, and hence the ones who make and mark the standards by which dancesport is assessed, almost always start quite young. Dancesport's mixed-gender base is thus quite different from junior league baseball, for example, and in connection with which Fine comments on 'the distinctive maleness of these leisure settings' (1987: 2) for young boys' socialization. According to Fine, junior league functions as a vehicle for moral socialization relative to the

12.2. Dancesport socialization – as seen in a social dance between 2006 and 2007 US Junior I Latin Champion (with partner Kiril Kulish), Natella Devitskaya social dancing a rumba with international coach and judge Victor Kanevsky at the 2007 United States Dance Championships in Orlando, FL. ©2007 Jonathan S. Marion

concerns of both adults and peers (1987, chapters 3 and 4 respectively), and in the abstract this is true of dancesport as well. In the details, however, dancesport tells a very different story, with the two people most deeply implicated in a young dancer's (dancesport) socialization being (a) their opposite gender partner and (b) an adult coach. The point here is that much of dancesport's socialization takes place in close physical contact with the opposite gender and among adults, generating poise, presence and sophistication in young dancers that often belies their years (Figures 12.2 and 12.3).

As demonstrated throughout this book, the complex, multidimensional facets of dancesport are many, with dichotomies present at every turn. It would be arrogant of me, and show a lack of appreciation for the competitive ballroom culture, were I to summarize this fascinating world in such a way as to provoke controversy intentionally or reduce it to a phrase which captures but a part of this lived world. Instead of presenting any final closure or resolution, then, my concluding remarks have capitalized on dancesport as a concentrated microcosm for exploring the myriad

12.3. Poise, presence and sophistication – as displayed by 16-year-old amateur 10-Dance competitor Nadiya Bychkova at the 2005 British Open Dance Championship in Blackpool, England. ©2005 Jonathan S. Marion

interconnections of ballroom dress, body and culture. As with this book though, such considerations are not only, or ultimately, about competitive ballroom dancing, but also about people's activities, values and lives. In the end, this book provides significant evidence of many points of departure inquisitive students and other scholars may pursue. I believe this is inevitable as ballroom engages so many aspects of the human experience.

NOTES

PROLOGUE

1. Doré Designs Inc. is one of the premiere ballroom dress companies in the United States, also providing costumes for ice dancers such as 2006 Olympic Silver medallist Tanith Belbin.
2. A word of clarification regarding terminology is in order here. Eicher and Roach-Higgins (1997) use the term 'dress' to designate all clothing, adornments and body modifications used to enhance personal identity, reserving the term 'costume' for that which is not about personal identity but is dress for stage, theatre, Halloween, masquerades and suchlike. This distinction is an important one, but problematic with the ballroom context. On the one hand, ballroom dancers compete *as themselves*, suggesting that their attire is, in fact, 'dress'. On the other hand, 'costume' is the popular-use term within ballroom. As such, I elect to use 'costume' in order to best reflect the understandings and thinking common among ballroom personnel.
3. The term 'dancesport' is widely used to designate competitive (versus social) ballroom dancing.

INTRODUCTION

1. Plural for kibbutz as transliterated from the Hebrew.
2. Knowing what I do now, I would take this to mean flamenco or Paso Doble but, at the time, I honestly had no clue.
3. The area was a commercial one with numerous shops and eateries on the ground floors, so that that the first stories were actually quite high.
4. Formation ballroom dancing was once described to me as a cross between ballroom dancing and synchronized swimming, with up to eight couples dancing as the entire formation constantly shifts between various lines and geometric shapes, much like a marching band on a football field or a drum and bugle corps competition.
5. Dancing with multiple partners in different divisions, levels and styles is fairly common within the collegiate circuit in the US, especially at lower levels and especially for men who are usually in short supply relative to the number of women.
6. Most 'salsa clubs' are really mainstream clubs or restaurants that have designated salsa nights one or more nights a week.
7. This section is based on and expanded from a research report published in *Suomen Antropologi* (Marion 2007).
8. *Dance Beat* is the specialized industry newspaper for competitive ballroom dancing in the US.
9. Throughout this book I use dancers' full names (first and last) for specific public figures or where I am citing with permission. In all other cases I use pseudonyms to protect confidentiality in accordance with the accepted ethnographic practice, and do so using only first names in order to avoid any confusion with last-name-only citations.
10. USABDA's name was changed to USA Dance in 2004.

11. Chapter 3 discusses some of the specific values being evaluated and judged in ballroom competitions while Chapter 5, on ballroom as sport, looks at some of the ramifications of the subjectivity in ballroom dancing.

12. Although a lower model, my 35mm SLR camera, vertical grip, flash bracket, shoe-mounted flash, and external battery pack closely resembled the equipment of the official professional event photographers. (For much of my fieldwork I was still shooting film, using a Cannon A2 with a VG-10 grip and a 540EZ flash. Just prior to Blackpool in 2005 I made the switch to digital, in the form of a Cannon 20D – upgraded to a 30D just prior to Blackpool in 2006 – with a BG-E2 grip and a 580EX flash with a Quantum Turbo battery pack.)

13. What constitutes 'good-sized' is rather relative, especially given the vastly different amounts of space typically utilized between spot Latin dances such as the Rumba versus space intensive Standard dances, such as the quickstep, which progress around the floor. Also worth recognizing in this regard is the vastly different amount of floor space required for the volume and shape generated by elite competitors (relative to that required and utilized by lower-level dancers' versions of the exact same figures).

14. While it is true that ballroom camps offer the option of private lessons with the various instructors, which many camp attendees pursue, the general camp schedule is built around the group class schedule and activities.

15. This is not to suggest that individual dancers may not prioritize the improvement of their own dancing when at a club, but to highlight that such self-development is generally understood to be the purpose of studios and not of clubs.

16. It is also worth noting that the typically far more crowded social conditions at a club constrain the amplitude of movement and gestures relative to competition and performance-based dancing.

17. I have encountered both physical and social salsa clubs but only social ballroom clubs in the United States. Also important to note in this regard is that the nomenclature I am using suits the US usages of these terms, as many European countries – at least as far as ballroom dancing is concerned – reference "studios" as the places where people learn to social dance and 'clubs' as the institutions fostering competitive dancing (i.e. competitive sports clubs).

18. Despite common uses for meetings and banquets, most hotels still have 'ballrooms' (labelled as such) which serve as the locations of most ballroom competitions in the United States. The majority of European ballroom competitions, in contrast, are held in sports halls. While this variation between venues relates to aesthetic and structural differences, there remains a larger ballroom 'world' that transcends such distinctions. As elite competitors travel from continent to continent, the same dances are done in the same ways by largely the same people.

19. Bolin makes a parallel case for bodybuilding, noting that 'bodybuilding competition, while only occupying a small part of the bodybuilders' total training, serves to create seasons of training' (Bolin 2004: 121).

20. This section is reworked from '"Where" is "There"?: Towards a Translocal Anthropology in Competitive Ballroom Dancing' (Marion 2005a) and 'Which Way to the Ballroom?' (Marion 2007).

CHAPTER I   WHAT IS COMPETITIVE BALLROOM DANCE?

1. For example, by the late sixteenth century, couples' dances commenced and concluded with a bow (Hammond 2000: 142).

2. It is worth noting that the Latin ballroom division is not seen as 'Latin' by many ballroom people, but as inspired and derived from a variety of (primarily) Latin rhythms. This point remains problematic, however, both for those from Latin America who often decry 'that's not Latin!', and for the unfamiliar

who are misguided by the title of 'Latin' dancing. Thus, while there is a reasonable history of how the Latin (or Latin American) division came by its name, the co-optation of the title of 'Latin dance' – and the authority to codify what counts as appropriate technique therefore – reflects a troubling pattern of Western colonialism (e.g. McMains 2007: 128, 131, 156, 169).

3. The divisions presented in Table 1.1 are largely specific to the United States because outside the United States the American Style is seldom taught or competed. This model is slowly changing, however, especially with the expansion of the Arthur Murray International® franchise into numerous overseas markets. Similarly, Table 1.2 focuses on the dominant styles most common to my research.

4. Although the word 'amateur' was removed to bring the IDSF into compliance with International Olympic Committee standards, this terminology is still used by the majority of ballroom dancers. For more on the histories of the IDSF and WDC, see Chapter 2.

5. This section includes substantially revised and rewritten materials from Marion 2005a, 2006 and 2007.

6. More technically there is a larger shared range here, that of modern industrialized society. Within the larger framework of modern globalization perhaps there are shared elements that would suggest a shared culture. I would contend, however, that in fact there are many similar or parallel forms at this scale that are not truly shared. While 'modern industrialized culture' may serve as convenient terminology, it remains overly reductionistic.

7. National culture is, by no means, the only separate (if intertwining) culture. Ethnic, religious and occupational cultures are but a few of the other hubs of typical cultural identification and elaboration.

8. For other examples, see Chaiklin and Lave 1993; Cole 1996; Engeström 1993; Forman, Minnick, and Stone 1993; Hutchins 1995; Lave 1988; and Rogoff 1990.

9. Geertz 1973a: 15; Goodenough 1981: 105; Schneider 1968: 6; Stromberg 1986: 8, 13; also see Wallace 1961: 42.

10. Ward 1993: 27.

11. Savigliano 1998: 103.

12. E.g. Anderson 1991 [1983]; Greider 1997; Horn 1998; Mankekar 1999; McKinley 1997.

13. E.g. Clifford 1988, Clifford and Marcus 1986, Fischer and Abedi 1991, Marcus 1992, Marcus and Fischer 1986, Marcus and Myers 1995.

14. E.g. Taylor 1998. Also, the efficacy of dance as a socially levelling and formative arena of human activity (Spencer 1985: 28), while always taking place within larger social contexts – which must themselves be looked at in any analyses of dance – is also generative of its own collectivities (Hanna 1988). This phenomenon is particularly telling in modern ballroom and salsa dance communities, which do not readily fit conventional models and understandings of community.

15. Savigliano 1998: 105–108.

16. E.g. Sumner 1906: 12

17. For examples of this phenomena, see Chaiklin and Lave 1993; Cole 1996; Engeström 1993; Forman, Minnick, and Stone 1993; Goodnow, Miller, and Kessel 1995; Hutchins 1995; Lave 1988; Lave and Wenger 1991; and Rogoff 1990.

18. E.g. Offen 2000.

19. Mobile in that they re-coalesce from night to night – in different locations with different permutations – while, simultaneously, being non-transient in that their core constituency remains stable over time, albeit in varying permutations.

20. Polhemus 1993: 4; e.g. Bateson and Mead 1942; Mead and McGregor 1951 regarding Bali.

21. Thomas 1993; see also Geertz 1973; Hanna 1979b, 1988; Radcliffe-Brown 1922.

22. An earlier version of this section appears in my research report 'Which Way to the Ballroom?' (Marion 2007).

23. This section draws from materials in my article 'Beyond Ballroom: Activity as Performance, Embodiment, and Identity' (Marion 2006).

24. For Turner these genres serve as a 'temporal structure which interdigitates constant with variable features' (1987: 26), and which simultaneously work to both sustain and challenge their social and cultural surrounds.

CHAPTER 2   A BRIEF HISTORY OF BALLROOM

1. This historical background regarding the ISTD is adapted from information at the ISTD website at www.istd.org and the USISTD website at www.usistd.org. For a slightly more in-depth history of the ISTD, especially concerning the people involved, see http://www.usistd.org/society_objectives/istd_uk/.

2. The Latin American division of the ISTD was actually first started by Monsieur Pierre, Doris Lavelle (Monsieur's partner), and Doris Nichols who were later joined by Gwenethe Walshe and Dimitri Petrides.

3. This information about the WDC was compiled from their website at www.wddsc.com.

4. International Amateur Dancers Federation.

5. This information is condensed from the 'History of International Organized DanceSport' as first published on the IDSF website, www.idsf.net, 25 August 1995.

6. *Reichsverband zur Pflege des Gessellschatstanzes* (Empire Association for the Promotion of Social Dancing).

7. Additional national organizations that soon joined were Finland (6 December 1953), Switzerland (15 August 1954) and the Netherlands (1 March 1955).

8. Although the term 'amateur' has been removed from the organizational materials of the IDSF and USA dance in order to comply with IOC standards, the overwhelming majority of competitors, officials and judges still use this term, as do the event listings in most competitions where both 'amateurs' and 'professionals' are present.

9. This material is condensed from information available at the NDCA website at www.ndca.org.

10. The North American Treaty of 1981 between the NDCA and the Canadian Dance Teachers Association was later reinforced and expanded with the signing on 19 November 2004 of the North American Dance Sport Alliance (NADSA) between the NDCA and the Canadian Dance and Dance Sport Council (previously the Canadian Dance Teachers Association).

11. The membership of the Asian-Pacific Council is Australia, Canada, Hong Kong, Indonesia, Japan, Korea, Malaysia, New Zealand, Singapore, Chinese Taipei, Thailand and the United States.

12. This information is condensed from the USABDA website at www.usabda.org.

13. The World Games include sports that are not in the Olympic Programme but which are recognized by the International Olympic Committee.

14. Adapted from the pamphlet *Winter Gardens, Blackpool, 125 Years Souvenir History*.

CHAPTER 3   JUDGING BALLROOM DANCE

1. This example speaks succinctly to the way in which 'politics' are often used as a scapegoat for unpopular or unwelcome results, and is also the reason there are eleven judges or more at many of the more prestigious competitions – to minimize aberrations statistically.

2. The obvious exceptions to this are other athletes, such as ice skaters, from whom the same type of posture-based poise, balance and control are also required.

3. While I could still see this same element in later visits, it no longer stood out in my mind the way it did the first time I went to Blackpool. Now that I am far more accustomed to seeing and interacting with elite dancers regularly, I take such posture for granted, no longer noticing it within ballroom settings.

4. The fact that only the gentlemen's names are used for referring competitive couples is a fairly common practice within ballroom, one with significant implications for gender I discuss in Chapter 9.

5. One of the stranger comments I encountered concerning timing comes from Dan – a popular coach, adjudicator and previous Blackpool champion – regarding music selections used for mambo at many US competitions. The issue was that a number of the songs played called for a break – a reversal of direction and body weight – on the '1' whereas ballroom mambo specifies breaking on the '2'. Dan conceded that this was often true, but went on to say that this just made it 'a better challenge for them [the couples] to dance on time' (to the dancesport prescribed 'on2'). The fact that Dan evaluates this simply as 'a better challenge' is deeply telling of how myopic the focus on 'correct' timing has become in ballroom – developing an autonomy separate from the musicality of actually dancing to the music.

6. It also strikes me that (aside from the directly visual disruption in shape provided by a poor hold), as experienced dancers and teachers themselves, most judges are also probably reacting to a poor hold based on their own experiences and understanding of how this diminishes and disrupts the bodily communication between partners.

7. Causing a collision, or not avoiding an easily circumvented one, is an issue of floorcraft; a separate variable of evaluation.

CHAPTER 4   BALLROOM AS SPECTACLE

1. Here I use the American labelling of MC, or Master of Ceremonies, but it is really the role I am referring to, whether performed by a designated coordinator/announcer or the Chairman of Judges (such as at Blackpool).

2. The person responsible for tabulating the judges' marks in establishing the outcome of a ballroom competition.

3. While some events are now starting to use hand-held electronic marking, pen and paper remain the dominant norm.

4. The 'deck' area, borrowing from baseball, is a designated location just off the dance floor, where those in the next event are lined up to enter the floor.

5. The 'International' is the common use slang for the Ellsa Wells International Dance Championships.

6. This competition was last danced in 2003, the last year before Sunday events were added to the Blackpool competition schedule.

7. Since events repeat annually, part of being a seasoned competitor includes learning the general conditions of each event and location.

8. In reference to floor conditions, dancers use 'fast' to mean a comparatively slick surface which their shoes easily glide over, while 'slow' is used for a floor with greater traction. Although preferences vary by individual, as a rule of thumb Standard and Smooth dancers tend to prefer 'faster' floors which better suit the progressive nature of their dances, while Latin and Rhythm dancers prefer 'slower' floors for the better grip it gives them to work off for the short, fast, sharp movements and actions of their dances.

9. For the dance context in question, 'excessive' should be understood relative to daily non-dance practices.

10. Private video recording is prohibited at all NDCA sanctioned competitions (some exceptions are made for children's events), and official videography companies do a very brisk business selling dancers videotapes (and now DVDs) of their dancing.

11. Contradictorily, Wilson argues that 'glamour is not about consumption in the consumer society, although the word has come to be continually misused to suggest that it is' (2007: 98).

CHAPTER 5   BALLROOM AS ART

1. Some might argue that music is as ephemeral as dance or, at most, only slightly less ephemeral. Certainly neither dance nor music produce physical objects of art such as painting, photography, pottery, or sculpture (just to provide a few of the more common examples) which can continue to be perceived, evaluated, and appreciated as created by the artist. But there are differences between dance and music as well. Much of the music produced today is, for instance, actually composed to be recorded. This is in drastic contrast to dance, where only a small fraction is primarily choreographed for the sake of reproduction. More importantly, however, music is still perceived as it was created and intended, through sound waves entering the ear and then being 'understood' as music. Recorded dance is different in that the light being reflected into the observers eye does not come from the three dimensional source of dancers but, instead, from a two dimensional depiction of three dimensional artistry.

2. This is not to say that photographs and video fail to capture anything of value or cannot evoke responses similarly to a painting or sculpture, only that the art and what it conveys are of a different order than as-danced-in-the-moment.

3. To be sure there is some similarity in this to sports as well, wherein players and athletes often also want to 'put on a show' for their audiences, and whereby future evocations (be they replays on TV, photos in magazines, and the like) may trigger partial re-livings of the moment.

4. Charlotte is also one of the judges shown for the children's ballroom competition in New York that was the subject of 2005's hit documentary film *Mad Hot Ballroom*.

5. I should point out that at least some competitors' assertions of their preference for performance quality over results proved false. For example one couple who expressed the 'performance is what matters' opinion to me during an interview, before I then overheard them talking about how 'great' they had danced and how 'worthless' that was (in light of their unwelcome placement) at the same competition. Just to be clear, I am not suggesting that these dancers were necessarily being insincere in their comments to me. I am only pointing out that, at least for some, the asserted values of what they intellectually found preferable may turn out to be at odds with their experiential evaluation in at least some situations. For many of the competitors I interviewed, however, their real world reactions matched their original assertions.

6. Following Schechner (e.g. 2002), the same person can be both actor and audience to his or her own performance. The key being that it is only in so far as one *is* an audience to one's self that activity becomes performance. For the point at hand then, if one merely moves it is not art, but if one is audience to one's own movement then it may become so.

7. The prominent place of ballroom on mixed-dance-genre TV show like *So You Think You Can Dance* may indicate the beginning of a shift in this general trend, but does not belie the long-standing pattern of denigration to accorded dancesport by the various forms of theatre-dance.

CHAPTER 6   BALLROOM AS SPORT

1. Aside from the seven league sports Christenfeld examined, he also finds the same dynamic at work in tournament-based contests when rankings are used to predict success.

2. The complete judging system is somewhat more complex and includes rules for when none of the couples receive a majority of ordinal placements as well as several tie-braking stipulations.

3. Here I use one-on-one to describe the binary competitive scenario – be it between two individuals or teams – versus the many-at-once model of a track or swimming heat. While any pair of couples, say, first and second, or fourth and fifth, might all be in one-on-one competitions with each other for their respective positions for all effective purposes – or two couple in any earlier round may effectively be in one-on-one competition for a slot in the next round. Such head-to-head contests 'in practice' are different in both character and implication from structurally defined one-on-one competitions.

4. The exceptions to this are the various formation and show dance divisions which do employ point systems.

5. An abundantly clear and public example of the emphasis on artistry in judged competitions came in the 1994 Olympics when, with tied overall scores, Oksana Baiul won the gold medal in women's figure skating over Nancy Kerrigan by dint of a higher artistic mark.

6. This is not to say that these young ballroom dancers, themselves, originally hail from outside the United States but, rather, that their parents are typically émigrés from former states of the USSR.

7. The very lack of ethnographic focus on dance in its own right (as noted in Chapter 1) highlights the marginalization of dance (and the arts in general) in academia which, unfortunately, is far from surprising in light of both the colonial heritage of Western social sciences and the Cartesian dualism of Western academia wherein the body is understood as separate from and even antithetical to the intellect.

8. For example, all ballroom dancers share an understanding of what constitutes a waltz versus a foxtrot, whereas a cha cha variation I learned in a franchise studio in California was unfamiliar to that franchise's studio I visited in Pennsylvania.

9. This same dynamic is most evident in the United States in Utah, where the dominant Latter Day Saints' faith concomitantly facilitates prolific dancesport participation and very conservative standards of bodily display therein (my thanks to Robert Bunnett for suggesting the use of this example).

CHAPTER 7 COMPETITIONS AS FESTIVAL AND CELEBRATION

1. Vending fees can be on a straight vendor fee basis or, more commonly, on a base fee plus a percentage of each vendor's sales at that event. Vendors are also typically required to purchase a full-page advertisement in the event programme for that competition. Since the price of both vending fees and programme advertisements tend to vary according to the appeal and size of various competitions, the fees associated with vending at larger competitions do actually tend to run higher than for smaller events. Still, vendors are required to pay some type of fee regardless of the size of the competition they are vending at, and whether or not they make any sales.

2. Food costs at a competition tend to be rather high as hotel restaurants are not typically bargain eateries and as room service charges—when there is insufficient time to sit down for a meal—tend to drastically inflate these meal expenses.

CHAPTER 8 COMPETITIONS AS RITUAL

1. Clearly the music, technique and performance of ballroom competition lack the meanings typically implicated in religious ritual, as does the prize structure. Nonetheless, dance can, and for many does, serve as an orientating system of meanings and motivations, albeit not ones that 'speak' to the existential concerns typically addressed in and by religion.

2. For several examples of non-religion-based ritual, see Bergesen 1996 [1984], Davis-Floyd 1996 [1994], Goffman 1996 [1967], Grimes 1996 [1990], Kertzer 1996 [1988], Wallendorf and Arnould 1996 [1991], Winn 1996 [1991].

3. Some IDSF events switch this ordering of the first two dances, running samba first and cha cha second.

4. I also want to point out that it is not only the competition venue itself that represents a known quantity at Blackpool, but also everything from surrounding lodgings and food options to the size of the floor and the type of music played. Also worth noting, the procedures for judging, for advancing to further rounds, the roles of the judges, DJ, scrutineer and MC all unfold in exactly this type of way as well.

5. While a few competitions have started using wireless PDA-type devices for judges' markings, the ritualized symbol, function and effect are all still (largely) the same.

6. There are a couple of reasons why Standard and Smooth competitors can usually be differentiated from each other based on costuming alone (at all but the lowest ages and levels, where costuming is not allowed), whereas Latin and Rhythm cannot. Probably the most obvious discrepancy between the costuming of Standard dancers versus Smooth dancers is that Standard dresses almost always have some type of floats, and typically offer the most coverage of any ballroom costuming, while Smooth dresses do not have floats and often seem to represent a cross between Standard and Latin dresses in both cut and design (although favouring Standard). The same floats that provide additional movement and shape in Standard – where partners never break the hold of their frame – would quickly emerge as impediments of the highest order in Smooth where partners' transition in and out of frame amidst numerous side-by-side and individual elements, spins and turns. Similarly, Standard men's attire is a ballroom tail suit while the Smooth men's costuming is a specially tailored waistcoat or dinner jacket (in order to provide a straight shoulder line while the arms are raised, into dance frame, and not when hanging at the sides, as is the case with commercial garments). Additionally, the shoes designed to be worn for Standard and Smooth are different (although much closer to each other than either is to Latin/Rhythm shoes). It is also worth noting here that, just as with the dresses, Smooth shoes are a cross between Standard and Latin footwear, but leaning towards Standard. Simply stated, there are no parallel points of comparison to differentiate between Latin and Rhythm competitors' costumes or footwear.

7. The only exception to the ordering comes when a podium is used for the first-, second- and third-place finalists, in which case the first-place couple is elevated the highest in between the second- and third-place couples.

8. There are exceptions to this inverse ordering, Blackpool being the most notable amongst them.

9. Except, perhaps, for the usually greater clapping, hooting and hollering for the higher placements (a point I thank Robert Bunnett for bringing to my attention).

10. In saying that competitions are publicly accessible even if expensive, I am not discounting the often tremendously great weight of economic reality. To be sure there are probably many people who would have enough interest to go and watch a competition – at least insofar as the recent success of ballroom-themed movies and TV shows would seem to suggest – if price was never an obstacle. The point I am making, however, is just that no group of people are excluded from being in a ballroom audience as a matter of principle.

11. As with any meaning system, which elements get internalized, and to what extent, are never given. Yet the more involved one becomes with any meaning system the greater the likelihood that, especially with exposure over time, more and more commitment will engender more and deeper internalizations.

CHAPTER 9   COSTUMES AND CONDUCT

1. As has already been noted in earlier chapters, various countries have additions of their own – such as the New Vogue and Street Latin categories in Australia – but Standard and Latin dominate the world scene while the American styles, already dominant in the United States, have some exposure via franchise studio instruction abroad.

2. Martin is making a similar point in noting that 'dress mediates how we see ourselves and how others see us, and if we want to pass muster we had better make the right choice' (Martin 2001: xv).

3. The differences between afternoon and evening sessions is actually an interesting intersection of social, cultural and psychological variables – of which attire is but one small piece.

4. Since then, also South African Professional Latin Champion.

CHAPTER 10   PERFORMING GENDER

1. As Wulff points out (1998: 110), however, there have been a few recent works on dance focusing on men, such as those by Burt (1995) and Franko (1995).

2. Annick Prieur's understanding that appearance, at least within appropriate contexts, is considered reflective of sexuality (1996: 88) seems to be based on this same dynamic.

3. Feelings and beliefs matter to people, and thus to their lives, since 'human social life', as Michelle Rosaldo points out, 'depends upon our forms of feeling and belief' (1980: 408).

4. That men's costuming offers more coverage than women's is a separate issue, but a longstanding one, that is not dancesport specific. As Harvey notes: 'Women's dress . . . has tended, historically, to reveal more than men's' (2007: 71).

5. Here I follow D'Andrade's framing that far from being a default setting for mental processes, consciousness represents an arena of upper level trouble-shooting (2000: 66, based on Minsky 1986).

6. Feelings and beliefs matter to people, and thus to their lives, since 'human social life', as Michelle Rosaldo points out, 'depends upon our forms of feeling and belief' (1980: 408).

7. Each a facet of social life refracting a variety gender implications as well.

8. But see Bellman 1974; Blacking 1973 (passim); Gell 1979; Hanna 1979a and 1979b (passim); Kaeppler 1972; Martin and Pesovar 1961; Metheny 1965; Royce 1977:192–211; Singer 1974; Spencer 1985:35; Williams 1978, 1982; and Woodward 1976.

9. Ballet, for instance, has been critiqued as males' view of females in contrast to modern dance as females' view of females (e.g. Blackmer 1989: 35; Hanna 1988: 132); with ideals of antigravity and ethereality versus gravity and natural movement at issue (Blackmer 1989: 37). Also see 1988:128–9 regarding the misogynism of contemporary ballet (e.g. Gordon 1983).

10. For more on the distribution of statuses culture (such as between men/women as leaders/followers) within a culture – and their influence on those who agree and disagree, acknowledge or do not acknowledge, and are aware or oblivious to such distributions – see Swartz and Jordan 1976, and Swartz 1991.

11. Biological sex is not, of course, the only filter of this type. Indeed, it is only in interaction with culture that biological factors function 'as predispositions that may or may not be transformed into manifestations through the mediation of culture' (Ardener 1993: 3). As Lorber well notes, then, 'gendered people emerge not from physiology . . . but from the exigencies of the social order hormones' (1994: 35).

12. Spiro makes this same point in *Gender and Culture* (1979) in noting that a person's physical body provides the primary filter for all of their experiences; a stance mirrored by Ortner's (1974) understanding that a woman's physically embodied experiences are part of what shapes her psychic structure.

13. There are partial exceptions to this, of course, such as the inclusion of dancesport in the Gay Games, a robust gay dancesport circuit in Europe, and the acceptance of same sex couples in many US college competitions. The larger point remains, however, that heteronormative gender roles serve as the overarching umbrella under which the most prestigious competitions (e.g. Blackpool) are conducted.

14. An alternative view on this is not that Standard is resistant to accepting gay men, but that gay men prefer and enjoy the style and movement of Latin. The limited interview data I have on this does suggest that there is a preference trend in this direction, *but* also indicates a less hospitable cultural landscape. To wit, the very lyrical and Broadway-like character of Smooth should, in theory, offer some of the same appeal as Latin; but because Smooth is grounded in the conventions in Standard (even if highly divergent in many ways), it too lacks known gays amongst the ranking professional competitors.

15. As per note 14, some people have argued that gay men are not in Standard because of their choice and preference. While certainly viable on a person-by-person basis, the scale of disparity between the two styles strikes me as too overwhelmingly systematic to be accounted for by personal preference alone. Add to this Standard's origins as the oldest of the dancesport styles, and its stylistic identity as the most traditional of the disciplines, and I think that a lack of 'fit' for out gay men stems from cultural norms at least as much as personal preferences.

16. Danced in all ballroom styles, pivots demand such shared responsibility as the man and the woman must alternately exert the same powerful energy in counterpoint to each other – one 'pulling' and then relaxing while the other 'pulls'. This coordination is complicated by a man's typically greater weight and a women's typically lower centre of gravity, suggesting that the woman may be doing more than her share for the pivots to be smooth and balanced. (Thanks to Robert Bunnett for suggesting this example.)

CHAPTER 11   LIVING THE DANCESPORT LIFE

1. The prevalence of competition videos (and now DVDs) has proved to be an interesting twist on this: new dancers actually get to 'see' and 'discover' the greats of the past for themselves, on the one hand, while, on the other hand, the mythologizing of specific performances facilitated by purely oral tradition has diminished. Both of which are dynamics that continue multiplying (in both degree and kind) as more and more clips from major dance competitions and showcases become regularly available on YouTube™ and other such video-sharing services (despite restrictions against private videotaping at most major competitions).

2. In all fairness, however, I should point out that there are those within the dancesport industry who perpetuate such misunderstandings, with announcements such as 'and now the dance from Argentina, the Tango', 'the dance from Cuba, the Rumba', 'the dance from Spain, the Paso Doble', 'the dance from Brazil, the Samba', and other such assertions. Certainly each of these dances is inspired by and has historical roots in the respective countries, but asserting that the ballroom version is *from* these countries is misinformed at best, and either ignorant or deceptive at the worst.

3. As an important point of clarification, I do not mean to suggest anything inherently problematic with all such teaching. Some ballroom instructors are true 'cross-over' dancers and teachers, being equally proficient in different dance styles and genres (both 'ballroom' proper and others). The point I am making is simply that many teachers and studios will teach an array of dances *as* ballroom dances, simply because the market allows (and as attested to by my first unwitting foray into a ballroom studio to learn salsa).

4. This is not to say that some professionals do not develop (and deserve) reputations as partiers, but only to point out that developing such a reputation works against how seriously he or she may be taken as a competitor.

5. I did not feel at liberty to bring up this specific incident without breaching the confidentiality of my discussions and interviews with Jacqueline.

6. This is not to say that money is not an end in itself to many involved with the ballroom industry. Both embedded within a larger modern market-driven sociocultural surround, and an arena in which many (aficionados or not) conduct business, the ballroom world is also a 'place' where people make their professional lives.

7. While not a topic I have had the chance to pursue, I think that this dynamic, especially as most readily seen in the US ballroom scene, is related to a general US discomfort with nudity. Whether as a means of diversion from otherwise discomforting nudity, or resonating with the Western linking of nudity and intimacy and privacy, the extent to which customers disclose to dress vendors while being fitted in a dress, and the frequency with which this happens, indicates an interesting and structurally coherent pattern for future investigation and explication.

8. There is also a status bias here, as only the best of competitors or those otherwise well connected with studio owners will ever have exclusive access to such private floor time.

9. This dynamic is, of course (and like many others), one that is being transformed by the continuing growth, emergence and popularity of the Internet, mobile phones, text messaging and related mass communications.

CHAPTER 12   CONCLUSION

1. Just as Moore notes that soccer 'does not have the same status everywhere it is played' (2004: 40), the same certainly holds true for dancesport. For preliminary data regarding class and ballroom participation in Britain, see Penny (1999). For comments on race and class in US ballroom dancing, see McMains (2006) and Picart (2006).

2. When I voiced my dual reaction of being disappointed not to be able to go yet relieved not to be seen in bathing suit within that grouping, one of my ballroom friends, Emily, said 'you sound like a girl'. Highlighting the typically made association of bodily concerns as women's concerns, Emily's response underestimates the prevalence of men's concerns with body image, both within the United States in general and within the ballroom world in particular. From the many meals I have shared with both male and female competitors—for whom the body is a vehicle of personal and cultural identity—it is clear that body-image concerns exist for both men and women.

REFERENCES

Aldrich, Elizabeth (1998), 'Western Social Dance: An Overview of the Collection', Library of Congress, 8 June 2004, accessed 6 February 2006, http://memory.loc.gov/ammem/dihtml/diessay0.html.

Alter, Joseph S. (2000), '*Kabbadi*, A National Sport of India: The Internationalism of Nationalism and the Foreignness of Indianness', in Noel Dyck (ed.), *Games, Sports and Cultures*, Oxford: Berg.

Anderson, Barbara Gallatin (1990), *First Fieldwork: The Misadventures of an Anthropologist*, Prospect Heights, IL: Waveland Press.

Anderson, Benedict (1991 [1983]), Imagined Communities: Reflections on the Origin and Spread of Nationalism, New York: Verso.

Appadurai, Arjun (1995), 'Playing with Modernity: The Decolonization of Indian Cricket', in Carol A. Breckenridge (ed.), *Consuming Modernity: Public Culture in a South Asian World*, Minneapolis: University of Minnesota Press.

Arbeau, Thoinot (1967 [1589]), *Orchesography*, Mary Stewart Evans (trans.) Julia Sutton (ed.), New York: Dover.

Ardener, Shirley (ed.) (1993), *Defining Females: The Nature of Women in Society*, Oxford: Berg.

Bailey, F.G. (1993), *The Kingdom of Individuals: An Essay on Self-respect and Social Obligation*, Ithaca, NY: Cornell University Press.

Bakhtin, Mikhail (1984), *Rabelais and His Words*, Helene Iswolsky (trans.), Bloomington: Indiana University Press.

Banet-Weiser, Sarah (1999), *The Most Beautiful Girl in the World: Beauty Pageants and National Identity*, Berkeley: University of California Press.

Barnes, Ruth and Eicher, Joanne B. (eds.) (1997 [1992]), *Dress and Gender: Making and Meaning*, Oxford: Berg.

Barthes, Roland (1957), 'The World of Wrestling', in *Mythologies*, Paris: Granada/Editions du Seuil.

Bartky, Sandra Lee (1979), *Femininity and Domination*, New York: Routledge.

Bateson, Gregory and Mead, Margaret (1942), *Balinese Character*, Vol. II, New York: New York Academy of Sciences Special Publications.

Baudelaire, C. (1964), *The Painter of Modern Life an Other Essays*, New York: Da Copa.

Becker, Howard S. (1984), *Art Worlds*, Berkeley: University of California Press.

Becker, Howard S. (2001), 'Art as Collective Action', in C. Lee Harrington and Denise D. Bielby (eds), *Popular Culture: Production and Consumption*, Malden, MA: Blackwell.

Bellman, B. (1974), *The Language of Secrecy: Symbols and Metaphors in Poro Ritual*, New Brunswick, NJ: Rutgers University Press.

Bergesen, Albert, (1996 [1984]), 'Political Witch-Hunt Rituals', in Ronald L. Grimes (ed.), *Readings in Ritual Studies*, Upper Saddle River, NJ: Prentice Hall.

Birrell, Susan and McDonald, Mary G. (2000), 'Reading Sport, Articulating Power Lines', in Susan Birrell and Mary G. McDonald (eds) *Reading Sport: Critical Essays on Power and Representation*, Boston: Northeastern University Press.

Blacking, John (1973), *How Musical is Man?*, Seattle, WA: University of Washington Press.

Blacking, John (1981), 'Political and Musical Freedom in the Music of Some Black South African Churches', in L. Holy and M. Stuchlik (eds), *The Structure of Folk Models*, London: ASA monograph 20: 35–62.

Blacking, John (2001), 'Making Artistic Popular Music: The Goal of True Folk', in C. Lee Harrington and Denise D. Bielby (eds), *Popular Culture: Production and Consumption*, Malden, MA: Blackwell.

Blackmer, Joan Dexter (1989), *Acrobats of the Gods: Dance and Transformation*, Toronto: Inner City Books.

Blackwood, Evelyn (2000), *Webs of Power: Women, Kin, and Community in a Sumatran Village*, New York: Rowman and Littlefield.

Bolin, Anne (1998), 'Muscularity and Femininity: Women Bodybuilders and Women's Bodies in Culturo-Historical Context', in Karina A.E. Volkwein (ed.), *Fitness as Cultural Phenomenon*, New York: Waxmann Münster.

Bolin, Anne (2004), 'Bodybuilding', in Gary S. Cross (ed.), *The Encyclopedia of Recreation and Leisure in America*, Vol. 1, Detroit, MI: Scribner, pp. 120–4.

Bordo, Susan (1993), *Unbearable Weight: Feminism, Western Culture, and the Body*, Berkeley: University of California Press.

Bourdieu, Pierre (1977), *Outline of the Theory of Practice*, Richard Nice (trans.), Cambridge: Cambridge University Press.

Bourdieu, Pierre (1980), 'The Aristocracy of Culture', *Media, Culture, and Society* 2: 225–54.

Bourdieu, Pierre (1984 [1979]), *Distinction: A Social Critique of the Judgement of Taste*, Richard Nice (trans.), Cambridge, MA: Harvard University Press.

Bourdieu, Pierre (1986), 'The Biographical Illusion', *Actes de la recherche en sciences sociales*, numéro 62/63.

Brinson, Peter (1985), 'Epilogue: Anthropology and the Study of Dance', in Paul Spencer (ed.), *Society and the Dance: The Social Anthropology of Process and Performance*, Cambridge: Cambridge University Press.

Brownmiller, S. (1984), *Femininity*, New York: Linden Press/Simon and Schuster.

Burt R. (1995), *The Male Dancer: Bodies, Spectacle, Sexualities*, London: Routledge.

Business Wire (2000), 'Ballroom Dancing Fans Outraged at NBC Olympic Coverage; New Internet Dance TV Network to be Launched in Response', 9 October 2000, accessed 31 August 2000, http://www.findarticles.com/p/articles/mi_m0EIN/is_2000_Oct_9/ai_65835953

Butler, Judith (1990),*Gender Trouble: Feminism and the Subversion of Identity*, New York: Routledge.

Castle, Vernon and Castle, Irene (1914), *Modern Dancing*, New York: Harper.

Castro, D. (1991), *The Argentine Tango as Social History: 1880–1955*, Lewiston: Edwin Mellen.

Chaiklin, Seth and Lave, Jean (eds) (1993), *Understanding Practice: Perspectives on Activity and Context*, New York: Cambridge University Press.

Chernin, Kim (1981), *The Obsession: Reflections on the Tyranny of Slenderness*, New York: Harper and Row.

Christenfeld, Nicholas (1996), 'What Makes a Good Sport?', *Nature* 383: 662.

Clifford, James (1988), *The Predicament of Culture: Twentieth-century Ethnography, Literature, and Art*, Cambridge, MA: Harvard University Press.

Clifford, James and Marcus, George E. (eds) (1986), *Writing Culture: The Poetics and Politics of Ethnography*, Berkeley: University of California Press.

Cole, Michael (1996), *Cultural Psychology: A Once and Future Discipline*, Cambridge, MA: Belknap Press of Harvard University.

Coleridge, Samuel Taylor (1817), *Biographia Literaria*, ch. XIV.

Comaroff, Jean and Comaroff, John (1992), *Ethnography and the Historical Imagination*, Boulder, CO: Westview.

Connerton, Paul (1989), *How Societies Remember*, Cambridge: Cambridge University Press.

Craik, J. (1994), *The Face of Fashion: Cultural Studies in Fashion*, London: Routledge.

Craine, Debra and Mackrell, Judith (2000), *The Oxford Dictionary of Dance*, New York: Oxford University Press.

Crawford, R. (1984), 'A Cultural Account of "Health": Control, Release, and the Social Body', in J.B. McKinlay (ed.), *Issues in the Political Economy of Healthcare*, New York: Tavistock.

Csordas, Thomas (1993), 'Somatic Modes of Attention', *Cultural Anthropology* 8: 135–56.

D'Andrade, Roy (2000), *A General Action Theory Primer*, unpublished manuscript: University of California, San Diego.

Davis, Helene (1923), *Guide to Dancing*, Chicago: Regan Publishing.

Davis-Floyd (1996 [1994]), 'Ritual in the Hospital: Giving Birth the American Way', in Ronald L. Grimes (ed.) *Readings in Ritual Studies*, Upper Saddle River, NJ: Prentice Hall.

Disch, Lisa and Kane, Mary Jo (2000), 'When a Looker Is Really a Bitch: Lisa Olson, Sport, and the Heterosexual Matrix', in Susan Birell and Mary G. McDonald (eds), *Reading Sport: Critical Essays on Power and Presentation*, Boston: Northeastern University Press.

Downey, Greg (2005), *Learning Capoeira: Lessons in Cunning from an Afro-Brazilian Art*, New York: Oxford University Press.

Eicher, Joanne (2004), 'Clothing, Costume, and Dress' in Valerie Steele (ed.) *Encyclopedia of Clothing and Fashion*, Vol. 1, Charles Scribner's Sons.

Eicher, Joanne B. and Roach-Higgins, Mary Ellen (1997 [1992]), 'Definition and Classifications of Dress: Implications for Analysis of Gender Roles', in Ruth Barnes and Joanne B. Eicher (eds), *Dress and Gender: Making and Meaning*, Oxford: Berg.

Engeström, Yrjö (1993), 'Developmental Studies on Work as a Testbench of Activity Theory' in S. Chaiklin and J. Lave (eds), *Understanding Practice: Perspectives on Activity and Context* New York: Cambridge University Press.

Faller, G.S. (1987), 'The Function of Star-Image and Performance in the Hollywood Musical: Sonja Henie, Esther Williams, and Eleanor Powell', PhD Dissertation, Northwestern University.

Feder-Kane, Abigail M. (2000), '"A Radiant Smile from the Lovely Lady"', in Susan Birell and Mary G. McDonald (eds), *Reading Sport: Critical Essays on Power and Presentation*, Boston: Northeastern University Press.

Fine, Gary Alan (1987), *With the Boys: Little League Baseball and Preadolescent Culture*, Chicago: University of Chicago Press.

Fischer, Michael M.J. and Abedi, Mehdi (1991), *Debating Muslims: Cultural Dialogues in Postmodernity and Tradition*, Madison: University of Wisconsin Press.

Ford, Nick and David Brown (2006), *Surfing and Social Theory: Experience, Embodiment and Narrative of the Dream Glide*, London: Routledge.

Forman, E.A., Minnick, N. and Stone, C.A. (eds) (1993), *Contexts of Learning: Sociocultural Dynamics in Children's Development*, New York: Oxford University Press.

Franko, M. (1995), *Dancing Modernism/Performing Politics*, Bloomington: Indiana University Press.

Frederik, Laurie Aleen (2005), 'Competition Ballroom Dancing: The Native's Point of View', *Anthropology News* 46(9): 19–20.

Geertz, Clifford (1973 [1966]), 'Religion As a Cultural Symbol' in *The Interpretation of Cultures: Selected essays by Clifford Geertz*, New York: Basic Books.

Geertz, Clifford (1983), *Local Knowledge*, New York: Basic Books.

Gell, Alfred (1979), 'On Dance Structures: A Reply to Williams', *Journal of Human Movement Studies* 5: 18–31.

Glassner, B. (1988), *Bodies: Why We Look the Way We Do (and How We Feel About It)*, New York: Putnam.

Goffman, Erving (1976), 'Performances', in Richard Schechner and May Schuman (eds), *Ritual, Play, and Performance: Readings in the Social Sciences/Theatre*, New York: Seabury Press.

Goffman, Erving (1996 [1967]), 'Interaction Ritual: Deference and Demeanor', in Ronald L. Grimes (ed.), *Readings in Ritual Studies*, Upper Saddle River, NJ: Prentice Hall.

Goodenough, Ward H. (1981), *Culture, Language and Society*, 2nd edn, Menlo Park, CA: Benjamin/Cummings.

Goodnow, J.J., Miller, P.J. and Kessel, F. (eds) (1995), 'Cultural Practices as Contexts for Development' in *New Directions for Child Development*, vol. 67, San Francisco: Josey-Bass.

Goodrum, Alison, (2001), 'Land of Hip and Glory: Fashioning the "Classic" National Body', in William J.F. Keenan (ed.), *Dressed to Impress: Looking the Part*, Oxford: Berg. pp. 85–104.

Gordon, Suzanne (1983), *Off Balance: The Real World of Ballet*, New York: Pantheon.

Graham, Martha (1991), *Blood Memory*, New York: Doubleday.

Greider, William (1997), *One World, Ready or Not: The Manic Logic of Global Capitalism*, New York: Simon and Schuster.

Grimes, Ronald L. (1996 [1990]), 'Ritual Criticism and Infelicitous Performances', in Ronald L. Grimes (ed.), *Readings in Ritual Studies*, Upper Saddle River, NJ: Prentice Hall.

Gupta, Akhil and Ferguson, James (eds) (1997), *Anthropological Locations*, Berkeley: University of California Press.

Hammond, Sandra Noll (2000), *Ballet Basics*, 4th edn, Mountain View, CA: Mayfield Publishing.

Hanna, Judith Lynne (1979a) 'Movements Towards Understanding Humans through the Anthropological Study of Dance', *Current Anthropology*, 20: 313–39.

Hanna, Judith Lynne (1979b), *To Dance is Human: A Theory of Nonverbal Communication*, Austin: University of Texas Press.

Hanna, Judith Lynne (1988), *Dance, Sex and Gender: Signs of Identity, Dominance, Defiance, and Desire*, Chicago: University of Chicago Press.

Hannerz, Ulf (2003), 'Being there … and there … and there!', *Ethnography* 4(2): 201–16.

Hansen, Karen Tranberg (2004), 'The World in Dress: Anthropological Perspectives on Clothing, Fashion, and Culture', *Annual Review of Anthropology* 33: 369–92.

Hargreaves, J. (1994), *Sporting Females: Critical Issues in the History and Sociology of Woman's Sports*, New York: Routledge.

Harvey, John (2007), 'Showing and Hiding: Equivocation in the Relations of Body and Dress', *Fashion Theory* 11(1): 65–94.

Hastorf, Albert H. and Cantril, Hadley (1954), 'Case Reports: They Saw a Game: A Case Study', *Journal of Applied Sport Psychology* 4: 129–34.

Heng, Geraldine and Devan, Janadas (1992), 'State Fatherhood: The Politics of Nationalism, Sexuality, and Race in Singapore', in Andrew Parker, Mary Russo, Doris Sommer and Patricia Yaeger (eds), *Nationalisms and Sexualities*, New York: Routledge.

Holland, Dorothy and Quinn, Naomi (eds) (1987), *Cultural Models in Language and Thought*, New York: Cambridge University Press.

Horn, Stacy (1998), *Cyberville: Clicks, Culture, and the Creation of an Online Town*, New York: Warner Books

Hutchins, Edward (1995), *Cognition in the Wild*, Cambridge, MA: MIT Press.

Ingold, Tim (2000), *Perception of the Environment*, New York: Routledge.

Jackson, Phil (2004), *Inside Clubbing: Sensual Experiments in the Art of Being Human*, New York: Berg.

Kaeppler, Adrienne (1972), Method and Theory in Analyzing Dance Structure with an Analysis of Tongan Dance', *Ethnomusicology* 16: 173–217.

Kaeppler, Adrienne (1985), 'Systems in Tonga', in Paul Spencer (ed.), *Society and the Dance: The Social Anthropology of Process and Performance*, Cambridge: Cambridge University Press.

Keenan, William J.F. (2001a), 'Introduction: "Sartor Resartus" Restored: Dress Studies in Carlylean Perspective', in William J.F. Keenan (ed.), *Dressed to Impress: Looking the Part*, Oxford: Berg, pp. 1–49.

Keenan, William J.F. (2001b), 'Dress Freedom: The Personal and the Political', in William J.F. Keenan (ed.), *Dressed to Impress: Looking the Part*, Oxford: Berg, pp. 179–96.

Kertzer, David I. (1996 [1988]), 'Ritual, Politics, and Power', in Ronald L. Grimes (ed.), *Readings in Ritual Studies*, Upper Saddle River, NJ: Prentice Hall.

Klepp, Ingun Grimstad and Storm-Mathisen, Ardis (2005), 'Reading Fashion as Age: Teenage Girls' and Grown Women's Accounts of Clothing as Body and Social Status', *Fashion Theory* 9(3): 323–42.

Lave, Jean (1988), *Cognition in Practice: Mind, Mathematics and Culture in Everyday Life*, New York: Cambridge University Press.

Lave, Jean and Wenger, Etienne (1991), *Situated Learning: Legitimate Peripheral Participation*, New York: Cambridge University Press.

Leach, Edmund R. (1954), *The Political Systems of Highland Burma*, Boston: Beacon Press.

LeDoux, Joseph E. (1996), *The Emotional Brain: The Mysterious Underpinnings of Emotional Life*, New York: Simon and Schuster.

Lin, Yu-Ling (1996) 'The Ideal of Slenderness in Taiwan's Diet Ads From Foucault's Framework of Power/Knowledge', *Journal of Women and Gender Studies* (7): 1–24.

Lorber, Judith (1994), *Paradoxes of Gender*, New Haven, CT: Yale University Press.

MacAloon, John J. (1984), 'Olympic Games and the Theory of Spectacle in Modern Societies', in John J. MacAloon (ed.), *Rite, Drama, Festival, Spectacle: Rehearsals Toward a Theory of Cultural Performance*, Philadelphia, PA: Institute for the Study of Human Issues.

MacClancy, Jeremy (1997), 'Anthropology, Art, and Contest', in Jeremy MacClancey (ed.), *Contesting Art: Art, Politics, and Identity in the Modern World*, Oxford: Berg.

Mandler, George (1984), *Mind and Body: Psychology of Emotion and Stress*, New York: W.W. Norton

Mankekar, Purnima (1999), *Screening Culture, Viewing Politics: An Ethnography of Television, Womanhood, and Nation in Postcolonial India*, Durham, NC: Duke University Press.

Marcus, George (1986), 'Contemporary Problems of Ethnography in the Modern World System', in James Clifford and George Marcus (eds), *Writing Culture*, Berkeley: University of California Press, pp. 165–93.

Marcus, George (1995), 'Ethnography in/of the World System: The Emergence of Multi-sited Ethnography', *Annual Review of Anthropology* 24: 95–117.

Marcus, George E. (1992), *Reading Cultural Anthropology*, Durham, NC: Duke University Press.

Marcus, George and Fischer, Michael (eds) (1986), *Anthropology as Cultural Critique: An Experimental Movement in the Human Sciences*, Chicago: University of Chicago Press.

Marcus, George E. and Myers, Fred R. (1995), *The Traffic in Culture: Refiguring Art and Anthropology*, Berkeley: University of California Press.

Marion, Jonathan S. (2000), 'Deep-Meaning: The Nexus of Lived Lives', MA Thesis, Department of Anthropology; University of California, San Diego.

Marion, Jonathan S. (2005a) ' "Where" is "There"?: Towards a Translocal Anthropology in Competitive Ballroom Dancing', *Anthropology News* 46(5): 18–19.

Marion, Jonathan S. (2005b), 'Why "Ballroom" is Bigger than the Studio Floor', *Anthropology News* 46(9): 20.

Marion, Jonathan S. (2006), 'Beyond Ballroom: Activity as Performance, Embodiment, and Identity', *Human Mosaic* 36(2): 7–16.

Marion, Jonathan S. (2007), 'Which Way to the Ballroom?', *Suomen Antropologi: Journal of the Finnish Anthropological Society* 32(2): 110–23.

Martin, David (2001), 'Foreword', in William J.F. Keenan (ed.), *Dressed to Impress: Looking the Part*, Oxford: Berg.

Martin, G. and Pesovar, E. (1961), 'A Structural Analysis of the Hungarian Folk Dance', *Acta Ethnographica*, 10: 1–40.

Mauss, Marcel (1973), 'Techniques of the Body', *Economy and Society* 2(1): 70–89.

McKinley, E. Graham (1997), *Beverly Hills, 90210: Television, Gender, and Identity*, Philadelphia, PA: University of Pennsylvania Press.

McMains, Juliet (2006), *Glamour Addiction: Inside the American Ballroom Industry*, Middletown, CT: Wesleyan University Press.

Mead, Margaret and Macgregor, F.C. (1951), *Growth and Culture*, New York: Putnam.

Mentore, George (2000), 'Society, Body and Style: An Archery Contest in Amerindian Society', in Noel Dyck (ed.), *Games, Sports and Cultures*, Oxford: Berg.

Metheny, E. (1965), *Communication of Movement in Sport and Dance*, Iowa: Brown.

Minsky, Marvin (1986), *The Society of Mind*, New York: Simon and Schuster.

Mitchell, T. (1994), *Flamenco, Deep Song*, New Haven, CT: Yale University Press.

Moor, Philip (2004), 'Scouting an Anthropology of Sport', *Anthropologica* 46: 37–46.

Myerhoff, Barbara G. (1974), *Peyote Hunt: The Sacred Journey of the Huichol Indians*, Ithaca, NY: Cornell University Press.

Myerhoff, Barbara G. (1986), '"Life Not Death in Venice": Its Second Life', in Victor Turner and Edward Bruner (eds), *The Anthropology of Experience*, Chicago: University of Illinois Press.

Myerhoff, Barbara G. (1996 [1984]), 'Death in Dues Time: Construction of Self and Culture in Ritual Drama', in Ronald L. Grimes (ed.), *Readings in Ritual Studies*, Upper Saddle River, NJ: Prentice Hall.

Nadel, S.F. (1954), *Nupe Religion*, London: Routledge and Kegan Paul

Nicholson, Linda J. (1986), *Gender and History: The Limits of Social Theory in the Age of the Family*, New York: Columbia University Press.

Offen, Julia Lynn (2000), 'Beyond the Ring: The European Traveling Circus', PhD dissertation: Department of Anthropology; University of California, San Diego.

Ortner, Sherry (1974), 'Is Female to Male as Nature Is to Culture?', in Michelle Zimbalist Rosaldo and Louis Lamphere (eds), *Women, Culture and Society*, Stanford, CA: Stanford University Press.

Ortner, Sherry (1995), 'Resistance and the Problem of Ethnographic Refusal', *Comparative Studies in Society and History* 27(I): 173–93.

Pandolfi, Mariella (2000), 'Body', *Journal of Linguistic Anthropology* 9(1–2): 16–19.

Parish, Steven M. (1996), *Hierarchy and Its Discontents: Culture and the Politics of Consciousness in Caste Society*, Philadelphia: University of Pennsylvania Press.

Penny, Patricia (1999), 'Dancing at the Interface of the Social and the Theatrical: Focus on the Participatory Patterns of Contemporary Competition Ballroom Dancers in Britain', *Dance Research: The Journal of the Society of Dance Research* 17(1): 47–74.

Picart, Caroline Joan (2006), *From Ballroom To Dancesport: Aesthetics, Athletics, And Body Culture*, Albany, NY: State University of New York Press.

Polhemus, Ted (1993), 'Dance, Gender and Culture' in Helen Thomas (ed.), *Dance, Gender and Culture*, New York: St. Martin's Press.

Popper, Karl R. (1966), *The Open Society and Its Enemies* 2, Princeton, NJ: Princeton University Press.

Prieur, Annick (1996), 'Domination and Desire: Male Homosexuality and the Construction of Masculinity in Mexico' in Marit Melhuus and Kristi Anne Stolen (eds), *Machos, Mistresses, Madonnas: Contesting the Power of Latin American Gender Imagery*, New York: Verso.

Radcliffe-Brown, A. R. (1922), *The Andaman Islanders*, Cambridge: Cambridge University Press.

Radler, Dan (1996) 'How a Dance Competition is Judged', 4 November 2003. http://www.ballroomusa.com/radham/howjudged.htm

Rappaport, Roy A. (1996 [1979]), 'The Obvious Aspects of Ritual', in Ronald L. Grimes (ed.), *Readings in Ritual Studies*, Upper Saddle River, NJ: Prentice Hall.

Reischer, Erica and Koo, Kathryn S. (2004), 'The Body Beautiful: Symbolism and Agency in the Social World', *Annual Review of Anthropology* 33: 297–317.

Richardson, Philip J.S. (1946), *A History of English Ballroom Dancing (1910–45): the Story of the Development of the Modern English Style*, London: Herbert Jenkins.

Rogoff, Barbara (1990), *Apprenticeship in Thinking: Cognitive Development in Social Context*, New York: Oxford University Press.

Rosaldo, Michelle Z. (1980), 'The Use and Abuse of Anthropology: Reflections on Feminism and Cross-cultural Understanding', *Signs* 5(3): 389–417.

Royce, Anya Peterson (1977), *The Anthropology of Dance*, Bloomington: Indiana University Press.

Ruby, Jay (2000), *Picturing Culture: Explorations of Film and Anthropology*, Chicago: University of Chicago Press.

Savigliano, Marta E. (1995), *Tango and the Political Economy of Passion*, Boulder, CO: Westview Press.

Savigliano, Marta E. (1998), 'From Wallflowers to Femmes Fatales: Tango and the Performance of Passionate Femininity', in William Washabaugh (ed.), *The Passion of Music and Dance: Body, Gender, and Sexuality*, Oxford: Berg.

Schechner, Richard (2002), *Performance Studies: An Introduction*, New York: Routledge.

Schneider, David M. (1968), *American Kinship: A Cultural Account*, Englewood Cliffs, NJ: Prentice-Hall.

Singer, A. (1974), 'The Metrical Structure of Macedonian Dance'. *Ethnomusicology*, 18: 379–404.

Skinner, G. William (1985), 'Presidential Address: The Structure of Chinese History', *Journal of Asian Studies* 44(2): 271–92.

Sosis, Richard (2004), 'The Adaptive Value of Religious Ritual', *American Scientist* March–April 2004: 166–72.

Spencer, Paul (1985), *Society and the Dance: The Social Anthropology of Process and Performance*, Cambridge: Cambridge University Press.

Spiro, Melford E. (1979), *Gender and Culture: Kibbutz Women Revisited*, Durham, NC: Duke University Press.

Stewart, John (1986), 'Patronage and Control in the Trinidad Carnival', in Victor Turner and Edward Bruner (eds), *The Anthropology of Experience*, Chicago: University of Illinois Press.

Strathern, Andrew (1985), '"A Line of Boys": Melpa Dance as a Symbol of Maturation', in Paul Spencer (ed.), *Society and the Dance: The Social Anthropology of Process and Performance*, Cambridge: Cambridge University Press.

Strathern, Andrew (1997), *Body Thoughts*, Ann Arbor, MI: University of Michigan Press.

Stromberg, Peter G. (1986), *Symbols of Community: The Cultural System of a Swedish Church*, Tucson, AZ: University of Arizona Press.

Sumner, W.G. (1906), *Folkways*, Boston, MA: Ginn.

Swartz, Marc J. (1991), *The Way the World Is: Cultural Processes and Social Relations Among the Mombasa Swahili*, Berkeley: University of California Press.

Swartz, Marc J. and Jordan, David K. (1976), *Anthropology: Perspectives on Humanity*, New York: Wiley.

Taylor, Julie (1988), *Paper Tangos*, Durham, NC: Duke University Press.

Thomas, Helen (ed.) (1993), *Dance, Gender and Culture*, New York: St. Martin's Press.

Turner, Victor W. (1987), *The Anthropology of Performance*, New York: PAJ Publications.

Turner, Victor W. (1995 [1969]), *The Ritual Process: Structure and Anti-Structure*, New York: Aldine de Gruyter.

Vermey, Ruud (1994), *Latin: Thinking, Sensing and Doing in Latin American Dancing*, Munich: Kastell Verlag.

Wachs, Faye Linda (2005), 'The Boundaries of Difference: Negotiating Gender in Recreational Sport', *Sociological Inquiry* 75(4): 527–47.

Wacquant, Loïc (2004), *Body and Soul: Notebooks of an Apprentice Boxer*, New York: Oxford University Press.

Wallace, Anthony F.C. (1961), *Culture and Personality*, New York: Random House.

Wallendorf, Melanie and Arnould, Eric J. (1996 [1991]), 'Consumption Rituals of Thanksgiving Day', in Ronald L. Grimes (ed.), *Readings in Ritual Studies*, Upper Saddle River, NJ: Prentice Hall.

Ward, Andrew H. (1993), 'Dancing in the Dark: Rationalism and the Neglect of Social Dance' in Helen Thomas (ed.), *Dance, Gender and Culture*, New York: St. Martin's Press.

Williams, D. (1978), 'Deep Structures of the Dance', *Yearbook of Symbolic Anthropology* 1: 211–30.

Williams, D. (1982), 'Semasiology: A Semantic Anthropological View of Human Movements and Actions' in D.J. Parkins (ed.), *Semantic Anthropology*, London: Academic Press.

Willis, P. (1982), 'Women in Sport in Ideology', in J. Hargreaves (ed.), *Sport, Culture, and Ideology*, London: Routledge and Kegan Paul.

Wilson, Elizabeth (2007), 'A Note on Glamour', *Fashion Theory* 11(1): 95–108.

Wilson-Kovacs, Dana (2001), 'The Fall and Rise of Erotic Lingerie', in William J.F. Keenan (ed.), *Dressed to Impress: Looking the Part*, Oxford: Berg, pp. 159–77.

Winn, Peter A. (1996 [1991]), 'Legal Ritual', in Ronald L. Grimes (ed.), *Readings in Ritual Studies*, Upper Saddle River, NJ: Prentice Hall.

Wolf, Naomi (1991), *The Beauty Myth: How Images of Beauty Are Used Against Women*, New York: William Morrow.

Woodward, S. (1976), 'Evidence for a Grammatical Structure in Javanese Dance', *Dance Research Journal* 8: 10–17.

Wulff, Helena (1998), *Ballet Across Borders: Career and Culture in the World of Dancers*, Oxford: Berg.

INDEX

Page numbers in *italic* refer to tables and illustrations